I0881216

SPIRITS OF THE ROCKIES

Reasserting an Indigenous Presence in Banff National Park

The Banff–Bow Valley in western Alberta is the heart of spiritual and economic life for the Nakoda peoples. Beginning with the Treaty 7 agreement (1877), the Nakoda were displaced from the region by the reserve system and the creation of Canada's first national park. In the twentieth century, the Nakoda reasserted their presence in the valley through their involvement in local tourism economies and the Banff Indian Days sporting festivals.

Drawing on six years of ethnographic research, extensive oral testimonies from Nakoda elders, and detailed analysis of archival records, *Spirits of the Rockies* is a sophisticated account of the the Nakoda peoples' colonial encounters with missionaries, government agents, tourism entrepreneurs, and park officials. The Nakoda strategically built relationships in order to gain access to their sacred sites that were redefined as protected areas. These Indigenous communities creatively responded to colonial policies that were designed to repress their subsistence practices and assimilate their cultures. Using an innovative Foucauldian approach, Mason examines the power relations that shaped racial discourse within the Rocky Mountains during this dynamic period of Western Canadian history.

COURTNEY W. MASON is a postdoctoral research fellow with the Indigenous Health Research Group at the University of Ottawa.

Spirits of the Rockies

Reasserting an Indigenous Presence in Banff National Park

COURTNEY W. MASON

UNIVERSITY OF TORONTO PRESS
Toronto Buffalo London

Toronto Buffalo London
utppublishing.com

ISBN 978-1-4426-4930-9 (cloth)
ISBN 978-1-4426-2668-3 (paper)

Library and Archives Canada Cataloguing in Publication

Mason, Courtney W., 1979–, author

Spirits of the Rockies : reasserting an indigenous presence in Banff National Park / Courtney W. Mason.

Includes bibliographical references and index.

ISBN 978-1-4426-4930-9 (bound). – ISBN 978-1-4426-2668-3 (pbk.)

1. Assiniboine Indians – Alberta – Banff National Park – History. 2. Assiniboine Indians – Colonization – Alberta – Banff National Park. 3. Assiniboine Indians – Alberta – Banff National Park – Social conditions. 4. Assiniboine Indians – Alberta – Banff National Park – Economic conditions. 5. Aboriginal tourism – Alberta – Banff National Park – History. 6. Banff National Park (Alta.) – Economic conditions. 7. Banff National Park (Alta.) – Social conditions. 8. Banff National Park (Alta.) – Ethnic relations – History. 9. Banff National Park (Alta.) – History. I. Title.

E99.A84M38 2014 971.23'3200497524 C2014-903670-1

This book has been published with the help of a grant from the Federation for the Humanities and Social Sciences, through the Awards to Scholarly Publications Program, using funds provided by the Social Sciences and Humanities Research Council of Canada.

University of Toronto Press acknowledges the financial assistance to its publishing program of the Canada Council for the Arts and the Ontario Arts Council, an agency of the Government of Ontario.

Canada Council for the Arts | Conseil des Arts du Canada

ONTARIO ARTS COUNCIL
CONSEIL DES ARTS DE L'ONTARIO
an Ontario government agency
un organisme du gouvernement de l'Ontario

University of Toronto Press acknowledges the financial support of the Government of Canada through the Canada Book Fund for its publishing activities.

To my parents, Morgan and Judy Mason, for giving us all that we needed in life.

To the memory of my grandfather, James D. Eamer, who passed away while I was completing the final stages of this book. You instilled in me an appreciation and respect for nature, which eventually included both national parks and mountains.

Contents

Figures and Illustrations

Colour Illustrations

Foreword

ROLAND ROLLINMUD AND IAN A.L. GETTY

The Bow Valley and Bow River, called Mînî Thnî Wapta or Cold Water River, has been the traditional spiritual centre of the Nakoda People since time immemorial. As the giver of life, the river provides us with traditional foods, medicinal plants, shelter, animals to hunt, as well as sacred areas and vision quest sites. Indeed, the river forms the centre of our culture, our economy, our families, and our way of living off the land. According to Nakoda elders, the location of the Banff Indian Days is called Mînî hrpa (waterfalls). The Nakoda camped at the foot of Cascade Mountain, which served as a gathering place for meetings, for healing, as a place of worship, for sweat lodges, and for access to the sacred waters of the hot springs for spiritual cleansing. After the Banff Hot Springs Reserve was established, each summer our people would visit the area as a special retreat. This is where we would celebrate our culture and renew our special relationship with Mother Earth.

This book by Dr Courtney Mason is an evocative analysis by the scholar into the history and the cultural heritage of the Stoney Nakoda people who have made the Bow Valley corridor and Rocky Mountain headwaters their homeland for centuries. He takes us on a personal and historical journey that is often ignored, or unwittingly passed, by travellers going through the Stoney Nakoda Indian Reserve on the Trans-Canada Highway, situated midway between Calgary and Banff National Park. This is partly a journey of personal awareness and contact with the Nakoda; the story of the early history of the Nakoda in Banff National Park and the importance and celebration of their culture as reflected through the Banff Indian Days festivals; and a narrative of Nakoda historic and contemporary way of life in the Bow Valley and foothills of Alberta.

Mason neatly ties together his personal experiences in meeting and gaining the trust of Nakoda community members as he sought out their perspectives on their historic roots in Banff National Park. The park was created in 1885 to protect and to exploit the hot springs that were (and are) the spiritual essence of the Nakoda's relationship with the land. This is meticulously demonstrated in the book using the oral-history testimony of elders. His decision to collaborate with the Nakoda community and individuals with whom he worked while volunteering in the community gave him rare access to the oral history of Banff National Park and its central role in Nakoda spirituality and cultural activities. Perhaps by serendipitous convergence, we met Courtney through our involvement in cultural events such as the Banff Indian Days, which are held annually near the Banff townsite.

Mason has skilfully combined this personal authenticity with the extensive archival research he conducted in local archives and data gleaned from newspapers. Based on the special request from elders, he has already deposited with the Stoney Nakoda Nation archives a condensed history of Nakoda communities and the Banff Indian Days festivals. Based on his primary evidence, this history will enable other researchers to instantly undertake additional analysis on Indigenous participation in this century-old event that predates even the Calgary Stampede. Mason's work is in direct contrast to that of many previous researchers, who have conducted fieldwork with community members and not shared their original notes, and sometimes even their results, with the community. Mason's research into the history of the Banff–Bow Valley region, the traditional homelands of the Nakoda people, incorporates their oral histories at the heart of his narrative. His approach challenges the many authors who ignore or in only a token fashion acknowledge local Indigenous peoples. By centring the Nakoda experience in his narrative, he offers fresh insight into the impact of government officials and policies, missionaries, the tourism industry, and the surrounding communities that now encircle the Stoney Indian Reserve at Morley.

This history of the Nakoda people is also analysed through the theories of Michel Foucault to demonstrate how the Nakoda people have survived culturally, linguistically, and spiritually despite the colonial, bureaucratic structure we know as the Indian Act. The application of the theoretical power constraints developed by Foucault and other theorists is found throughout the text in each chapter. While inevitably this does interrupt the narrative flow, this approach adds an intellectual dimension which demonstrates that the colonial experiences of the Nakoda were a common experience within colonial power relations and its objectives to assimilate, conform, and repress Indigenous rights and cultural practices. Mason blends this academic approach, along with his personal observations and experiences, into the historical narrative in order to demonstrate how Nakoda society has been impacted by government policies ranging from conservation laws to changes brought about by economic enterprises like the Banff Indian Days. He describes how the colonizing priorities and the political-economic imperatives of the Dominion government were able to sideline and ignore the treaty rights of all First Nations people in Canada. Yet despite the constraints of the colonial administration, the Nakoda people were able to adapt to the restrictions and preserve their language, customs, and spiritual ceremonies. This complex personal and historical journey has given us new understandings of the rich human histories of the Banff–Bow Valley region by centring it around Nakoda perspectives of their experiences.

Roland Rollinmud is a Chiniki Nation artist and elder activist, who spearheaded the revival of the Banff Indian Days cultural traditions in 2004. Part of his artistic vision is to carry on his family's tradition of storytelling and portraying Nakoda history and legends through his artwork. His recent and most significant work is a large mural depicting the original state of the Banff hot springs cave and basin, which first attracted Euro-Canadian attention in the 1880s and prompted the establishment of Banff National Park in 1885.

Ian A.L. Getty is a research director with the Stoney Nakoda Nation in Morley, Alberta, having served in that position since 1980. He has authored many articles on Stoney Nakoda history and leadership for the *Canadian Encyclopedia* and the *Dictionary of Canadian Biography*. He has also co-edited two books in the field of native studies: *One Century Later: Western Canadian Reserve Indians since Treaty 7* (1978) and *As Long as the Sun Shines and Water Flows* (1983).

Acknowledgments

There are many individuals who have supported me over the years. Quite simply, without their encouragement, knowledge, and generosity, this book would not have been possible. I thank all of them for their individual contributions.

Elders and residents of Nakoda communities at Morley and Banff collaborated with me on this project. I would like especially to acknowledge Roland Rollinmud, Lenny Poucette, Margaret Snow, Jackson Wesley, Ralphine Locke, and Ian A.L. Getty for facilitating aspects of this research, building connections between cultures, and teaching me how to listen.

A number of colleagues have contributed to this work. Debra Shogan, Andie Palmer, Pirkko Markula, Tom Hinch, Ian MacLaren, Vicky Paraschak, Michael Robidoux, and the late Rod Murray deserve special mention due to their reviews of content and shaping of ideas. As undergraduate students, Erin Flaherty, Leslie LeMoal, and Jayn Villetard helped with early archival data collection.

Valuable support was provided by the following institutions: the University of Alberta, the Social Sciences and Humanities Research Council of Canada, the Eleanor Luxton Historical Foundation, Parks Canada, the Glenbow Museum, the Whyte Museum of the Canadian Rockies, the Canadian Pacific Archives, and the Banff Public Library. I would like to recognize the three anonymous reviewers, as well as the staff at the University of Toronto Press, for their commitment to this project.

Numerous friends have shaped aspects of this book. To childhood friends, the Laurier crew, and fellow grad students over the years, thank you for being there along the way. Thanks to my friend Sabrina Russo for her photographic expertise.

I am fortunate enough to come from a large and caring family. My Mason/Bilmer cousins, aunts, uncles, and grandparents have taught me much about the social world. Support from the Howitt/Bruce families is also appreciated. The unconditional love and encouragement of my family (Mom and Dad, Emily, Todd, Kaley, Laure, Andie, Tia, and Alienor) constantly gives me meaning and direction in life.

My partner Josephine has shared much of this journey and subsequently there is a part of her in everything I do. This book has also benefited from her fine editing skills and comments.

A portion of the royalties for this book will be donated to the Stoney Health Centre in Morley, Alberta, which provides critical health services to local youth and families.

SPIRITS OF THE ROCKIES

Reasserting an Indigenous Presence in Banff National Park

Introduction

A number of years ago, I sat listening to the life history of elder Roland Rollinmud in the Chief Chiniki Restaurant on the Nakoda reserve in Morley, Alberta. During what was our second meeting, he told me that as a storyteller you should convey your personal experiences, as any listener needs to hear a bit about your life in order to understand where the story comes from and why the telling of it may be of importance.[1] For him, the contexts that frame the life of a storyteller were as essential as the details of any narrative that could be shared. He clearly expressed that weaving in your own experiences was the responsibility of any good storyteller. Appreciating Roland's insight and advice, I open this book in this very spirit.

The Oka Crisis (June 1990)

Surprisingly, after all these years, it remains a vivid memory as these images are etched into the very fabric of my existence. I was in the grade 6 classroom and my desk was positioned adjacent to the south-facing window. In many ways it was similar to a lot of afternoons at that time of year. By the middle of June, all I could focus on was being outside, and when in class, all I thought of was how terrible it felt in comparison to running outdoors with the warm breezes and the smells of summer. I sat at my desk, glaring out that window onto the view it afforded of the local sports grounds. This lazy afternoon should not have been different from any other. However, on this particular afternoon those athletic grounds were full of activity of a different sort. As a tank pulled onto where we had been playing baseball over the lunch hour, I remember being filled with mixed emotions: bewilderment, excitement, but most notably fear. For the next few hours I watched intently as the Canadian Armed Forces assembled their barracks and worked on their equipment. I had never seen a tank, an army truck, or perhaps even a soldier before. Finally, as the activity and noise increased, the curiosity of my classmates was piqued and the situation required a bit of explanation. I remember the teacher saying that the army was here to "take care of those troublemakers over in 'Kwa-bec.'" Growing up on the border of eastern Ontario and western Québec, I had heard mention of such troubles before, but this time the trouble concerned, not the sovereignists, but the Indigenous communities located near the border between the two provinces.

Although school let out a few days later, the army's presence in our small village, situated on the banks of the St Lawrence River, lasted all summer. They were there for the duration of a seventy-eight-day standoff with the Mohawk residents of the Kanesatake reserve near the town of Oka, Québec. The decision to expand a golf course onto a Mohawk burial site triggered a conflict that pulled Indigenous land rights and claims into the public spotlight in both national and international contexts. As a consequence of its strategic location, our village's police station became the base for the Canadian military. In a region often starved for activity, our local newspaper followed every detail of the event, sometimes offering captivating images. Few conversations that summer went without mention of the dynamic and fragile situation that seemed to implicate us all. It was some time during this summer that I first became interested in the issues and challenges that impact Indigenous communities in Canada. Although I cannot trace it to an exact moment, what I saw from the window that afternoon deeply influenced me in a way that I did not fully understand until well over a decade later.

I grew up in a mixed Anglo, Franco, and Mohawk community, but I do not draw on these experiences to specifically situate myself as a researcher working with Indigenous peoples, as that will be addressed later in this book. The importance of sharing these memories simply emphasizes that there was no event, either before or after the Oka crisis, that shaped me in such a manner. These experiences also clearly marked the gross inequalities that exist in the Canadian nation state that stem from its histories of colonial violence. My memories of the Oka crisis, albeit through the eyes of a child, became the genesis of this research project, including its broader political and scholarly objectives.

While these recollections trace an aspect of my own personal history, which as this book will reveal has become entangled with the histories of others, they primarily serve as an entry point into a discussion about why Indigenous histories matter and what implications the telling of them may have for contemporary Canadian society.

It was not until I was in graduate school that I developed a more profound political interest in the distinct challenges that Indigenous communities encounter. My master's research, which involved community-based work on the history of Euro-Canadians in this region of Eastern Ontario and Western Québec (Mason, 2005, 2007), was complicated through the often-dismissed regional presence of Iroquois peoples by historians. After completing this degree, I headed out west to pursue my joint interests in Indigenous histories, mountains, and national parks. I was particularly intrigued by the conflicts that emerged between Indigenous communities and governments in Canada's iconic Banff–Bow Valley.[2] Many of these disputes were directly related to Nakoda subsistence land uses in regions redefined as parks and protected areas.

This book explores Nakoda histories of the Banff–Bow Valley by focusing on their experiences of being excluded from the region. The Banff–Bow Valley is located in the province of Alberta on the eastern slopes of the Canadian Rocky Mountains and represents the most developed part of Banff National Park (BNP) as it includes the urbanized townsite (see plate 1).

As a unique montane ecoregion, this valley is part of a critical ecosystem and wildlife corridor that supports a large diversity of species. The valley also contains an incredible amount of human history. For millennia before 1000 CE, diverse groups of Indigenous peoples[3] lived, fished, hunted, gathered, and traded throughout the Banff–Bow Valley (Fedje et al., 1995; Langemann, 2011). By the late eighteenth century, the arrival and presence of Europeans in the mountains altered the well-established trade networks and ways of life that had supported extensive networks of Indigenous groups. Despite these abrupt changes, Nakoda communities continued to live and work on the eastern slopes of the Canadian Rockies, including the lands currently regarded as BNP, until the last quarter of the nineteenth century. Following the Treaty 7 agreements of 1877, Indigenous peoples were relocated to reserves outside what would become the national park, and over the ensuing decades their access to the region was increasingly restricted. For Nakoda First Nations (NFN) communities,[4] which had been the most active group in this region before the European presence, these restrictions severely altered their socio-economic, political, and cultural ways of life. Even though their access to the lands assumed by the new national park drastically changed Nakoda ways of living, they strived to maintain connections to the lands that were intricately linked to their subsistence and cultural practices by adopting numerous adaptive strategies.

One of the ways local Indigenous communities responded to colonial constraints was through their selective engagement in the local tourism industry. Beginning at the turn of the twentieth century, Nakoda communities collaborated with local tourism producers in what would turn into a burgeoning tourism economy in the nearby Banff townsite. For many decades thereafter, one festival in particular became the centrepiece of these productions. The Banff Indian Days, which ran from 1894 to 1978, was an incredibly successful cultural event that annually attracted tens of thousands of tourists from North America and around the world. Showcasing the cultural practices of local Indigenous peoples, this festival has a fascinating history that has almost entirely escaped the attention of popular historians and scholars.

When I first began to examine the published cultural histories of the Banff–Bow Valley, it became apparent that there are a plethora of works that have investigated a variety of topics. I think that it would be a difficult task to identify any other place in the country (acre for acre) that has been the subject of so many high-quality popular and scholarly histories. This is one of the reasons why the Banff–Bow Valley represents such a unique location in the Canadian imaginary and has been used so successfully to market the country as an international tourist destination. This book will reveal that these published histories, along with the captivating photographs and images that often accompany them, have formed a powerful platform to produce Canadian identities and shape international perspectives of the nation state.

Any comprehensive analysis of the many published cultural histories of Banff will reveal a number of notable anomalies. When I first examined this literature, it became painfully clear that the lion's share of this material was centred on Euro-Canadian histories. Despite the relatively recent arrival of Europeans to the region, many aspects of their cultural histories have been extensively explored by historians.[5] In direct contrast, it was apparent that there were very few publications concentrated on the histories of Indigenous peoples. Perhaps even more troubling, some histories failed to recognize the previous and current Indigenous presence in the valley. Even though some accounts do include histories of local Nakoda peoples, most authors did not directly consult individuals or communities for their perspectives on their own histories and cultures.[6] While many aspects of Indigenous histories of the region have not been comprehensively investigated or published, there are a few works that do cover specific topics by consulting local Nakoda peoples.[7] Based on the existing gaps in the literature and the advice of Indigenous scholars and community members, I decided that it was critical for my research to collaborate with members of Nakoda First Nations to understand their personal and collective experiences. The collaborative methods that informed the latter group of works on local Indigenous histories assured me that this type of project was possible and that it could fill a significant gap in the human history of the region.

I defined this project based on two important foundations: the current absences that exist in the published literature and my personal interest in the issues that face many Indigenous communities throughout Canada. In this book, I explore histories of the Banff–Bow Valley by privileging local perspectives. I centre on Nakoda experiences of first their exclusion from the lands in the making of parks and later their return to the region through their engagement in the tourism industry. This research examines the ways Nakoda peoples interacted with missionaries, government officials, tourism producers, and local Banff residents. This also includes the instrumental roles Nakoda peoples played as leaders, participants, performers, and producers in local tourism economies. Of most interest is how Nakoda peoples contributed to the production of discourse through their participation in tourism industries. Paramount in this analysis of prevailing discourse are understandings of how Nakoda participants created meanings for themselves and partly shaped what was possible to know about Indigenous peoples in the region and the province of Alberta throughout the twentieth century.

Situating Research and Understanding Evidence

It is imperative to discuss the research design of this study, including some detail on the methods that I employed and information on how evidence was produced as well as reviewed. This book is the product of over five years of ethnographic based research in the province of Alberta's Banff–Bow Valley. In the spring of 2006, I began volunteering in the Nakoda community at Morley. With no prior contacts or research relationships that I could pursue, volunteering was the main forum through which I got to know and interact with community members. I was fortunate to meet several welcoming and generous Nakoda elders who shaped the remainder of my experiences in the community. My initial entry point was through volunteering at a Nakoda cultural gathering that is held annually near the Banff townsite. A few months later, I was invited to join the organizing committee of a group that facilitates opportunities for Nakoda youth, mainly through music gatherings. This soon developed into further commitments and relationships that fostered an important learning process for me while I simultaneously built trust with local people and contributed to broader community initiatives. As a result of developing relationships over the years, I began to be invited to community events such as rodeos and powwows as well as sweat-lodge ceremonies and other private cultural practices. I was always honoured by these types of invitations and attended as often as I could. It was only through several years of volunteer work that I was able to understand, and eventually meet, some of the expectations of reciprocity that were expressed by elders who participated in my research. All of these experiences facilitated meaningful relationships that extended beyond research interests into the realm of my personal life.[8]

Through the entirety of this project a mixed-methods approach has been used that involved oral history interviews and various aspects of archival analyses. Oral history interviews with Nakoda elders complicated my understandings of the cultural histories of the Banff–Bow Valley and provided the main thrust of historical evidence that guided this research. The texts produced from these accounts offered different and at times contradictory perceptions of the prevailing discourse. While privileging oral histories, this research also draws from archival documents and ethnographic observations. Formal documents concerning park policy, including national parks acts, park warden reports, and municipal, provincial, and federal government policies were included. These documents gave insight into how policies and laws implicated Nakoda peoples and contributed to circulating discourse. In addition to art and photography related to the tourism industry and Indigenous peoples, I also examined all Canadian Pacific Railway (CPR) images concerning travel in the Canadian Rocky Mountains. Produced in Canada and distributed internationally to Europe, Asia, and the United States, these images offered important perspectives on how cultures, landscapes, and technologies were used to market travel in the Canadian Rockies to diverse audiences. Personal collections of tourism entrepreneurs and guides, who sometimes had extensive relations with Nakoda communities, are another group of documents that were considered. Newspaper reports also provided key information on the prevailing discourse of a particular period, and it is for this reason that they were crucial as evidence. Two local weekly newspapers (*Banff Crag and Canyon* and *Stoney Country*) and two regional newspapers (the *Calgary Herald* and *Edmonton Journal*) were analysed.[9]

During the research and writing of this book, a number of key objectives remained foundational, as it was imperative that this study address the absence of published Indigenous histories of the Banff–Bow Valley. This also included a commitment to collaborating with participants and communities to represent Nakoda experiences and histories from their perspectives. The focus of these histories was on how Indigenous actors responded to the colonial constraints that attempted to restructure their lives. In other words, instead of just identifying assimilatory and at times racist policies by tracing the history of colonial bureaucracy and speculating on the impacts in communities, it was of primary significance to this project to determine how local Nakoda peoples negotiated this terrain and managed colonial influences. This book also forwards a theoretical argument that advocates for scholars to consider more flexible understandings of (post)colonial power relations within the context of the Canadian nation state. By engaging with both postcolonial and post-structural conceptualizations of how power is exercised, I consider the effectiveness of various models for interpreting the complexities and contradictions of colonial relationships. Critically, I assess how colonial power can be theorized through different lenses to account for the ability of Indigenous communities to contest, manage, and respond to colonial processes of repression and assimilation.

While this book does have a significant theoretical component, my hope is that it will also speak clearly to a general audience of those interested in Indigenous histories and cultural practices, parks or protected areas, and, more generally, Western Canadian histories. Foremost among this audience are the individuals and community members who participated in this research, many of whom have anxiously awaited this written and interpreted account of their personal histories, perspectives, and stories. The task of speaking to diverse audiences is a difficult one that introduced several overt challenges throughout the research, but especially in the analysis of the material and the writing of these histories. It is my goal that this book contribute to the diverse fields of history, anthropology, and critical works in the sub-disciplines of tourism, sport, and health, as well as Indigenous and Canadian studies. While the focus is on Canadian contexts (and I heed caution in extending evidence beyond this), where appropriate I also regularly draw on international examples. This serves to broaden the scope of this study to connect with relevant theoretical paradigms and historical perspectives about the colonial experiences of Indigenous peoples.

I am aware of the inherent limitations, challenges, and problems associated with a Euro-Canadian researcher writing about Indigenous histories, and I expect that a critical dialogue will emerge from this book. In fact, that is, at least in part, my intention in producing and publishing this research. My hope is that this book contributes to analytical discussions among both Indigenous and non-Indigenous scholars on the theoretical perspectives and the methodological approaches that shaped this historical analysis and underlying processes involved in producing such a text. Ultimately, my personal and scholarly objectives in this research project were to offer understandings of the complicated histories of Indigenous peoples in this region and of the colonial experiences that impacted their communities.

Overview

This book is divided into three distinct components. In the first, which consists only of chapter 1, I establish the theoretical lens that shaped my interpretations of local history and colonial contexts. I centre on the divergent ways in which power relations and the production of colonial identities can be conceptualized. In particular, I engage with the works of Michel Foucault and other related theorists to identify my theoretical perspectives, noting the advantages and limitations of adhering to them. I situate this book in the relevant disciplines and sub-disciplines that it contributes to and exists within. There is a specific focus on how this research addresses some of the significant gaps in scholarship that persist related to the analyses of racial discourse through applying the works of Foucault.

In the second section, which includes chapters 2 and 3, I begin the analyses of local cultural histories with attention to the early historical period, the 1870s to 1920s. In chapter 2, I investigate the incredible changes that Nakoda peoples experienced in the second half of the nineteenth century. Through the history of missionary movements, treaty agreements, and the establishment of the reserve systems, I map the emergence of colonial power structures and the subsequent destructive consequences in Nakoda communities. I argue that introduced regulations furthered cultural assimilation processes through a regime of disciplinary power. Using Foucault's theorizing of disciplinary technologies, more specifically the art of distributions, I demonstrate how the manipulation of time, space, and movement altered the structure of Indigenous lives. The chapter assesses how power was exercised through these colonial systems, but also how some community members at times refused these structures. In chapter 3, I examine the conditions that led to the formation of Canada's first national park and the development of the region. The creation of Rocky Mountains Park (the precursor to Banff) and related conservation discourse had numerous impacts in Nakoda communities. Besides greatly restricting access and curbing subsistence land uses, the exclusion from the park lands also produced another rung of discipline designed to repress cultural practices. Race as a normalizing and dividing practice is considered in theorizing how disciplinary technologies furthered government assimilation strategies.

In the third section, which consists of chapters 4 and 5, a chronological shift occurs to centre on a later period of history, 1894–1980, with an analysis of the development of tourism economies in the Banff–Bow Valley. In chapter 4, the focus is on the various capacities through which Nakoda peoples participated in the tourism industry and contributed to the production of "naturalness" discourse. This chapter details their involvement in the tourism industry and the use of representations of their cultural practices in tourism promotions. I concentrate on the Banff Indian Days sporting and tourism festivals (1894–1960s), which evolved into the region's most important tourist attraction. Along with providing an overview of which events occurred at the Indian Days, I highlight the interactions between tourists, participants, organizers, and performers. In addition to conceptualizing power as a productive, relational, and omnipresent force, I emphasize the importance of consulting Indigenous perspectives to understand power relations in the contexts of colonial societies. In chapter 5, I assess how the Indian Days reinforced, temporalized, and exoticized images of local First Nations and informed the production of "Indigeneity" from 1911 to 1980. While attention is directed to prevailing discourse, this research is also concerned with how Nakoda participants responded to this discourse through their involvement in tourism industries. As well as facilitating a process whereby Nakoda peoples returned to important sites within the parks and reasserted their cultural links to these landscapes, the Indian Days offered unique socio-economic, political, and cultural opportunities. Interpreting the discursive production of Indigenous identities reveals how some community members refused colonial structures and defied limiting definitions of their cultural practices. The festivals are established as key spaces of exchange that fostered identity-making possibilities for Nakoda peoples.

While advocating that scholars take into account particular theoretical perspectives and methodological approaches, the conclusion (chapter 6) offers insight on why the telling of Indigenous histories is so significant in contemporary multicultural Canada. This discussion considers the consequences and contestations that the sharing and learning of these histories may have at localized levels and within the broader Canadian nation state. Finally, I assert that Indigenous histories play a crucial role in building cultural bridges, advancing the objectives of some communities, and recognizing pressing Indigenous land and human rights issues. Acknowledging these histories of colonial violence and repression, which continue to have a devastating legacy in many Indigenous communities, is a foundational step in the processes of pushing forward while simultaneously owning our past.

Chapter One

Theorizing Power Relations in Colonial Histories

Colonial Power Relations

Following from Hall's contention that theory is always a detour on the way to something more important (1997), this research relies on social theory to interpret larger systems of power relations that impacted the experiences of Indigenous peoples. This book is especially indebted to the works of French philosopher, sociologist, and historian Michel Foucault. While I also rely on various other theoretical tools from post-structuralist and postcolonial thought,[1] Foucault's works provide a foundational framework that shapes numerous aspects of this research. Over the last decade, I have become increasingly interested in Foucault's critical studies of social institutions. Most notably, his conceptualizations of power relations, disciplinary practices, and the discursive production of subjectivities have been of importance.

Foucault's understandings of power as a productive force, not just a repressive mechanism that controls and prohibits, has been extremely influential. His conceptions of productive power relations have been especially useful in theorizing how Indigenous leaders and participants in the tourism industry strategically took up various positions to play with cultural forms in stereotypical representations of their cultural practices. Moreover, Foucault's view of power as relational and bottom-up is central to my interpretations of colonial histories. From this perspective, power lies in the articulation of distinctive forms of social life, not in the control of resources by some to affect the lives of others. Power does not only reside with individuals and groups in authority, it manifests itself in a multitude of ways and at different points simultaneously. For Foucault, everyone is part of power relations. Power is not held by one group as it is part of all human interactions – radiating and penetrating throughout all of society (Foucault, 1987). In an effort to undermine the idea of power as a possession, Foucault notes that the state does not have a monopoly over power, because power relations are unstable and fluid. Rather, "one impoverishes the question of power if one poses it solely in terms of legislation and constitution, in terms solely of the state and the state apparatus. Power is quite different from and more complicated, dense and pervasive than a set of laws or a state apparatus" (1980: 158). In theorizing the impacts of state power in Indigenous communities, Mohawk scholar Alfred argues that Foucault's "approach is particularly useful for analyzing the relationship between the state and Indigenous peoples" (2009b: 72). Alfred's research also refers to the effectiveness of Foucault's productive and omnipresent perspectives of power relations when theorizing colonial contexts in Indigenous communities: "This conception of power is not predicated on force. It does not involve coercing or inducing other beings ... Nor does it require a contractual surrender of power, leading to continuous tension between the individuals and the state" (ibid.).

As Markula and Pringle (2006) indicate in their seminal work in sport studies, Foucault's project in the 1970s was to re-conceptualize the notion of power in order to understand the lived experiences of humans and broaden the field of political analyses. This offered new interpretations of the political significance of cultural activities and provided a framework for interrogating the workings of power in specific locations. This view of power did not focus on laws, gender, class, or state apparatuses:

> Foucault was not undermining the social influence of governments, dominant groups or laws, nor neglecting the massive social inequalities that exist yet he thought it more important to understand how power was exercised with respect to the formation and legitimation of these influential social phenomena. He asserted that dominant individuals, groups, corporations and states do not arrive at their position because they have power, but they become influential due to the contingent workings and, at times, tactical usages of "discourses." (Markula and Pringle, 2006: 34)

However, Foucault does acknowledge that patterns of domination do exist in society. For example, the power to punish was established through the actions of the human sciences and put into practice by the state and other corroborating institutions (Foucault, 1977). Despite common misconceptions of his work, Foucault did not ignore these patterns of domination, as he viewed power as a multiplicity of complex force relations that are "embodied in the state apparatus, in the formulation of the law, and in the various social hegemonies" (Foucault, 1978: 93).[2] Relational notions of power are also crucial for understanding how power was exercised in diverse ways in multiple locations. This supports the analysis of power relations on an individual basis and offers a more sophisticated model to theorize the colonial milieu. If power is seen as productive, relational, and bottom-up, a comprehensive appreciation for the complexities of colonial relationships is encouraged. This is exemplified in the actions and opportunities created by Nakoda participants in local tourism economies.

Foucault's notions of power also demonstrated how resistance and refusals could be accounted for in colonial interactions. While postcolonial scholars have become more cautious about rendering colonial histories too simply as uncomplicated narratives of domination and resistance, many representations of such encounters continue to replicate these binaries. In his research on the experiences of First Nations athletes in the sport of ice hockey in Canada, Robidoux (2012) argues that it is no longer useful to focus on resistance to dominant cultural forms in colonial contexts. He suggests moving beyond these dichotomous relationships in order to avoid reducing human experiences. Bhabha (1994) asserts that the problem with using Marxist-based theories in examinations of power in colonial societies is that they reduce the complexities of the sites of struggle and subsequently also the possibilities within them. Rather than emphasizing the oppositions between colonizer and colonized, Bhabha argues, that it is more progressive "to concentrate on the fault lines themselves, on border situations and thresholds as the sites where identities are performed and contested" (1994: 142). From this point of view, the colonizer and the colonized cannot be conceptualized as separate entities that are defined independently. In his comprehensive examination of the networks of surveillance that were implemented by the government to monitor Indigenous communities and repress their cultural practices in Alberta and British Columbia, Smith (2009) also discusses the importance of uncovering these aspects of colonial rule, and of not "examining Euro-Canadian colonialism only to chronicle its history of domination. Rather it is the inconsistencies, the contradictions, the fractures, and the failures of liberalism and colonialism that [should] be examined. The intent in exploring these fault lines [should be] to investigate the possibility of divergent understandings that were never allowed to surface" (24). As Smith and others contend, Foucault's more flexible notions of power relations provides a model for these multiple sites of interaction and exchange.

Problematizing the Use of Foucault

Foucault's understandings of power relations have provided a foundation for some of the most influential postcolonial works (Said, 1978, 1993; Bhabha, 1994). In this respect, Foucault's studies, which examined the processes that produced discourses in Europe, have the potential for further contributions to help unravel the intricacies of colonial power relationships. Despite these significant contributions, the shortcomings of applying Foucault to colonial contexts need to be highlighted up front by specifically defining how I engage Foucault's theoretical tools in this project and the distinct limitations of doing so. Foucault's glaring Eurocentrism means that his scholarship fails to problematize colonialism or understand colonial experiences. Stoler (1995) views this oversight as a missed opportunity. She explains that by short-circuiting empire, Foucault's histories of European sexuality ultimately miss key sites of discourse production and the practices that racialized bodies and produced related fields of knowledge. It is imperative to further unpack this common, but compelling criticism of Foucault. In her infamous critique, Spivak (1988) admits that postcolonial scholars are indebted to Foucault for his innovative approaches to conceptualizing discourse, but she argues that he ignored colonial expansion, its impacts on European society, and how colonialism contributed to the production of distinctly European power/knowledge systems. Loomba (2005) expands this by suggesting that because Foucault's own theories are Eurocentric, they are of limited use in understanding colonial societies. While I agree with Spivak's reading, I differ with Loomba's point, despite the fact that many postcolonial scholars have latched onto this critique over the decades. Claiming that Foucault's works have little or no relevance in colonial contexts discounts the multitude of ways that the disciplinary technologies and practices that were honed in Europe formed the basis of disciplinary institutions in the colonial empire. These institutions were often designed to repress and assimilate Indigenous populations. For example, there are an incredible number of similarities between the ways that space, time, and movements were structured to optimize surveillance and discipline in European schools, prisons, and hospitals and how colonial institutions were organized on reserves for the same purposes by French and British colonial influences in Canada. The fact that colonial disciplinary strategies did not all necessarily follow the same trajectory as European ones – first through physical punishment and other spectacular forms of the state's power over the human body and later more obliquely through the prison and the asylum – does not mean that Foucault's theories of structural and discursive power relations have no relevance in colonial settings. As shown by both Indigenous and non-Indigenous scholars studying colonial relations in North America (Biolsi, 2001; Deloria, 2004; Alfred, 2009b; Smith, 2009; Mason, 2012), Foucault's theories are in fact very effective for understanding particular types of power relations because these colonial structures of power often mirrored European models.

However, not all of Foucault's tools are useful for interrogating colonial institutions, structures, and inequalities, because they centre on European histories and experiences. This is precisely why his theories of discursive power in Europe cannot be directly mapped onto the colonies and the colonial milieu. For example, while Foucault's understanding of how power is exercised through various spatial and temporal arrangements was a valuable contribution, these need to be complemented by postcolonial scholarship that specifically theorizes colonial contexts. Importantly, from my point of view, they should also be accompanied by, and are most effective with, Indigenous perspectives and voices. While the political and cultural configurations of Europe were also worked through in the colonial projects, the challenge for scholars is to avoid uncritically positioning marginalized peoples as simply the product of colonial rule. The key is to demonstrate how these individuals and communities negotiated the colonial constraints they encountered.

Loomba summarizes how postcolonial scholars have developed central aspects of the critique of Foucault's Eurocentric analyses:

> By pointing out how deeply its knowledge systems were imbricated in racial and colonialist perspectives, scholars such as Bernal, Said or Spivak have contributed to, indeed extended, the discrediting of the project of the European Enlightenment by post-structuralists such as Foucault. The central figure of Western humanist and Enlightenment discourses, the humane, knowing subject, now stands revealed as a white male colonialist. (2005: 60)

As alluded to above, this critique most certainly has merit, but many fruitless postcolonial studies have often reified Western subjectivity simply because they are ineffective in presenting marginalized positions and voices. The supposed strength of postcolonial theory is its insistence on offering analysis from the viewpoint of the marginalized, and several key scholars argue that this is necessary when examining the production of identities in colonial histories (Spivak, 1988; Prakash, 1994). However, Jacoby (1995) states that postcolonial theorists constantly accuse each other of complicity with colonial structures of thought, and subsequently their intentions to allow the voices of colonized peoples to be heard are often lost in the rhetoric, as are any legitimate places from which critics can speak. Other scholars have advanced this critique of postcolonial studies. Sivaramakrishnan argues that "postcolonial theory has attended more to elites, ideation, and representations, at the expense of changes in the economic and political spheres – especially everyday practices, micro-political economies, and cultural politics" (2004: 367–8). Specifically referring to Said, Loomba succinctly supports my earlier point concerning marginalized peoples and their perspectives:

> Colonial authority, like any other, is legitimized through a process during which it constantly has to negotiate with the people it seeks to control, and therefore the presence of those people, oppositional or otherwise, is a crucial factor in studying authority itself. Foucault's own work suggests that domination and resistance are inextricably linked. So Said's story about how texts constructed the East is necessarily incomplete without some sense of the specific peoples and cultures it re-wrote, and situations into which it intervened. (2005: 48)

In advocating for a Foucauldian approach, Māori sport studies scholar Hokowhitu extends this critique of Said: "The 'other' in Said's *Orientalism* has no materiality; s/he is a text that is constructed through dominant discourse, whilst the alternative Indigenous discourse is obscured" (2013: 227). As Cruikshank (2005) notes in her renowned anthropological study of Indigenous histories of the Saint Elias Mountains of northern North America, postcolonial histories often provide compelling analyses of imperial institutions and their contradictions, but they have less space for narratives documenting the experiences of individual participants. Responding to Cruikshank's assertion, this book concentrates on and privileges the experiences of Indigenous peoples. Even though I am interested in the experiences of individuals, the focus is on how they have come to have certain experiences. A key component of this analysis is investigating the prevailing discourse and the related production of identities that were shaped in this period of colonial history.[3]

Importantly, I do not draw on Foucault's Western European–centred analyses of discursive knowledge production to understand the experiences of Nakoda peoples. I rely on the diverse postcolonial theories of Indigenous and non-Indigenous scholars and especially the stories of Nakoda peoples to examine these experiences. However, as will be shown through the interpretation of the colonial histories presented in this study, Foucault offered a nuanced tool kit for analysing the links between the production of knowledge or discourse and the exercise of power. Moreover, his understandings of how individuals and groups are positioned in oppressive structures of power relations are also relevant in some colonial contexts. This research specifically borrows from Foucault for these two significant components.

Racial Discourse and Foucault

While some of the works that emerge from postcolonial studies can seem to stand in theoretical opposition to post-structural accounts, as Stoler (1995) asserts, the field of postcolonial studies is greatly indebted to Foucault for broadening the conceptions of racial discourse and related subjectivities.[4]

In contrast to Said (1991), who contends that Foucault ignored racial discourse, Stoler argues that he was deeply interested in the nature of modern racism and the sustained power invested in it. By relying on archival evidence on the colonial control of the Dutch East Indies, she reveals how forms of nationalist discourse drew on and gave force to a wider politics of exclusion. She assesses how racial politics shaped what was possible to know about the boundaries of race in European bourgeois society. As noted, some postcolonial scholars discount Foucault in their analyses of racial discourse because his works focused so intently on Europe and are more clearly linked to discourses of sexuality. However, Stoler provides a convincing argument that reveals why Foucault's writings are relevant in examinations of racial discourse and power relations. Following her contention that Foucault's works on power relations could extend the field of analysis to interpret racial discourse, it is key to indicate where these potential contributions could fit in with the existing scholarship. Before applying specific theoretical tools to localized cultural histories, it is necessary to discuss why the use of Foucault to examine racial discourse is a unique, and potentially controversial, undertaking.

This book attempts to address a significant gap in theoretical scholarship by applying a Foucauldian interpretation of racial discourse through analyses of historical texts. As Rabinow (1984) indicates, history as a discipline has been reluctant to accept the work of Foucault, and as a result, few historians seriously consider his contributions or apply his concepts in their research. In his two most influential genealogies (1977, 1978), Foucault reveals the discontinuities and breaks in discourse as he adopts an anti-hermeneutic approach that rejects the concept that you can determine from fragments a picture of the whole. This positions him in direct opposition to many in the discipline of history (Markula and Mason, 2013). However, there are some historians who have taken up the Foucauldian project in their historical interpretations and analyses of racial discourse (Butchart, 1998; Deloria, 2004; Smith, 2009). Foucault maintained that his works were studies of history, but he was not necessarily a historian. In some respects, this sentiment also articulates my discomfort with locating my research and interests solely in history. This "history of the present" flows in an alternative stream to many historical analyses. As a consequence, I understand that this study will not be easily read by some historians or other scholars deeply invested in Marxism or liberal-humanism traditions.

In response to Foucault's *History of Sexuality Volume I: An Introduction*, Baudrillard (1977) urged us all to "Forget Foucault" in his scathing critique of Foucault's foundational text. Fortunately, many scholars have ignored Baudrillard's facetious contention and have continued to take up Foucault in their analyses of numerous subjects. The most significant examinations of racial discourse that have shaped my perspectives of power relations in colonial contexts come from sociology (Wetherell and Potter, 1992; Jiwani, 2006), anthropology (Stoler, 1995), and history (Butchart, 1998; Deloria, 2004; Alfred, 2009b; Smith, 2009). Following the use of Foucault's writings in various mother disciplines, scholars in the sub-disciplines of tourism, physical activity, and sport studies have also drawn upon Foucault's works. It was through tourism and sporting festivals that Nakoda peoples strategically built relationships with broader Euro-Canadian society and also returned to sacred locations inside Banff National Park during the twentieth century. In tourism studies, which overlaps considerably with the research on parks and conservation, the works of Foucault have surprisingly received little attention despite scholars' interests in the conditions that maintain inequalities and related power relations (Hollinshead, 1999).[5] Until relatively recently, the works of Foucault have also been underused in physical activity, exercise, and sport studies, despite the probability that these subjects lend themselves well to Foucauldian interpretations (Andrews, 2000). There were a number of important foundational works that introduced sport scholars to Foucauldian analyses (Hargreaves, 1987; Andrews, 1993; Rail and Harvey, 1995; Markula, 1995; Cole, 1996; Rinehart, 1998; Shogan, 1999).[6]

Despite the fact that a number of disciplines and sub-disciplines have welcomed Foucauldian-based analyses over the last two decades, significant gaps remain on a plethora of issues. Most notably, there are few principal studies that have used Foucault's theoretical directions in their research on racial discourse. His writings have been widely used in studies on sexuality and gender, but much less frequently in works on racial discourse. By highlighting the more influential studies that have shaped my thinking throughout the research and writing of this book, I identify how this work addresses a significant void in scholarship. The number of studies applying Foucault's theoretical tools and methodological approaches to examinations of racial discourse is limited and there are only a handful of researchers relating this material to their research with Indigenous peoples or, even more generally, in colonial contexts. I have pointed to some of the researchers who provide potential models to take up the Foucauldian project in my analysis of colonial encounters. Through the interpretation of the colonial histories that follow, this book will assess the production of racial discourse related to Nakoda experiences in the Banff–Bow Valley.

Chapter Two

Colonial Encounters: Treaty 7, Missionaries, and the Constraints of the Reserve System

Beginning with the arrival of Europeans to the Banff–Bow Valley in the late eighteenth century, Indigenous peoples began to undergo a series of significant changes that would alter aspects of a well-established way of life that had persisted for millennia. Through the landmark 1877 Treaty 7 Agreement that established the reserve system and missionary movements, a disciplinary power regime emerged that had subsequent consequences for Nakoda communities. Partly through the enforcement of the written terms of Treaty 7, which was instituted by the Canadian government and fostered by agents of the colonial bureaucracy, forms of disciplinary power disrupted the lives of local peoples. Regulations extending from seemingly independent colonial policies worked in conjunction to further cultural assimilation processes. Using Foucault's theorizing of disciplinary technologies (Foucault, 1977), more specifically the art of distributions, I investigate how the manipulation of space, time, and movement altered the structure of Indigenous peoples' lives in ways that attempted to increase visibility, economic productivity, and docility. Assessing the ways in which power was exercised through these colonial systems reveals not only the effectiveness of the disciplinary regime, but also how some community members continued to refuse these constraints by pursuing opportunities to sustain their cultural practices.

Histories of Indigenous Peoples in the Banff–Bow Valley

The Banff–Bow Valley includes the area between the headwaters of the Bow River at Bow Lake and the Kananaskis River, which is south of the current boundary of Banff National Park and at the western border of the Nakoda reserve.[1] Diverse groups of Indigenous peoples lived in and migrated through what is now considered the Banff–Bow Valley. Evidence collected from archaeological research indicates that Indigenous peoples used this landscape for millennia before any European presence. Archaeological studies reveal evidence of semi-permanent settlements dating as far back as 11,000 years (Fedje et al., 1995; Langemann, 2004, 2011). The Nakoda (Stoney), Ktunaxa (Kootenay), Tsuu T'ina (Sarcee), Pikunni (Peigan), Siksika (Blackfoot), Kainai (Blood), Secwepemc (Shuswap), and members of the Cree Nations lived, fished, hunted, gathered, and traded throughout the eastern slopes of the Canadian Rockies for many centuries before the arrival of the first Europeans (Hungry Wolf and Hungry Wolf, 1989). Just before the turn of the eighteenth century, as a consequence of the massive fur-trading networks that were formed in Western Canada, members of other Indigenous groups, including the Iroquois, Nippissing, and the Saulteaux from the Great Lakes and St Lawrence River districts, also began to live and work in the region. While the Banff–Bow Valley has been of importance to diverse groups of Indigenous peoples, the region is of particular significance to the Nakoda peoples who inhabited the foothills and mountain ranges for several centuries and currently have reserve lands near both the northern and southern sections of the valley. Not only has this land been vital to Nakoda peoples for their subsistence land uses, but their spiritual and cultural practices are also anchored in these landscapes (see plate 2).

The Nakoda peoples were members of the Sioux Nation and Assiniboine groups who lived primarily throughout the plains of North America. It is difficult to pinpoint exactly when, many centuries ago, Nakoda peoples split from the larger Sioux Nation and began to migrate towards the plains in the southern sections of what are now considered the Canadian provinces of Saskatchewan and Alberta (Dempsey, 1998). Although it is unclear what motivated the split with the Sioux Nation, it is likely that sickness or migrating bison herds were factors (Whyte, 1985). Later, Nakoda peoples also separated from the larger Assiniboine groups and began to live closer to the foothills and mountain ranges of the eastern slopes of the Canadian Rockies. The Nakoda peoples broke into three bands as they moved west. The Chiniki, Jacob (later Wesley), and Bearspaw bands, as they eventually became known, all preferred to occupy the foothills and mountain ranges. This gave

Nakoda communities access to both the plains and mountain regions for seasonal encampments and hunting grounds.

Oral accounts from members of Nakoda First Nations reveal similar migration histories, but they also emphasize the established presence of their communities in this region. These oral histories reinforce the idea that Nakoda peoples have been living in the Banff–Bow Valley for a significant period of time. As one Nakoda elder explains, "We have been living here on this very land ... from the beginning of time."[2] Another elder provided a bit more detail on their presence in the valley:

> While at times my people did not permanently reside in this area, as for centuries we followed the buffalo herds throughout the plains of North America ... in years of drought or when we had troubles finding the herds ... we would rely on food sources closer to the mountains ... you know like the bighorn, elk and goats.[3]

As the bison herds were severely threatened by the late 1870s, Nakoda peoples began to rely more heavily on mountain ecosystems for their main forms of subsistence. This partly explains why they adapted so well to mountain ecosystems after the bison no longer provided their principal source of food. Their transition to hunting and gathering in the mountains was successful because of their previous experiences of seasonal or periodic reliance on this region for subsistence. Compared to many of the Plains peoples who were forced to make drastic changes to their hunting practices after the collapse of the bison herds, as skilled hunters and gatherers Nakoda peoples adapted well to alternative resources (Snow, 2005). Like the Nakoda, the Shoshone and the Ute also shifted their focus to Rocky Mountain ecosystems when life on the prairies became difficult in the United States due to shrinking bison herds and pressure from Euro-American settlers. In particular, the equestrian Shoshone developed a hybrid lifestyle based on hunting bison in the plains and alpine/subalpine hunting, fishing, and gathering (Spence, 2009).

The arrival of Europeans in the region through the fur trade in the late eighteenth century created new rivalries between Indigenous groups over control of fur markets. This facilitated a shift in balances of power between communities that, through conflict, rapidly extended the territories of some groups while displacing those of others. As Hart (1999) notes, "the period of first white contact was one of jealousy, rivalry and sometimes open hostility at the mountains' foot" (15). This shift of power accounts for the successful transition of the Nakoda to the Banff–Bow Valley. Although the Cree encroaching from the north and the Pikunni from the south had already encouraged the Ktunaxa to spend more time over the continental divide on the western slopes of the Rockies before the presence of Europeans, disputes sparked by the fur trade ensured more conflict in the area (Hart, 1999). Also a consequence of the European explorers and fur traders heading west, the smallpox epidemic ravaged the plains and eventually reached the mountains by the late eighteenth century. This impacted all groups, but especially affected the Pikunni, and they subsequently were not able to assert their presence in the region. These shifts of influence allowed the Nakoda to actively inhabit the Banff–Bow Valley and adjacent regions (Whyte, 1985).

In addition to these factors, the Nakoda also made alliances with neighbouring groups, including the Cree who occupied land north of the Banff–Bow Valley. One Nakoda elder's explanation of this process is related to his peoples' knowledge in producing medicines from plants and animals found in the mountains. At times Nakoda peoples shared some aspects of this knowledge with local groups and often made alliances through these processes.[4] Despite the European presence in the mountains that altered the well-established trade networks supporting extensive networks of Indigenous peoples, Nakoda communities continued to successfully live and work on the eastern slopes of the Rocky Mountains and in the Banff–Bow Valley by assuming numerous adaptive strategies. In the last quarter of the nineteenth century, however, Nakoda peoples began to face additional threats to their ways of life.

Missionary Movements and Treaty 7

The Wesleyan minister Robert Rundle first had contact with Nakoda communities in 1840 and remained in the region for eight years, but it was not until the 1870s that a permanent mission was founded in the Banff–Bow Valley (Dempsey, 1997). Methodist missionaries George McDougall and his son John visited the Banff–Bow Valley in 1873 to determine a suitable location to set up a mission. While the McDougalls were motivated by their desire to "improve" the lives of local peoples, Nakoda perspectives suggest that the missionaries did not really understand their cultures, but coveted their ways of life. In reference to the McDougalls, Hungry Wolf and Hungry Wolf state: "Like those before them, they came with good intentions, but they looked at Stoney

[Nakoda] ways only through European eyes" (1989: 53). Although at times the McDougalls did express a genuine concern for the welfare of the Nakoda communities within which they worked and lived, the "civilizing" and assimilating elements of their mission created several problems for Nakoda peoples.[5]

In 1875, with the help of Nakoda peoples, the McDougalls built a settlement and church on the valley bench of the Bow River at the junction of Jacob's Creek. Although the Nakoda communities welcomed the McDougalls into the area, they sometimes did not comprehend the "civilizing" and Christianizing intentions of their work (Hildebrandt et al., 1996). In addition, Nakoda peoples had difficulty understanding both the missionaries' objectives as well as how they were related to the emerging governments of the new nation. Nakoda chief John Snow explains:

> The government was to educate and civilize the savage. The Church was to Christianize the savage. These three words, educate, civilize, and Christianize, were used synonymously by both the state and the Church. Sometimes it was difficult for my people to recognize whether they were talking to government representatives or Church personnel because it was almost impossible to distinguish between the two. (2005: 28)

Although the relation was not entirely apparent to local peoples, there was a clear alliance between the missionaries and governments in the Banff–Bow Valley. As well as the education and conversion principles that inspired the missionary movements, missionaries sometimes served as conduits connecting government interests with Indigenous communities. Furniss (1995) reveals that similar alliances between missionaries and the federal government also existed in British Columbia during this period. In 1874, John McDougall accepted a government commission to explain to local Indigenous communities the treaty processes and the benefits of agreeing to treaties (Hildebrandt et al., 1996). There was a definite need for governments to exploit the established relationships between missionaries and Indigenous peoples of the west. Their primary concern was the introduction to and preparation of Indigenous peoples for the treaty agreements that would be pursued throughout the decade. Missionaries played significant roles in brokering these arrangements. This was of particular importance in the west, as fewer Euro-Canadians had established relationships with Indigenous communities in comparison to the prairie and Great Lakes regions of the country. This was the case in the Banff–Bow Valley, where the McDougalls used their experience with Nakoda peoples to perform this brokerage function. The McDougalls were viewed by Nakoda peoples as men of God, but not necessarily representatives of the state. They had earned the respect of many community members and were entrusted with negotiating on behalf of the Nakoda peoples in several critical circumstances throughout the ensuing decades (Snow, 2005).

After the Confederation of Canada in 1867, a number of events in the western part of the nation would further shape the lives of Indigenous peoples. In 1870, the Red River Rebellion of the Métis in southern Manitoba raised the consciousness of governments and Indigenous leaders to the growing potential of conflict over control of and access to land and its resources (Pannekoek, 1996).[6] The final sale of Hudson Bay Company lands to the emerging Dominion of Canada in 1870 and the start of construction of the national railway in the early 1870s also had major impacts on Indigenous groups as more Europeans began to frequent their territories. In the autumn of 1874, the North-West Mounted Police (NWMP) added to the European presence in the region. Nakoda peoples initially welcomed the police to the Banff–Bow Valley, as they brought some safety and security by managing the conduct of new settlers as well as reducing the impact of the illegal whisky trade that had plagued some communities (Snow, 2005).[7] When the mounted police were first introduced, their role in the area was not clearly outlined to Indigenous leaders. They were representatives of the government, but they often acted to help local Indigenous peoples. The appreciation and respect that the mounted police had gained in many communities was another factor that encouraged some chiefs to sign the Treaty 7 Agreement (Hildebrandt et al., 1996). Within two decades of Treaty 7, the relationships between the mounted police and local Indigenous communities would be strained as the police eventually came to be viewed as a critical arm of the colonial bureaucracy that greatly restricted the rights and cultural practices of Nakoda peoples.

These significant developments, in combination with the rapid decline of bison herds, caused great concern for Indigenous leaders in the west as well as for government officials in Ottawa. In September of 1877, following decades of abrupt changes that had altered Nakoda ways of life, representatives of the three bands of Nakoda peoples along with John McDougall went to Blackfoot Crossing to negotiate a treaty with David Laird, the lieutenant-governor of the North-West Territories and James Macleod, the superintendent and inspector of the

NWMP. The Nakoda representatives signed Treaty 7 and, under the direction of John McDougall, agreed to several terms that would become the subject of confusion, dispute, and conflict over the coming decades. For years the McDougalls had been trying to convince Nakoda peoples to give up their subsistence land-use practices of hunting, trapping, gathering, and fishing in the foothills and mountains to settle near the mission and pursue a life of ranching and agriculture (Whyte, 1985). Thus, the McDougalls had a vested interest in the Nakoda chiefs signing the treaty. When referring to John McDougall's role as an interpreter for the treaty agreement, Nakoda elder Archie Daniels explicates: "It is thought that McDougall voiced his own ideas, not those of the Stoney" (Hildebrandt et al., 1996: 132). The Treaty 7 Agreement would further reveal the underlying "civilizing" intentions of the missionaries and the colonial bureaucracy. Moreover, the agreements would introduce multiple problems for the Nakoda peoples as the first of the formal policies that would try to specifically limit their practices and rights.[8]

From the perspective of Nakoda communities, Treaty 7 had a number of important components. While Indigenous groups agreed to share land and resources with new settlers, the government secured some land for Indigenous communities and provided critical support in the form of food rations, payments, health care, education, and protection. While some farming infrastructure was included in the case of the agreements with Nakoda communities, they were permitted to continue their subsistence land-use practices on their long-established migrations through the foothills and mountains. As Laird stated, when referring to the rights of Indigenous communities at the time of individual treaty signings, "they would be free to hunt and fish after the treaty as they would be if they never entered into it" (Fumoleau, 1973: 84). Referring to Nakoda understandings of how the treaty would implicate their hunting and subsistence practices, Nakoda elder Lazarus Wesley explains: "If the land for growing wheat was all they wanted, there was no problem. If the Stoneys could continue to hunt as they always had, there was no problem" (Hildebrandt et al., 1996: 79). The groups who participated in Treaty 7 unanimously asserted that they always interpreted the agreement as a peace treaty not a concession of their lands and resources. Nakoda peoples viewed the treaty as an opportunity to protect their cultural practices and decrease the amount of conflict with other Indigenous groups and new settlers, not as a surrender of their lands. In reflecting on the conditions that led to the treaty's signing by their chiefs, Nakoda elders emphasize this point: "They went to Blackfoot Crossing intent on an alliance of peace, to safeguard their territory and to protect their way of life. This would last for as long as the sun will shine, and as long as the rivers flow" (Hildebrandt et al., 1996: 25). While this summarizes some of the key aspects of Nakoda leaders' interpretation of the treaty, not long after it was signed, it became evident that there were several critical discrepancies between the government's and First Nations' understandings.

Part of the confusion around Treaty 7 was a consequence of fundamental differences between British common law and Nakoda understandings of individual ownership of land and its resources. A Nakoda man expresses this differing perspective by stating: "We've never owned the land ... The land always has and it always will own us."[9] Nakoda elder Lenny Poucette explains this perspective, which reflects the conflict between contrasting interpretations of the land and its resources:

> We had very different ideas about the land than the White men that settled here ... You see we shared the land and everything on it with other Native peoples ... like when we would invite the Kootenays [Ktunaxa] from over the mountains to come meet us and go hunting ... We would camp at Banff and they would meet us to hunt in the surrounding areas ... We were happy to share with people that respected the land.[10]

Furthermore, there are numerous discrepancies between the oral and written versions of the agreements because of different cultural practices. As Stanley (1983) suggests, the differences between written and oral cultures can account for many of the inconsistencies that have arisen through informal and formal treaty agreements between North American governments and Indigenous peoples. This can also be seen in the land and resource agreements involving Indigenous peoples internationally (Tuhiwai Smith, 1999; Little, 2004; Stewart-Harawira, 2005). Elder Poucette alludes to some of the important distinctions between oral and written documents:

> It may have caused a bit of problems in the past with the treaties, but our traditional history is not written down you see ... nor are the methods of using and collecting herbal medicine or other important cultural information ... It's not written down ... The true story of all these methods is in our hearts. You may read a book about a person ... you may read a book about how things happened, but it's when you can visualize it within your heart and mind ... that it becomes the truth.[11]

As well as cultural differences, there were also difficulties concerning the involvement of interpreters between the English and the Cree, Nakoda, and Tsuu T'ina languages that were present at the signing. According to Nakoda elders, in addition to being inadequate, no one interpreter fluently understood more than two of the languages. This meant that sometimes documents were translated and conversations interpreted into one language before they could be understood in another (Hildebrandt et al., 1996). All of these conditions contributed to the outright confusion over Treaty 7. These misunderstandings and discrepancies would become more apparent as the treaty began to impact local First Nation communities.

Even though cultural and linguistic differences can account for some of the initial confusion over aspects of the treaty, it is now clear that this agreement was not an attempt by the government to help communities manage the changes they were facing in the late 1870s. Rather, the treaties were opportunities for the government to secure Indigenous lands and to effectively resolve the question of their rights, in order to provide resources to mostly European settlers migrating west and prevent further conflict between groups (Tobias, 1983).[12] This coercion and manipulation by government representatives would have devastating consequences in Nakoda communities. Within a few decades, Nakoda peoples realized that "the treaties were the vehicle through which the government achieved its objective of opening up the west to settlement and commercial exploitation" (Snow, 2005: 33). In essence, the government's primary intentions concerning the treaties were to convince Indigenous peoples to relinquish their land rights and to assimilate them into broader Anglo and Franco Euro-Canadian society. While this became clearer to Nakoda peoples as the decades passed, there was also serious debate among leaders over the key issues at the signing of the treaty. It is important to recognize that all parties involved represented different sets of concerns and perspectives regarding how these agreements would affect their communities. Nakoda chiefs and the leaders representing the Plains peoples were not passive figures who were duped into signing their lands and resources away. Cardinal (1969) argues that Indigenous leaders had much to offer in return for the rights they expected. This position is also supported by the elders of Treaty 7 nations, who assert that their leaders knew that they were in a position to negotiate with the government and that they made significant efforts to improve what they were initially offered. The signing of the treaty did not represent a unanimous agreement by all individuals and groups involved, nor was it anticipated that it would be a peaceful panacea for Indigenous communities. Leaders were well aware of the broken promises made by the government to other Indigenous groups in central Canada, and they also anticipated many of the issues that would eventually develop with the treaty agreement (Hildebrandt et al., 1996). In the fall of 1877, Indigenous leaders demonstrated remarkable foresight regarding many of the issues that would impact their communities, as well as an acute awareness of the broader political and socio-economic conditions.

The Reserve Systems and Assimilationist Institutions

The reservation systems that were implemented across the North American continent had strong assimilatory principles. In referring to reservations in an American context, Field states that "the system incarcerated Native peoples in barracks-style living, instituted massive changes to diet and daily life ... The result was a profound hemorrhaging of their cultural, linguistic, social and economic structures and systems" (2008: 20). In Alberta, Treaty 7 directly targeted the very foundations of Indigenous ways of living by the relocation of their communities to relatively small tracts of land that were defined as reserves. At the signing of the treaty, this was not seen as a large problem for leaders, who were reassured that they could continue their long-established subsistence land uses (Hildebrandt et al., 1996). For Nakoda peoples, this meant that they could continue their seasonal migrations into the foothills and mountain ranges. It cannot be emphasized enough that Indigenous leaders were mostly concerned with access to lands and its resources. The treaty designated 640 acres at Morleyville (later renamed Morley), "conveniently" located around the McDougalls' mission, for each Nakoda family of five. While the size of each parcel of land was not an initial issue for the community, where it was located was most certainly a problem. Some Nakoda bands preferred different locations for their own reserves, but the treaty specified only the land adjacent to the current mission site. This would become the subject of much controversy that is yet to be properly resolved, even in the twenty-first century.[13] As some bands preferred other locations, for reasons that would become more apparent in the first few decades following the signing of treaty, they were deeply dissatisfied with being located at Morley (Snow, 2005).

Figure 2.1 The Morleyville settlement and mission site (1885). In the foreground of the picture is the McDougall ranch and in the background is the mission site near Jacob's Creek. Courtesy of the Glenbow Archives. NA-4967-69. (Photographer unknown)

By 1880, bison had almost disappeared from the Canadian prairies, but the implications of the treaty for Nakoda peoples had yet to fully emerge. Even though the First Nations that lived on the plains of southern Alberta, mainly the Tsuu T'ina, Pikunni, Siksika, and the Kainai, were forced to rely heavily on the government rations after the collapse of the bison herds, Nakoda peoples continued to hunt in the foothills and mountains, where large mammals were still prevalent. In the first few years following the treaty, Nakoda communities were actively encouraged by the government to continue to provide for themselves through their hunting, gathering, and fishing in order to save ration funds greatly needed in the south on the open prairies (Snow, 2005). The scarcity of bison actually facilitated the government's desire to relocate many communities onto the new reserves. In order for individuals or families to receive their food rations, they needed to remain on or in close proximity to the reserve. Although some Nakoda families did move to the allotted land near the missionary settlement on the Morley reserve to raise cattle and plant crops, in contrast to the Plains peoples, the majority of community members continued their migrations in the mountains and maintained their subsistence land-use practices.[14]

By the time of the complete collapse of bison populations, most of the Nakoda peoples had agreed to winter at Morley and would leave the reserve to hunt and gather throughout the spring, summer, and fall seasons. Despite the disapproval of the McDougalls and the Indian agent, there was also a small group of Nakoda peoples who preferred to live at the headwaters of the North Saskatchewan River on the Kootenay Plains, approximately 125 kilometres north of Morley (Snow, 2005). Led by John McDougall, the few budding agriculturalists who remained at Morley for the summer and fall seasons had serious difficulties raising crops due to poor soil and the late frosts that were so common in the foothills. Agricultural lifestyles were foreign to Nakoda peoples and few decided to conform to this way of life. As one Nakoda elder indicated, in addition to the extremely tough growing conditions on the reserve, the stationary aspects of agriculturalist living still had little appeal for most of the community.[15]

The 1885 completion of the national railway was the first in a series of events that would drastically constrain the possibility of Nakoda peoples continuing their subsistence land uses. The rail lines through the Banff–Bow Valley not only disturbed wildlife, but they also brought an influx of farmers, ranchers, and miners (Hart, 1999). Between 1885 and 1888, Nakoda hunters encountered significant challenges and the scarcity of large mammals made it increasingly difficult to feed community members. Even after the attempts to restrict Nakoda peoples to reserve lands, the government continued to use and abuse these lands to meet their development objectives. The experience of Nakoda peoples in Alberta was representative of many of the relationships between Indigenous communities and provincial or federal governments in Canada throughout the nineteenth and twentieth centuries. The seminal work of Alfred (1995) provides an excellent example of how these processes were a significant component of policy and approach by the Canadian nation state in its relations with Indigenous communities. In his research on the expropriation of Mohawk lands in western Québec as part of the international seaway development project of the late 1950s, Alfred effectively argues that these experiences not only further damaged relations between the federal government and Kahnawake Mohawk peoples, but also forever altered local relationships between them and their lands.

By 1885, the same year the railway was completed, the Indian agents who lived in the communities, both to provide surveillance and to serve the peoples' needs, were instructed by the Indian Affairs Branch to introduce a pass system in an attempt to restrict the movements of local peoples. The pass system threatened people with fines or even incarceration if they were found off the reserve without the proper documentation and this had consequences for local subsistence practices. While these regulations were enforced, Smith (2009) directly questions the legality of the pass system that was implemented at Morley and other Treaty 7 communities: "It was well known during the period, even not considering the promises guaranteed in the treaty signings, [that] the NWMP had no legal grounds to restrict the movements of local First Nations" (72). Despite the fear that the pass system introduced, individuals responded to the regulations that threatened their cultures in various ways. In Montana, at the turn of the twentieth century, even though Flathead Indian subsistence practices were rebranded as illegal, hunting was one of the most noticeable manners that Indigenous peoples expressed their opposition to many of the changes that were forced into their communities (Ross, 1998). Initially, the pass system was not strictly policed at Morley, and so, similarly to what occurred in Montana, many Nakoda groups ignored it and continued their seasonal hunting in the mountains. Nevertheless, by 1889 restrictions were tightened through a number of methods and it became progressively more complicated for community members to leave the reserve for lengthy periods (Snow, 2005). However, budget cuts that decreased the amount of government food rations and the low production from reserve lands from either agricultural or ranching endeavours gave Nakoda communities few options but to rely on hunting, fishing, and gathering. In the face of worsening conditions, decades after the signing of the treaty, some Nakoda peoples successfully continued their subsistence practices in the mountains. At times these practices took Nakoda individuals considerable distances away from the reserve.

The necessity of Indigenous communities remaining in the vicinity to collect their food rations allowed government agents and missionaries to pursue their assimilation strategies with a new level of intensity. Although severe cuts were made to the rations that were promised to communities in the treaty, there appeared to be a healthy budget committed to the promotion of the "civilizing" mission (Snow, 2005). Even though the missionaries had been performing services at the church and teaching classes at the school they built with community support since 1875, local participation in these institutions was not very high. By the late 1880s, with more Nakoda peoples forced to remain on reserve lands because of the strict pass system and their need for rations, the Indian agent and John McDougall eagerly encouraged local church and school attendance. By 1894, many community members were attending church services, and despite objections from Nakoda leaders, school attendance was made mandatory by the government. Tobias contends that "school attendance was of vital concern to the government, for education of the Indian child was the keystone of the 'civilizing' process the reserve was supposed to perform" (1983: 48). In addition to a Christian education, the Indian agent at Morley was directed to encourage local peoples to adopt more aspects of the lifestyles of European agriculturalists.

While the government and missionary objectives were often meant to improve the socio-economic and health conditions on the reserve, underlying assimilation intentions directed all of their initiatives. As a Nakoda elder indicates when specifically referring to the process at Morley:

> I think that the early government and the Indian agents … and definitely the missionaries generally had some good intentions … but they just did not understand our way of life … We lived in a similar way for a long time … and we did not really want to change our ways to be more like the Europeans.[16]

Figure 2.2 Instructors and students at the mission school in Morley (1885). Reverend John McDougall is in the centre of the front row. Courtesy of the Glenbow Archives. NA-1677-1. (Photographer unknown)

Snow reinforces this view:

> Granted they were trying to improve the conditions on the reserves, but at as little cost as possible and with no recognition of, much less respect for, our heritage. No attempt was made to suit goals to specific local needs and conditions ... Their policy was rooted in the nineteenth century white-man's assumption that his own civilization was far superior to any other lifestyle. (2005: 78–9)

Not only did the assimilation objectives of missionaries and government agents directly impact the livelihoods of Nakoda peoples in the last quarter of the nineteenth century, but the initiatives and policies that they put into action would become a major source of disruption and conflict for generations to come. These drastic changes contributed to considerable loss in Nakoda communities. Unfortunately, with the missionary movements and schools, some Nakoda individuals lost their names, which expressed meaningful aspects of their cultures. Their names were replaced with Christian, Hebrew, and western European monikers (Jonker, 1988). This symbolic renaming process was only the outer surface of what became a deeper rupture: the attempt to strike at the very core of Indigenous values and practices by targeting almost all aspects of their cultures and identities. Despite these colonial initiatives, Indigenous peoples all over the continent had to endure assimilationist strategies in order to continue to celebrate their cultural practices. Field's work with Hupa peoples in California emphasizes the collective resilience of Indigenous peoples:

> The allotment of reservation lands, boarding schools, officially managed agricultural and vocational training programs, aggressive Christian missionary activity, and the negative effects of well-intentioned white reformers were, however, unable to convince most of the Hupa to abandon their religion (at least not entirely) or their predilection to fish and gather other wild plant and animal foods. (2008: 110)

Treaty 7, and the colonial policies and institutions that followed it, enabled a system that was designed to erode Indigenous rights and cultural practices, with no regard for the fragmentation, repression, and loss in their communities. In spite of the powerful desire and concerted efforts of many Nakoda peoples to refuse the assimilation processes they encountered, these networks of colonial assimilation eventually changed some fundamental aspects of their ways of living, as important cultural knowledge was threatened and at times lost in these processes.

A Colonial Regime of Disciplinary Power

The histories of the colonial policies that Nakoda peoples confronted as a consequence of Treaty 7 and the implementation of the reserve system can be considered a form of disciplinary power. Disciplinary technologies, through the manipulation of time, space, and movement, produced a regime of disciplinary power that began to structure many aspects of Nakoda communities. In *Discipline and Punish: The Birth of the Prison*, Foucault examines how organizing and structuring space, time, and movement have shaped individuals and bodies with the values of discipline. He identified discipline as "neither an institution nor an apparatus; it is a type of power, a modality for its exercise, comprising a whole set of instruments, techniques, procedures, levels of application, targets, it is a 'physics' or an 'anatomy' of power, a technology" (1977: 215). By focusing on how disciplinary technologies were applied to various institutions in French society, including the medical and educational systems, the prison, the military, and the industrial complex, Foucault demonstrated the extent to which disciplinary power was exercised in a modern regime. His influential work can be considered a history of these different disciplinary institutions. The criteria put forth by Foucault regarding the emergence of disciplinary power can also be mapped onto the reserve in order to indicate how these technologies came to influence the lives of Indigenous peoples. Disciplinary technologies that formed aspects of colonial power produced a set of knowledges about where and how to live for the administrators of the reserves. Revealing Nakoda perspectives about how this occurred in their communities can show how the facilitation of policies and regulations represented different technologies of discipline that were designed to control the lives of Indigenous peoples within the matrix of broader "civilizing" and assimilating processes.

Foucault argued that the ordering of space was a key aspect in the production of disciplined bodies. He theorized the art of distributions, including the categories of enclosure, partitioning, and function, to further specify how space can be organized to facilitate the exercise of power through discipline (Foucault, 1977). Following Treaty 7, Nakoda peoples were relocated onto the reserve at Morley under the pretext that this would secure land, but this became a significant mechanism to enclose Nakoda communities and control the spaces where they lived. Foucault viewed enclosure as a critical aspect of discipline. He asserted that for discipline to be optimized, spaces needed to be enclosed. Enclosure was required to differentiate the purposes of one space over other similar spaces, or the "specification of a place heterogeneous to all others" (Foucault, 1977: 141). Reserves established what was considered Indigenous land and thus defined it from other properties that often bordered these newly formed spaces. For example, it was important to distinguish the reserve from lands that would eventually be situated along its edges, including territories that were designated for Euro-Canadian setters to establish farms or for government exploitation of natural resources. Tobias (1983) indicates that the reserve, which he considers the heart of Canada's policies regarding Indigenous peoples, was conceived of as a social laboratory where communities were confined to minimal spaces so they could be controlled and prepared to cope with Euro-Canadian ways of life. Smith (2009) supports this point in his analysis of how the reserve functioned in Treaty 7 communities, but also how surveillance was optimized in the Canadian reserve system:

> A fundamental difference in the Canadian case is the creation of isolated enclaves called Indian reserves which represent a degree of segregation and potential for surveillance unparalleled in the British empire ... These reserves created a physical geographic border in addition to the cultural and racial barriers in evidence elsewhere. (8)

The enclosure of space, which was achieved by the relocation of communities to the reserves, was a crucial aspect of exposing Indigenous peoples to disciplinary technologies. If reserves formed large tracts of lands that allowed Indigenous peoples to continue their migration patterns over considerable distances, their communities would not have been as susceptible to disciplinary technologies. Subsequently, enclosure was a key part of the assimilation tactics advanced by arms of the colonial bureaucracy.

It is also imperative to recognize that enclosure is not entirely about space. As Shogan (1999) notes, enclosures also reinforce hierarchical boundaries and to this effect can also serve to define peoples in spaces, as well as the spaces themselves. This is an important distinction, because the reserve systems not only designated spaces where Indigenous peoples would live, but as a consequence they also established barriers between these spaces and others which determined who could live within them and under what circumstances. These boundaries can be considered attempts to control the lives of Indigenous peoples, but also define the individuals who occupied these constructed spaces. The reserves marked Indigenous land from property occupied by settlers or the government, but this demarcation was one further step towards asserting control over the definitions of Indigenous cultures and identities.[17]

Foucault recognized that enclosure was merely one action in organizing space to facilitate disciplinary practices. After a particular space was enclosed, it would then have to be partitioned into micro spaces to optimize discipline. Foucault stated that partitioning spaces would "eliminate the effects of imprecise distributions, the uncontrolled disappearance of individuals, their diffuse circulation, their unusable and dangerous coagulation" (1977: 143). Although this reference was to spaces occupied by the military, health, and education systems, this description applies well to some of the government's imagining of the reserves, which were intended to erect spatial constraints for Indigenous communities and control how they lived in those spaces.

Reserves were eventually divided into multiple districts with meeting locations, a ration-distribution site, and subdivisions for church lands and schools. Where residents could live and work became increasingly constrained. The landscape was reordered, structured, and controlled. In reference to the reservations that were instituted throughout North America, Dakota Sioux scholar Phillip Deloria explains that Indigenous peoples who were "used to moving as they chose, found themselves confronting a far more static life, one in which they lived within a bounded landscape, among a web of centers established by church and state, in ways that could be tracked and restricted" (2004: 27). This was certainly the case at Morley, where the reserve was increasingly divided based on the activities that should be performed in such spaces. For example, the reserve was broken into property distributed to certain families where they could erect their tipis or build small cabins, lands designated for church and school activities, spaces for growing crops or ranching, and a location where rations were issued.[18] The disciplinary advantages of partitioning spaces are to discern "where and how to locate individuals, to set up useful communications, to interrupt others, to be able at each moment to supervise the conduct of each individual" (Foucault, 1977: 143). As Nakoda reserve lands were remade to facilitate this process, the church, school, and ration-distribution site took up central locations where they were woven into the centre of Nakoda communities.

According to Foucault, the objective of partitioning spaces was to increase the functionality of the enclosed sites and redefine them as productive or useful. Functional sites are spaces where efficiency can be optimized. As spaces and the activities to be performed within them are increasingly specified, the responsibilities of individuals occupying the particular places are more defined. Foucault described the changes instituted in French industrial workshops during the late eighteenth century: "Production was divided up and the labour process was articulated, on the one hand, according to its stages or elementary operations, and, on the other hand, according to individuals, the particular bodies, that carried it out" (1977: 145). Snow refers to how the reserve at Morley became a site to control and increase the efficiency of the activities of Nakoda peoples:

> The treaties all aimed at locating my people on reserves in order that we might be collected into easily controllable communities. Only there could we supposedly become self-supporting through agriculture, only there could schools be constructed for our children to teach them "industrial pursuits," to develop "moral improvements," and to learn "social grace." (2005: 35–6)

It is through constructing functional sites that discipline improves the productivity of peoples. After spaces are enclosed, partitioned, and their functionality is increased, the next level of asserting discipline involves attempting to control how time is spent in specific spaces.

Foucault asserted that discipline was almost always "adopted in response to particular needs" (1977: 138). Following the move of Nakoda peoples onto reserves, it was then essential to initiate a new way of life so that the reserves could become productive sites that would sustain local communities and thus save government funds designated for food rations (Hildebrandt et al., 1996). Foucault found that temporal limits were often asserted in conjunction with spatial constraints (1984). Beginning in the 1880s, there was pressure on Nakoda peoples to alter their long-established subsistence land-use practices, to remain on the reserves, and to conform to European agriculturist lifestyles. A considerable amount of effort by governments, missionaries, and Indian agents went into encouraging Nakoda peoples to assume these abrupt changes. This included training in agricultural techniques and Christian education. Under this new regime of disciplinary power, the lives of many community members were structured differently. It is important to recognize that before the arrival of Europeans on the eastern slopes of the Rockies, Nakoda peoples had structured lives that revolved around migrations associated with food sources, seasonal weather patterns, and significant cultural practices. As one Nakoda elder explained:

> Our lives were always organized by the seasons ... They determined when we would move in search of different game and when and even where we would set up our camps ... When we got together with other groups for social and cultural reasons ... it was the seasons that decided most aspects of our lives.[19]

The agricultural pursuits on reserves that were strongly encouraged by governments and their agents necessitated a restructuring of time and altered a way of life that Nakoda communities had developed through centuries of experiences and knowledge of the land, local conditions, and ecosystems.

The changes to lifestyle that were facilitated by the move to reserves had major implications for Nakoda peoples. Foucault argued that discipline was achieved by a rhythmics of time. This meant a structuring and refining of time with certain degrees of precision. On the Morley reserve there was a newly enforced temporal regime. Within a few short years of moving to the reserve, Nakoda peoples were confronted with a new set of time tables that were based on the lives of European agriculturalists and ranchers. These lifestyles were completely foreign to community members. Time was increasingly divided and specified by activities. Under this new structure, there was time allotted for planting and harvesting crops, for butchering domestic animals, for meeting with community members, for attending church services and schools, and for all other activities that were deemed important or appropriate by the colonial administration. Time was micromanaged in efforts to increase the productivity of life on the reserve. In addition to taking classes about how to improve agricultural techniques, Nakoda peoples were also instructed in domestic responsibilities and the appropriate uses of leisure time (Snow, 2005). There is an importance to not wasting time and maintaining high levels of productivity in a disciplinary regime: "In the correct use of the body, which makes possible a correct use of time, nothing must remain idle or useless" (Foucault, 1977: 152). Despite the extended periods over which Indigenous communities produced a particular structuring of activities that formed their quotidian lives, in the last two decades of the nineteenth century, the physical and cultural practices of Nakoda peoples were reinterpreted through a colonial lens as unimportant or wasteful of time.

The control of time was also linked to methods of exercising power by colonial agents. It was through this reorganization of the temporal constraints, which profoundly impacted community members, that power was exercised by colonial systems. Foucault explicitly indicated the connection between time and power: "Time penetrates the body and with it all the meticulous controls of power" (1977: 152). The reordering of time, which was fostered by the reserve system, extended the impacts of the spatial constraints that continued to expose Nakoda peoples to technologies of discipline.

The control of space, time, and movement were deeply integrated in disciplinary regimes. Controlling the modalities of movement were the consequences of space and time constraints. For Foucault, time and movement constraints are linked. Time considered of good quality was spent with the body constantly engaged in movement. Constraining the movements of individuals and groups was a crucial aspect of asserting discipline over bodies. Foucault describes the intentions of exercising discipline over the movement of peoples: "Discipline fixes; it arrests or regulates movements; it clears up confusion; it dissipates compact groupings of individuals wandering about the country in unpredictable ways; it establishes calculated distributions" (1977: 219). In her research on historical and contemporary experiences of Native women in the penal and legal systems in the United States, Salish scholar Ross (1994, 1998) indicates that restricting the movements of Indigenous peoples and the undermining and transforming of their cultures was a critical strategy of colonialism. She demonstrates how the pass system, instituted in 1877, not only helped Euro-American-controlled authorities imprison Flathead Indians and protect the interests of settlers and ranchers, but it also became a key method of social control and surveillance in the state of Montana. As in the United States, constraining the movements of Nakoda peoples was an important aspect of increasing surveillance and advancing colonial assimilation objectives. In addition to time and space controls, the movements of Nakoda peoples were reordered under the new regime of colonial discipline.

How did constraints to spatiality and temporality change the ways Nakoda peoples moved in and through landscapes? These constraints were attempts to structure when and how Nakoda peoples moved about reserve lands and even where they engaged in various activities. In this manner, they partly determined the distributions and micro movements of Nakoda peoples on the reserve, which, as indicated, had a series of consequences. However, perhaps more importantly, this structure also implicated the macro movements of Nakoda peoples to and from reserve lands. The pass system began to restrict the movements of individuals from and between reserves. This required Indigenous peoples to seek permission to leave their reserve to hunt or for any other purpose. A pass was then either granted or denied based on the subjective decision of the local Indian agent (Bracken, 1997). While, at least initially, the pass system was not strictly enforced at Morley, by 1889, under the direction of the government, the Indian agent and missionaries began to adhere to the system by discouraging Nakoda peoples from leaving the reserve through several methods, including refusing to provide rations to guests and visitors from other reserves. It was the opinion of the colonial administration that spending time off the reserve served as a distraction to local peoples and also a barrier to assimilation strategies (Snow, 2005). Foucault revealed how distractions impeded productivity and the functioning of discipline. As one would expect, the missionaries also had a vested interest in the reinforcement of regulations restricting the movements of Nakoda peoples. The pass system was implemented with these intentions, despite the fact that the hunting, fishing, and gathering practices of local Indigenous groups were supposed to be secured by the signing of Treaty 7.

The regulations constraining the movements of Nakoda peoples not only interrupted their subsistence land uses and cultural practices, but also altered their patterns of interaction with other Indigenous groups. Through a complex network of conflict, trade, and collaboration, over centuries Nakoda peoples had formed alliances with other Indigenous groups that were based on mutual respect and the sharing of knowledge, land, and resources. At times these alliances were actively improved and solidified with intermarriage between groups. Whyte (1985) notes that the positive relationship between the Stoney (Nakoda) and the Kootenay (Ktunaxa) was formed through hunting together in Ktunaxa territories on the western slopes and Nakoda lands closer to the plains during different hunting seasons. The Nakoda peoples also had similar relationships with members of the Cree Nations and other groups. As elder Poucette details:

> Over many generations we had become good friends with the Kootenay [Ktunaxa] and the Cree ... We even had relationships with the Blackfoot too ... who at times were our traditional enemies ... We would learn from each other ... hunt together, share knowledge about the mountains and ... also get together to celebrate our cultural practices ... These interactions were important for many reasons.[20]

These relationships between Indigenous peoples were formed over many centuries and were considered deeply sacred to all the groups involved. However, the government opposed such interactions between groups. Another elder expresses his opinion on the dual purpose of limiting the movement of Nakoda peoples through the pass system and other regulations:

> I feel that the Indian Act and all the restrictions … were about controlling the interactions between peoples as much as it was about assimilation … The outlawing of the Sun Dance and spiritual events was to do with limiting interaction between Native peoples as much as anything else … both on the individual reservations … and in the ways that they controlled how we lived and where we went … but maybe more importantly how we could communicate with the other tribes. I know I've read about the assimilation ideas … and that may be true … but I think that controlling the way we interacted with each other was also the intentions of the government's restrictions.[21]

Although the government was clearly not comfortable with large meetings where Indigenous groups could share their experiences, express forms of dissent over the treaty agreement, and discuss the various changes to their ways of life, discouraging their cultural practices was also a fundamental objective of limiting these interactions (Hildebrandt et al., 1996). In conjunction with the spatial and temporal constraints, limiting the movement and interactions of Nakoda peoples was also a significant component of exercising assimilation strategies through disciplinary practices. All the constraints produced by government policies and implemented by the agents of the colonial administration would fundamentally change many aspects of Nakoda cultures throughout the ensuing decades.

Refusing Constraints

Improving productivity, which is one of the main objectives of discipline, can only be accomplished if docility is increased and power is disassociated from the body. Foucault summarizes this point:

> Discipline produces subjected and practiced bodies, "docile" bodies. Discipline increases the forces of the body (in economic terms of utility) and diminishes these same forces (in political terms of obedience). In short,

> it dissociates power from the body; on the one hand, it turns it into an "aptitude," a "capacity," which it seeks to increase; on the other hand, it reverses the course of the energy, the power that might result from it, and turns it into a relation of strict subjection. (1984: 182)

This analysis of disciplinary power was derived from Foucault's studies of select disciplinary institutions in French society. Prisons, military operations, hospitals for the mentally ill, and industrial workshops, which certainly did not represent the most unruly of institutional locations in society, were all constructed spaces where the implementation of disciplinary technologies could be optimized. As Foucault indicates, carrying the exercise of power to bodies was also facilitated in such locations (1975). In contrast to the levels of discipline outlined by Foucault, this absolute position of strict subjection was not reached on the Morley reserve. Ultimately, the colonial assimilationist intentions that motivated policies during this period were only partly successful at conforming Indigenous peoples to European ways of thinking and living. In the case of Nakoda peoples, assimilation policies appeared to have been even less productive than they were in some other Indigenous communities. This is partly the consequence of the Nakoda peoples being allocated reserve lands that were incompatible with the agricultural objectives set out by the colonial administration, but also because of their desire and resolve to resume the physical, cultural, and spiritual practices that were established by generations of their ancestors.

As with many Indigenous communities throughout the country, Nakoda peoples continued to refuse some of the spatial, temporal, and movement constraints that the colonial administration attempted to assert over their ways of living. Despite the strength of the disciplinary technologies applied by the colonial presence in the region and its impacts on changing their ways of life, Nakoda peoples sought out opportunities to refuse this discipline and pursue their subsistence land-use practices. Far from occupying positions of complicity and docility, many Nakoda peoples continued to hunt, gather, and fish in the mountains as well as interact with other groups and celebrate their cultural practices. Referring to the regulations placed on aspects of their culture in the late nineteenth century, one Nakoda elder stated: "Even while the governments tried to change how we lived with their rules ... when there were opportunities ... or a need to do so ... many of us continued to hunt in the mountains like we'd always done."[22] Like the Nakoda in the Banff–Bow Valley, other Indigenous groups in the United States also used hunting as a form of resistance against various changes in their communities. As Spence (1999) suggests, in response to the presence of miners and settlers on their lands, the systematic attack on treaty rights, and the diminishment of reservations, some groups continued to hunt in parks. They used the park as a space to express their resentment to government policies that threatened their communities and ways of life. However, as Jacoby (2001) notes, by the turn of the twentieth century, Indigenous communities attempted to assert their subsistence rights in increasingly intolerant environments where Euro-American perspectives of conservation principles were dominant and governments were aligning with special-interest groups in their policies to limit Indigenous subsistence practices. In general reference to the often diverse constraints that were operating on reserves throughout North America, Deloria argues that "these structures represented a colonial dream of fixity, control, visibility, productivity, and, most importantly, docility" (2004: 27). He suggests that these dreams, which embodied the aspirations expressed by government assimilation policies, were only partially realized.

Despite the limiting aspects of constraints that did restructure the lives of Indigenous peoples, they also provided opportunities to reinterpret landscapes in manners that asserted them as their own. These new spaces and the conditions that shaped them certainly constrained Nakoda peoples, but they also produced opportunities to refuse these structures. As Foucault contends, increased levels of discipline also generate more possibilities to resist structures that produce disciplinary technologies (1978). Powwows, reunions, political meetings, hunting trips, and festivals such as the Banff Indian Days are only a few of the ways that some Nakoda peoples created openings to redefine their ways of living, their cultures, and the very lands they occupied. While seriously constrained by colonial structures, these opportunities also represented new forms of resistance and possibilities for many community members.

Conclusion

It must be emphasized that colonial power relations cannot be understood or interpreted through a one-dimensional lens. This analysis of a disciplinary regime only represents some of the colonial strategies that were employed and therefore only some of the levels of disciplinary power that were exercised over a particular socio-historical period.

There are several levels of discipline simultaneously operating in any given society at any time (Foucault, 1980). This chapter does not map the entire strategic field of power relations that impacted Indigenous peoples during this period. Conversely, it has examined some of the intricacies of colonial power and, importantly, the ways it was specifically exercised in relation to Nakoda peoples.

This research is more concerned with how technologies of discipline came to implicate Nakoda peoples than it is with specifying the sources of discipline. Thus, little attention is given to explanations of the philosophies behind the government policies designed to assimilate Indigenous peoples. Rather, the focus remains on how disciplinary constraints fundamentally altered a way of living in Nakoda communities. In order to properly outline how a disciplinary regime was established through the mechanisms of the colonial administration, it is necessary to determine how the treaty agreement, missionaries, and colonial institutions produced constraints on space, time, and the modalities of movement as part of a larger regime of disciplinary power.

The decades that passed from the initial contacts with Europeans until the impacts of the treaty agreement began to constrain the lives of Nakoda peoples represents a dynamic period of history for Nakoda communities and other Indigenous groups across the nation, one marked by interactions, exchanges, and negotiations. Nakoda peoples were faced with difficult circumstances that would alter many aspects of how they lived in the Banff–Bow Valley and the eastern slopes of the Canadian Rockies. Even though these changes would have serious consequences for their communities, throughout this period they managed these challenges with an incredible degree of adaptability and resilience. Unfortunately, in the following decades Nakoda communities would continue to encounter additional socio-economic, political, and cultural hardships in their complex and prejudicial relationships with the colonial bureaucracy.

Colour Illustrations

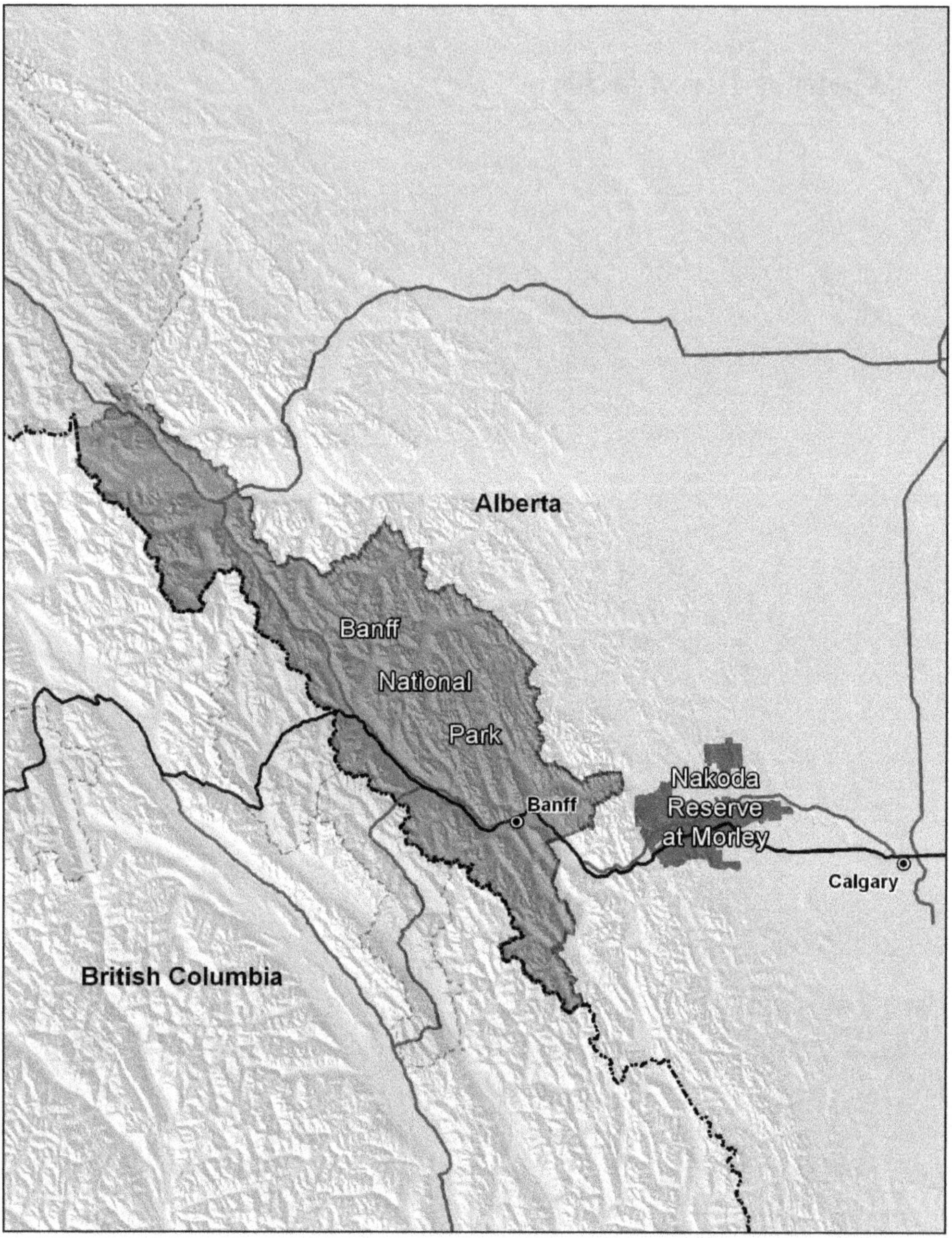

Plate 1. Current boundaries of Banff National Park and the Nakoda Reserve at Morley. The lighter shade of green denotes the boundaries of Jasper, Yoho, Kootenay, and Glacier National Parks. Map was created by Ali Buckingham, Parks Canada.

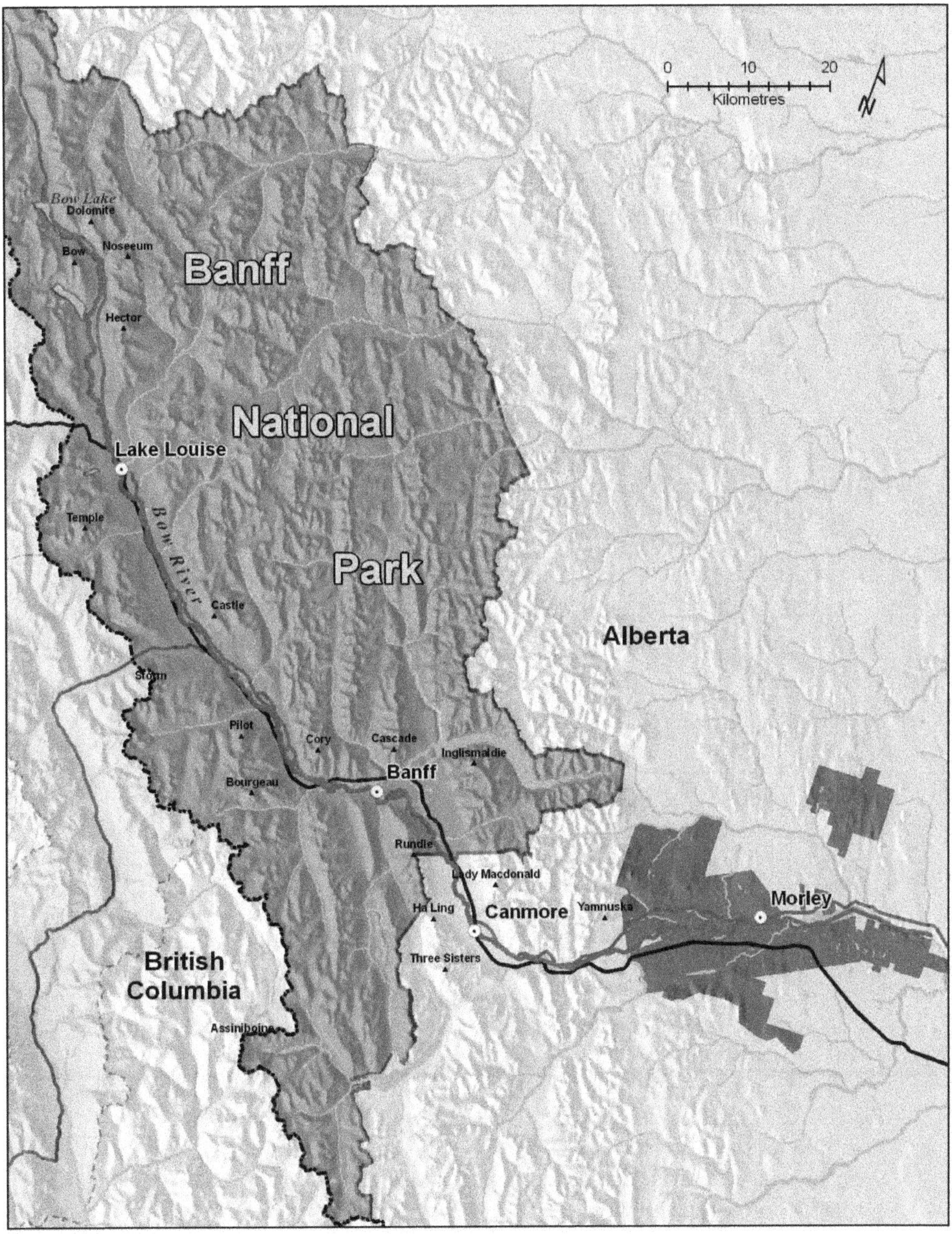

Plate 2. The upper section of the Banff–Bow Valley with current boundaries of Banff National Park and the Nakoda Reserve at Morley. Map was created by Ali Buckingham, Parks Canada.

Plate 3. CPR tourism poster (1897). This promotional material was clearly designed for an affluent tourism market. This scene features urban, sophisticated characters dressed in Victorian attire situated in a dominant position above nature in classic picturesque style. Their gaze is directed towards the Banff Springs Hotel. Courtesy of Canadian Pacific Corporate Archives. A. 20297. (Artist unknown)

Plate 4. CPR tourism poster (1928). This image promotes some of the expansion of accommodation infrastructure that occurred after 1914. In contrast to the Banff Springs Hotel, bungalow camps became affordable accommodation options for middle-class tourists. Meeting the demands of middle-class tourists also diversified the recreational opportunities offered in the region. Courtesy of Canadian Pacific Corporate Archives. BR. 176. (Artist: Charles J. Greenwood)

Plate 5. CPR tourism poster (1933). This promotional image featuring a precolonial representation of Indigenous peoples was internationally distributed to numerous markets on several continents. Courtesy of Canadian Pacific Corporate Archives. A. 6521. (Artist: Morley Rigal)

Plate 6. CPR tourism poster (1920). This promotional material is an example of a precolonial representation of Indigenous peoples. The image focuses on exotic regalia, the homogeneous label "Indian" is italicized, and the figure's off-centre position displaces analysis and avoids direct engagement with viewers. This image features Nakoda man John Hunter. Courtesy of Canadian Pacific Corporate Archives. A. 6517. (Artist unknown)

Plate 7. CPR tourism poster (1939). Focusing on exotic regalia, such as the peace pipe, this promotional image is an example of a representation that temporalizes Indigenous peoples as part of a bygone past. Courtesy of Canadian Pacific Corporate Archives. A. 6143. (Artist unknown)

Chapter Three

The Repression of Indigenous Subsistence Practices in Rocky Mountains Park

For centuries, Nakoda communities lived throughout the Banff–Bow Valley with established subsistence uses of the region. The emergence of Canada's first national park and the corresponding protected areas had significant consequences for local Indigenous communities. Through the formation of Rocky Mountains Park (RMP), conservation discourse was produced during the period from the treaty making until the early 1920s. This discourse was central to both the creation of the parks system and the extension of restrictions placed on the subsistence land uses of Nakoda communities. Conservation discourse was also intricately linked to the implementation of levels of discipline designed to foster the repression of cultural practices. Competing ideas of conservation and related knowledges informed dividing and normalizing practices that were used to further government policies designed to assimilate the cultures of Nakoda peoples.

The Formation of Rocky Mountains Park

Before we expand on the early history of RMP, which emerged through the federal government's efforts to secure lands surrounding a series of hot springs near the current location of the Banff townsite, it is critical to recognize that these unique geologic formations had significance to local Indigenous communities for many centuries before the arrival of Europeans to the region. Some early histories represent the late-nineteenth-century discovery of the Cave and Basin mineral hot springs by railway workers in a manner that attempts to erase the Indigenous presence in the Banff–Bow Valley by failing to acknowledge their extensive use of the region. While recognizing the presence of Indigenous peoples in the Banff–Bow Valley, some historians have claimed that it was only Europeans who understood the value of the hot springs. For example, in 1948, popular historian and park employee Mabel B. Williams wrote: "It is probable that the Indians had known of the existence of the springs for years, but as usual they ascribed their peculiar behaviour, as they did everything they could not understand, to evil spirits, and regarded the spot as a place that was wise to avoid" (1922: 11). In discussing Williams's histories of the parks and her failure to acknowledge the previous and current presences of Indigenous groups, MacEachern (2011) notes that she must have considered how her histories of presence or absence in the parks were incredibly convenient, as "erasing the native presence in the parks allowed her to start the parks' history with European exploration and the fur trade, better positioning the parks in the broader history of Canadian nation-building and so defining them more easily as part of our national birthright" (42). Since the 1960s, the majority of historians have acknowledged the long history of Indigenous peoples in the region. When discussing the first Europeans to locate the hot springs, historians often utilize the stylistic device of putting the words "discovery" into quotation marks. While this does underscore the arrogant and absurd notion that diverse groups of Indigenous peoples who had lived in the Banff–Bow Valley for millennia had not located the hot springs, this strategy does little to develop the histories of Indigenous use of the hot springs. In order to recognize the presence of Indigenous peoples in the region and respect their experiences, it is critical to consult local perspectives of their communities' historical uses of the hot springs.

In direct contradiction to what some Euro-Canadian authors contend, in addition to other Indigenous groups who at times have migrated through or lived in the Banff–Bow Valley, Nakoda peoples had significant cultural practices related to their multiple uses of the hot springs. Similarly to Canada, there were attempts to erase Indigenous presences near the hot springs in Yellowstone National Park in Wyoming, but it is clear that Indigenous peoples had diverse uses of the springs and the surrounding areas (Spence, 1999). In 1954, Nakoda Chief Tatanga Mani (Walking Buffalo), or George McLean, elaborated on the importance of the hot springs to local Nakoda peoples and how it was believed a great spirit lived in the waters:

> They would bathe in the springs because of the medicine in them. Then they would drop something in the water as a sacrifice, as a thank you to

> the spirits for the use of their water ... But since the white people came, the strength has gone out of the water. That mysterious power that comes from the spirits is there no more. Probably the white peoples do not pray to get well. In the old days, the Indians used to pray to the spirits to cure them of their sickness. Then they were healed by the mysterious strength of the waters. (Clark, 1960: 95–6)

Other oral accounts also suggest that the hot springs were sacred sites for Nakoda peoples. One elder indicated that, as a result of the unique microclimate produced by the warm waters, the lands surrounding the springs were vital locations for gathering herbal medicines.[1] Nakoda woman Margaret Snow stated that her grandparents told her of the important cultural significance of the hot springs for their communities. Marriage and initiation ceremonies, which celebrated young men and women reaching adulthood, were held at sites near the Cave and Basin mineral hot springs.[2] Nakoda elder Rollinmud also spoke of these sacred ceremonies:

> Yeah, the Cave and Basin was a place for baptisms that we would do. So the youth and the younger generations were blessed there ... Everybody was, but the young generations were blessed there to become an adult ... It was about getting as much knowledge for the journey of life and knowledge to understand the earth.[3]

Based on oral accounts, it is clear that the hot springs were important cultural sites for Nakoda communities in many respects. In addition to the significance of the area for its healing potential, medicines, and cultural ceremonies, the springs represented a key meeting location where Nakoda peoples, and sometimes other Indigenous groups, would gather at certain points throughout their seasonal migrations.[4] It is essential to establish Indigenous uses of the hot springs before elucidating the conditions that led to the formation of RMP. Nakoda perspectives of their histories provide understandings of why the creation of the park and the subsequent limitations on access to the region had implications that extended far beyond constraining their subsistence land uses in the Banff–Bow Valley.

Early Europeans in the region also visited the hot springs, including geologist James Hector in 1859 and prospector Joe Healy in 1874, but it was not until railway workers reported a series of hot springs in the fall of 1883 that the immediate vicinity would be of concern to the federal government (Hart, 1999). Recognizing the potential of the springs and the surrounding landscape, Frank McCabe, William McCardell, and Tom McCardell immediately made efforts to secure ownership of the hot springs and proximal lands by developing them as a homestead and a mineral claim. In 1885, following a dispute between several parties that lasted over a year, the federal government settled the conflicting claims by creating a 26-square-kilometre reserve surrounding the Cave and Basin mineral hot springs (Nelson, 1970). Direct parallels can be drawn between the foundation of national parks in the United States, as Spence (1999) details about the 1872 foundation of Yellowstone: "The creation of the first national park had less to do with ideas about undisturbed nature than a desire to keep the region's scenic wonders out of the hands of private interests" (55). Based on two earlier American examples, the Hot Springs Reservation in Arkansas (1832) and Yellowstone National Park (1872), the Banff Hot Springs Reserve was part of the Canadian government's first initiative to establish federal protected areas. Just two years later, on 23 June 1887, the area was expanded to 673 km^2 and Rocky Mountains Park, Canada's first national park, was formed. The expansion of the park would soon have important consequences for local Nakoda communities.

Conservation Discourse and Competing Knowledges

In 1885, the same year that the Banff Hot Springs Reserve was created, the pass system was introduced to monitor and restrict the migrations of Indigenous peoples across the country. In Nakoda communities, this was the beginning of a period where movements from their reserve were increasingly constrained. Although the pass system initially was not strongly imposed at Morley, a significant factor motivating the enforcement of these restrictions in years to come was the formation of the RMP. The Rocky Mountains Park Act specified that the forceful exclusion and removal of "trespassers" who did not adhere to the new park regulations was critical to the early development of the park.[5] Indigenous subsistence land uses, including hunting, gathering, trapping, and fishing, became a source of conflict between park managers and local Nakoda communities (Whyte, 1985). At the time of the creation of the Banff Hot Springs Reserve, the majority of Nakoda peoples continued their subsistence land uses in the mountains, as they considered them their right affirmed by the 1877 treaty agreement. Nakoda elder Lazarus Wesley explains their understandings of how the creation of the park infringed on their rights to hunt in the mountains: "At the time [1877] nothing was ever mentioned about the cutting up of the land here and there into recreational areas and parks. The government didn't tell them it would eventually be doing this. It is because of these special areas that we can't go hunting" (Hildebrandt et al., 1996: 90). The government never consulted with or informed Nakoda peoples about the formation of the reserve or the national park. This lack of consultation continued to bring Nakoda peoples into direct conflict with park policies and those who enforced them (Snow, 2005).

The knowledges that repositioned the hot springs as a potential tourism site were jointly produced by the government as well as individuals and organizations that held a vested interest in its development for this purpose. These knowledges stood in direct opposition to the ways local Indigenous communities imagined the hot springs. As demonstrated by their extensive uses of the location for centuries before the European presence in the region, Nakoda understandings of the springs as sacred spaces were informed by very differing foundations of knowledge. These contrasting conceptualizations of this site would be one of several conflicts between tourism producers and Indigenous peoples that would justify the dividing and normalizing practices throughout the coming decades.

In 1886, the government's Department of the Interior sent a biologist, W.F. Whitcher, to report on the state of the mountain ecosystems. The Whitcher report, as it was known, directly implicated the hunting practices of local Nakoda peoples, as well as depredations by foxes and wolves, in the decline of the large game mammals in the region. In addition, the report recommended the establishment of limited hunting seasons and the hiring of police officers and forest rangers who would strictly enforce regulations with fines and penalties (Foster, 1978). In his history of grass-roots conservation movements in Western Canada, Colpitts (2002) notes that Europeans were blaming local Indigenous hunters for the lack of big game as early as the late eighteenth century. When Whitcher made his recommendations in 1886, he did not consider the rights of Nakoda communities that were solidified through the treaty agreement, suggesting that "exceptions of no kind whatever should be made in favour of Indians. Those who now invade that territory are stragglers and deserters from their own reserves, where they are well cared for in food and clothing at the public expense" (Binnema and Niemi, 2006: 729).[6] The Whitcher report led to the first wildlife regulations in Canadian national parks. They did not, however, serve to maintain all mammal and fish populations. Instead, the regulations were designed to sustain the region as a sporting playground, rather than preserve a healthy and intact ecosystem. By the early 1890s, both CPR representatives and the government recognized the value of creating a sporting paradise to the development of local tourism economies. In 1895, partly based on Whitcher's assessment, Park Superintendent George Stewart recommended in his first official report that Indigenous peoples be excluded permanently from the park because of the threat to wildlife. Motivated by the creation of Algonquin Provincial Park in Ontario (1893), Stewart also asked for an expansion of RMP to protect wildlife especially around the southern section of the park, next to the Nakoda reserve.

With the completion of the railway, the increasing number of sportsmen and women attracted to the region created further interest in the restriction of Indigenous hunting and fishing in the park. Indigenous subsistence practices were in direct opposition to the sports code of etiquette that specified that "big game" was not to be eaten but used for sport and hunting trophies. The differing objectives for hunting often formed an entirely separate code for hunting practices (Bouchier and Cruikshank, 1997). Referring to the Western Canadian context, Loo contends that "with the recreational use of wildlife established as normative, wise use and waste were defined in different terms, ones that marginalized those who hunted to eat rather than those who hunted for trophies" (2006: 45). Not surprisingly, this sporting ethic, which originated in urban elite Euro-Canadian understandings of landscapes, was quite foreign to Indigenous peoples (Gillespie, 2002). The sporting ethic, which was inherently linked with conservation discourse, aimed to "conserve" large mammals for sportsmen and women. It was also this ethic that supported harsh and, at times, completely unfounded critiques of Nakoda hunting practices. Indigenous subsistence practices were regularly deemed wasteful by European standards. Based on cultural knowledges formed over millennia of experiences, hunters often took large quantities of game when opportunities were presented. It must be noted that many Indigenous peoples, but especially the Plains peoples, believe that animals offer themselves at key moments to hunters. Based on intricate relationships formed over millennia between mammal species and the people who rely on them, there are strong spiritual components to subsistence hunting practices and the ethics that guide them for Nakoda peoples.[7] In comparison to sport hunters, a differing sense of ethics directed their hunting practices. This made it easier for Euro-Canadians to portray Nakoda hunters' practices as wasteful or detrimental to conservation policies (Colpitts, 2002). While Krech (1999) contends that Indigenous peoples did significantly contribute to the demise of animal species like the bison and the beaver through their participation in colonial mercantile systems (and this is an important point), other research convincingly indicates that Indigenous knowledge systems had built in methods to ensure the conservation of animal and plant species, even though they were not characterized as "conservation" from a European lens (Field, 2008).

Drawing on examples across the country from this period, Loo (2006) notes that even though their rights to fish and hunt were guaranteed by treaties only a few years earlier, Indigenous peoples were targets of condemnation by sport and game clubs as well as related authorities. By 1893, strong opposition was mounted against Indigenous hunting in the mountains by gun and hunting clubs located throughout much of what would become the province of Alberta in 1905 (Dempsey, 1997). As Smith (1999) notes, in 1893 the Calgary Rod and Gun Club identified the importance of enforcing the pass system to conserve local game populations for the future use of Euro-Canadian hunters. The impact of the railway, increased numbers of sport hunters, as well as mining and timber operations were often discounted as factors in the decreasing populations of large mammals. Despite these influences, Indigenous peoples became the main target of sport-hunting organizations of the period. These organizations were powerful advocates that at the time outweighed any conservation voices in the region. As a result of their influence, sport hunting groups were able to lobby the federal government to increase hunting and fishing restrictions on local Indigenous peoples. The importance of sportsmen and women to the tourism economy, which was growing rapidly at the beginning of the twentieth century, aligned them with major tourism producers, such as local entrepreneurs as well as the CPR, and entrenched the power of sport-hunting organizations that had been established over several decades. This was clearly the case in the Banff–Bow Valley, as tourism entrepreneurs like Jim Brewster often complained about Nakoda peoples hunting in or near the park. In 1905, Brewster criticized the hunting practices of the Nakoda, claiming that "there is no discrimination in their shooting ... Rams, ewes, and lambs all look alike to the Indian and if a whole herd is cornered up they are all exterminated" (Loo, 2006: 44). He requested that the Nakoda bands be moved into the prairies away from the Rocky Mountains. The merit of Brewster's concerns do not, of course, warrant much consideration. He was deeply invested in protecting large game, as these resources were imperative to his own hunting and outfitting businesses, which he marketed to affluent sport hunters and tourists for many years.

Although produced two decades earlier, the Whitcher report is also part of the same stream of evidence during this period. The report not only condemned Nakoda hunting practices but also connected these practices to conservation discourse, situating Indigenous peoples as the central target of emerging conservation movements committed to preserve fish and mammal populations for the pleasure of sport hunters and the benefit of the tourism industry. In this case, biological science was taken up in ways that produced knowledges which contributed to conservation discourse that effectively excluded Indigenous peoples and their ways of knowing. The findings of the report, founded in the rigour of scientific inquiry, added to the support for the exclusion of Indigenous peoples from park lands and the repression and assimilation of their cultural practices. As Loo argues (2006), while wildlife management was highly localized until the late nineteenth century, the state took an increasingly active role in the twentieth century. Ecology and game management were powerful discourses that emerged out of the biological sciences and began to shape conservation practices and principles. Conservation policy effectively marginalized local uses of wildlife, and in this sense it was part of the colonization of Canada. Unfortunately, this would not be the last time that the rigours of scientific and ecological knowledge were used by the administration of parks and protected areas to exclude the presence of Indigenous peoples and their related subsistence practices. Throughout the twentieth century in Canada, due to conflicts with newly created conservation principles, Indigenous peoples have been effectively displaced by the foundation of a number of parks and protected areas.[8] As Sandlos reveals, even during the post-war period, the complex links between scientific discourse and state objectives were entangled as the Canadian Wildlife Service and "its scientists were more than willing to frame their scientific studies and management programs in terms of the administrative priorities of their bureaucratic masters" (2007: 241). This continued to ensure that Indigenous communities were displaced and their subsistence practices marginalized throughout Canada.

In his research on conflicts that arose in the formation of reserves and parks in the southern portions of Yukon Territory, Neufeld (2011) indicates that by the 1920s animals began to be commodified as an economic resource in the region. Big-game outfitting businesses were established and trapping permits were encouraged, but there was no acknowledgment of the subsistence reliance upon hunting of many local Indigenous communities. As early as the 1940s, the number of conflicts between Indigenous subsistence practices and the tourism industry increased, as big game needed to be protected for these developing businesses. While soldiers, construction workers, and prospectors were all depleting large mammal populations, the subsistence practices of Indigenous communities were targeted by conservation regulations. The Canadian government did set aside large tracts of land in the south-western portion of the territory for the protection of big game, but hunting was forbidden to preserve various species in anticipation that they would become tourist attractions. Consequently, Indigenous communities were displaced as the practices that sustained them were made illegal.

While no hunting was permitted in RMP in 1890, it was not until a few years later that the Indian commissioner notified the North-West Mounted Police (NWMP) about government and special-interest-group concerns over Nakoda subsistence hunting practices (Snow, 2005). Over the next few years, the movements of Nakoda peoples were more closely monitored. In 1893, the Indian agent was directed to inform the police if any individuals were missing from the reserve. Indian Affairs specified that Indian agents were to be very attentive to "the movements of their Indians," and the police were to investigate any anomalies (ibid.: 82).

While it is clear that several groups did combine their efforts with the objective of limiting Nakoda subsistence land practices in the mountains, there were certainly individual exceptions to the strident opposing voices that were so audible during this period. There are examples of government officials, police, and missionaries who openly defended Nakoda subsistence practices against the unjustified charges of stakeholder groups such as sport-hunting organizations (Binnema and Niemi, 2006). Of course, Nakoda peoples also greatly resented the manner in which their subsistence practices were (re)imagined as unethical and illegal. One example of their objection to these processes is in a 1907 letter to the federal government where Nakoda peoples express their resistance to the game laws and remind the government of its treaty commitments to protect their subsistence practices (Snow, 2005).

In 1902, the boundaries of the park were extended to cover 11,400 km^2. This massive expansion greatly affected Nakoda communities, as their hunting grounds were almost entirely swallowed up by the extension of park lands. Rollinmud explains the impact this began to have on their communities: "It cut off all the circulation that was providing us of life ... which is our game and berries ... Anything that's in the mountains is brought back and is preserved. When we lost access to the area this meant straying away from all of our roots and our physical and spiritual energy."[9] In the park's annual report in 1903, Nakoda hunters are directly blamed for decreases in populations of large mammals. By 1909, under rising pressure from sport-hunting organizations and stakeholders in the local tourism economy, the government introduced game wardens into the park. The government's keen interest in curbing Nakoda hunting in the region was exemplified by their selection of Howard E. Sibbald as the first park warden. In addition to being the Indian agent at Morley from 1901 to 1904, Sibbald was not an advocate for Nakoda subsistence land uses. His position on the issue is reflected in his annual report in 1903: "As long as they can hunt, you cannot civilize them ... With the exception of a few of the younger ones, they are no more civilized now than they were when I first knew them, and I blame hunting as the cause."[10] The selection of Sibbald as the first game warden is a clear indication that the government viewed Nakoda subsistence practices as a problem to be solved. Moreover, Sibbald's appointment also reveals that the government intended to prohibit the subsistence land uses of Nakoda peoples to appease the interests of sport-hunting organizations and, ultimately, the tourism industry. Finally, with the support of J.B. Harkin, the commissioner of Dominion Parks, in 1913 a game preserve was declared on the southern border of the park directly north of the Nakoda reserve. The preserve was designed to protect big-game populations, including deer, bighorn sheep, and goats. This severely inhibited Nakoda subsistence practices in one of the last remaining locations for Nakoda hunters (Foster, 1978).

Paradoxically, in 1912 the CPR actively began to promote the exceptional hunting and fishing opportunities in the park to international audiences. These opportunities became one of the region's largest draws for early tourists. Again, scientific-based studies and reports were used to document and provide support for discourse that subjugated Indigenous peoples and their ways of knowing. In this case, parks explicitly endorsed a conservation ethic that was deeply linked to knowledges produced by and through individuals who were invested in the tourism industry. These particular ways of understanding conservation later informed dividing and assimilating practices. The conservation ethic of the period was deeply connected to the discourse that positioned Indigenous peoples as illegal "trespassers" and "poachers" on their own land. The conservation of large mammals to satisfy sport-hunting organizations and tourism producers was a key objective of government policies designed to limit the subsistence practices of Nakoda communities. Ultimately, the expansion of the park and the enforcement of regulations greatly restricted access to the region for Indigenous peoples. Relying on the conservation discourse, tourism producers, government directors, and park officials excluded Nakoda peoples and other Indigenous groups from living in key protected areas on the continent and practising their subsistence land uses. Although it was in direct contradiction to the treaty agreement and it required several decades to implement, by the mid-1920s, the restrictions had ensured that few Nakoda community members relied on hunting, gathering, or fishing as their main forms of subsistence (Snow, 2005).

Conservation principles were also used to exclude Indigenous peoples in numerous national parks and protected areas throughout the United States from as early as the 1870s (Spence, 1999; Keller and Turek, 1999; Burnham, 2000; Jacoby, 2001; Cruikshank, 2005).[11] In the United States during this period, there were incredibly similar processes unfolding concerning Indigenous communities. As Spence meticulously details in his histories of the first US national parks, the parks were created because "outdoor enthusiasts viewed wilderness as an uninhabited Eden that should be set aside for the benefit and pleasure of vacationing Americans" (1999: 4). As a consequence, the foundation of the first national parks necessarily entailed the removal of Indigenous peoples, precisely because their subsistence and cultural practices did not align with Euro-American understandings of "natural" landscapes. In 1872, the Yellowstone Park Act incorporated lands where several Indigenous groups were exercising their off-reservation treaty rights to hunt, fish, and gather. Spence (1999) argues that the removal of Indigenous peoples from Yellowstone National Park set a precedent for the creation of further conservation spaces in the United States with the same founding principles. In this respect, Yellowstone not only was the first example on the continent of the removal of communities to preserve "nature," but it also provided a model for the displacement of Indigenous peoples from national parks in the decades to come. Parallels with the experiences of other Indigenous groups reveal a pattern of exclusion that was part of regional and national policies throughout the continent rather than an isolated occurrence in Yellowstone and the

Banff–Bow Valley. Also similarly to the Nakoda experiences in Banff, Spence demonstrates that park officials in the 1880s collaborated with the Indian Service, the military, and the federal judiciary to displace several groups of Indigenous peoples from Yellowstone. During the 1920s, cooperative efforts were also made by park rangers, Montana state game wardens, and reservation officials to remove the Blackfeet from Glacier National Park and restrict hunting practices in the park and on their reservation (Burnham, 2000). These collaborations among Euro-American individuals, groups, and institutions effectively displaced Indigenous communities and, at the very least, marginalized their subsistence practices.

To parallel what occurred internationally for Indigenous peoples, during this period colonial governments, particularly in Africa and Asia, were also pursuing similar policies concerning Indigenous peoples. Under the guise of "conservation" and "wildlife management," Indigenous communities were displaced, access to lands were denied, and their subsistence practices were either severely restricted or in some cases rebranded as illegal. In his analysis of conservation movements in Bengal, India, Sivaramakrishnan contends that "the colonial regime's policies for forest management, hunting regulation, and disciplining tribal people invented social categories and also filled them by means of criminalization, displacement, or paternalist isolation of specific groups" (2004: 370). There are a number of excellent international studies on the exclusion of Indigenous peoples from protected areas and parks (Rangarajan, 1996; Chatty and Colchester, 2002; Neumann, 1998). In most cases, their exclusion was precipitated by conflicts between their subsistence practices and the protection or management of wildlife. In an American context, Spence (1999) argues that the foundation of the first national parks occurred simultaneously with and was influenced by developments in nineteenth-century Indian policy, especially the creation of the reservation systems. In other words, the production of discourse around conservation and preservation supported the assimilatory objectives of the government by the ways "nature" and the spaces designated to preserve it were founded and exemplified in the first national parks. Consequently, it is crucial to link conservation processes to assimilation objectives that were concurrently pursued by governments and other collaborative members of the colonial bureaucracy. Across North America and in other colonial environments internationally, there were further rationales behind the intentions to limit the subsistence and cultural practices of Indigenous peoples.

Cultural and Subsistence Practices as Threats to the Colonial Bureaucracy

Tobias (1983) contends that the ability of Indigenous peoples in the Canadian west to continue subsistence land-use practices was particularly irksome to the federal government. As outlined above, although a number of factors led to the policies opposing Nakoda hunting practices in the Banff–Bow Valley, in most Indigenous communities in the west, the reasoning behind the government restrictions on their subsistence practices and seasonal migrations was less convoluted. If groups or individuals provided their own subsistence from hunting, gathering, and fishing, the ration system no longer functioned properly, as it was designed to ensure that Indigenous peoples needed to live close to, and rely on, ration sites. Hunting and subsistence practices also stood in direct opposition to the agricultural systems implemented by the government. Most important, if communities were left to move as they chose, they would not be as susceptible to the cultural repression and assimilation strategies that were under way on most reserves in the west by the 1880s.

In 1885, the government began to directly repress specific cultural practices of Indigenous peoples in the west. By prohibiting Sun Dances and Potlatch ceremonies, the government sought to reinforce capitalist notions of private property and discourage any practices that were viewed as "uncivilized" through a Euro-Canadian lens. Select cultural practices were seen as obstructing or opposed to a white way of living. As Bracken notes, "to be white is to reside in one place and practice agriculture. It does not include roving around and neglecting property" (1997: 72). If Indigenous groups placed value in or experienced pleasure from engaging in their own cultural practices, they may reject the structured and constrained lives that were instituted by assimilation policies. While initially government agents were apprehensive about military and physical uprisings, they eventually became just as concerned with political and cultural forms of resistance. While the banning of the Potlatch targeted the communities on Canada's west coast, the prohibiting of the Sun Dance impacted the Plains peoples, including the Nakoda. In the 1890s, Indian agents and the mounted police used section 114 of the Indian Act to ban the performing of Sun Dances. By 1914, stronger efforts were made to eradicate the cultural practices of the Plains peoples as it became illegal to wear Indigenous dress or perform traditional dances.[12] As well as prohibiting Indigenous forms

Figure 3.1 Nakoda hunters at the Banff Indian Days camp grounds near Banff townsite (1910). Pictured from left: John Simeon, Eli Rider, Eli Rider's mother, John Salter and Ben Kaquitts. Courtesy of the Whyte Museum of the Canadian Rockies. V263-na-3254. (Photographer: Byron Harmon)

of dance and music on reserves, government regulation also sought to strongly discourage cultural performances for tourists at festivals. The Department of Indian Affairs' 1914 amendment to the Indian Act was precisely designed to target the wearing of traditional dress and cultural performance as it related to attendance at festivals like the Banff Indian Days or the Calgary Stampede.

Through a Euro-Canadian government lens the Sun Dance was reinterpreted as a pagan festival where Indigenous peoples worshipped the sun and sometimes engaged in forms of self-torture. Government officials and agents of the colonial bureaucracy also viewed this particular custom as a barrier to their Christianizing procedures. Lazarus Wesley clarifies the purpose and significance of the Sun Dance to Nakoda peoples:

> It is a time of acknowledging our blessings and to give thanks. Just like the birds of feather who make their nests in the trees and sing their sweet songs praising the Creator, so do the Indian people. They make a nest in the Sun Dance tree. They think of it as representing the Creator. They see it as a tree of life. It is a family representation and they rejoice at these Sun Dances. They rejoice during the beautiful summer season that they survived another harsh winter. The Sun Dance was seen in this concept to give thanks and praise the benevolence of the Creator. (Hildebrandt et al., 1996: 153)

Rollinmud also shares his perspective of the Sun Dance: "The Europeans never really did understand it … It is a gathering to share the wealth of mother earth and to thank the creator for all that life is … It is sacred because it is believed that the creator could communicate to the people that are there."[13] The sweat lodges, which were also prohibited by the government, were important in Nakoda cultures. From his perspective, Nakoda elder Poucette explains the value of the sweat lodge: "We used the sweat lodges for spiritual guidance and cleansing for a long long time. It is about our spirituality, it is about renewal. For me it is all about opening up our hearts and having the opportunity to heal each other."[14]

In addition to disrupting long-established cultural practices that embodied profound cultural meanings that extended to all aspects of Nakoda ways of living, the bannings of the Sun Dance and the sweat-lodge ceremonies were extremely harmful in that they broke up the unity of communities and the relations between different Indigenous groups. As well as forming social gatherings around these practices, these ceremonies were important celebration and bonding opportunities for Nakoda peoples. Furthermore, hunting and other cultural practices such as the Sun Dance fostered interaction and meaningful relationships with other groups.[15] When movement between reserves was restricted and Nakoda cultural practices were prohibited, aspects of relationships were also severed in Nakoda communities and between Nakoda peoples and other Indigenous groups.

Ross's (1998) research reveals how the banning of the Sun Dance also became a major issue for Indigenous groups just south of the Canadian border. She documents how Indigenous peoples in Montana were denied their culture as well as material resources. Federal policy had outlawed Indigenous spiritual practices, and in the Northern Plains it was the Sun Dance ceremony that was targeted. However, similarly to the groups in the Canadian Rockies, Indigenous peoples in Montana also resisted these unjust policies. The regulations prohibiting Nakoda cultural practices eventually had calamitous impacts in their communities. However, throughout the first few decades of the twentieth century, Nakoda peoples continued to produce opportunities to celebrate their significant practices among themselves on or near the reserve. As seen in a 1915 photograph of Nakoda man John Hunter preparing for the Sun Dance ceremony on the Nakoda reserve (figure 3.2), many of these practices simply moved outside the gaze of missionaries and Indian agents. Despite the restrictions, Nakoda peoples also strived to maintain relationships with other groups by interacting with them as often as possible (Jonker, 1988). While these opportunities were considerably constrained by the regulations, and became less frequent for many decades, the prevalence of Sun Dances, sweat lodges, and other practices such as powwows at Morley in the twenty-first century, speaks to both the importance of these practices for Nakoda peoples and their determination to maintain them as a part of their communities.

In addition to viewing subsistence and cultural practices as a barrier to colonial processes to assimilate and repress Indigenous peoples, the federal government also recognized the importance of dismantling tribal political systems. According to federal policies, as early as 1869 Indigenous forms of government were intended to be replaced by elected councils. To encourage communities to adopt the council system, the government offered communities that agreed to elect councils a number of additional authorities (Hildebrandt et al., 1996). By the 1880s, the band council systems were strongly advocated by the government, and many communities did conform to them in order to secure more autonomy in decisions over local issues. The choice to adopt an elected council had a large impact on communities. As Tobias argues: "The elected band council was regarded as the means to destroy the last vestiges of the tribal life, the traditional political systems" (1983: 46).[16] Alfred (2009b) argues that the systematic attacks on traditional forms of government facilitated some of the most destructive consequences in communities throughout the entire colonial period.[17]

Reforming Indigenous communities to an elected council system was a key step in furthering government assimilation objectives and part of larger dividing and normalizing practices. Although Nakoda

Figure 3.2 Nakoda man John Hunter prepares for the Sun Dance ceremony near the Morley reserve (1915). Courtesy of the Whyte Museum of the Canadian Rockies. V263-na-3147. (Photographer: Byron Harmon)

peoples switched to an elected band council in the 1880s, they found that the government increasingly intervened in their local matters. Snow suggests that the government asserted a great degree of control over the councils, often determining who would be considered "acceptable" as elected members. This significantly altered the political structure in communities, as the government favoured individuals who represented its positions in the council. Through these processes the government not only devalued the established Indigenous political systems, but also gained insight and power over any political decisions that were made in Nakoda communities. The government facilitated a new system that was completely foreign to Indigenous peoples and then asserted a significant amount of control over political processes in communities by infiltrating the councils and influencing key decisions. Just a few decades following the signing of Treaty 7, the federal government systematically changed the political processes that shaped communities and used this influence to further its cultural repression and assimilation objectives. In his influential critique of political corruption on the Nakoda reserve at Morley, Reilly (2010) clearly links the federal government's late-nineteenth-century efforts to transform traditional political systems to many of the challenges that Indigenous governments encounter in the twenty-first century. He argues that the corruption of Indian agents and the favouritism they displayed towards certain family groups that supported their assimilating institutions ushered in new systems of local politics that would have severe consequences for generations to come as they eroded traditional methods of accountability in tribal governments. He states that an "extremely autocratic and unfair system of governance was the role model for future elected chiefs" (140). While it is clear that Reilly's research does present limited Eurocentric understandings of legal and political systems, he convincingly connects early colonial-government polices to contemporary political corruption in ways that recognize the disrupting impact of colonial assimilation strategies on Nakoda cultures and ways of life.

A Critique of the Panopticon and Surveillance

In his studies on the history of French disciplinary institutions, Foucault developed his theories around disciplinary power by using Jeremy Bentham's philosophy of the panopticon. Based on models of French prisons, the panopticon was a system for producing and maintaining power relationships. From Foucault's perspective, the panopticon was a "laboratory of power" with the primary objective of shaping more productive societies (1977: 204). The panopticon has two main criteria for how disciplinary power is exercised. According to Markula and Pringle (2006), Foucault specified that in the panopticon the source of power is omnipresent and constantly visible, but it is also simultaneously unverifiable. It is this second aspect that makes this disciplinary technology so effective. A key part of the panopticon model is that individuals become the source of their own discipline. Foucault explains this self-policing process:

> He who is subjected to a field of visibility, and who knows it, assumes responsibility for the constraints of power; he makes them play spontaneously upon himself; he inscribes in himself the power relation in which he simultaneously plays both roles; he becomes the principle of his own subjection. (1977: 203)

The main intention of the panopticon is to induce a state of consciousness and visibility that produces the automatic functioning of power. The omnipresent gaze is what brings discipline – and, in its ultimate form, docility – to bodies. However, it is the individuals' response to the panoptic gaze that constrains them through technologies of discipline (Foucault, 1984).

Foucault's adaptation of the panopticon is certainly a visually stimulating concept for theorizing levels of disciplinary power. What remains less clear is whether it is an effective tool when applied to understanding how disciplinary power functions in colonial societies. The panopticon has been widely used, and sometimes misused, by scholars attempting to understand how disciplinary power is produced and sustained in any given society (Arac, 1991). Despite Spivak's (1988) warning that Foucault's analysis itself reinscribes the West as the only subject as it fails to incorporate how colonial peoples responded to such disciplinary technologies, the panopticon has also been commonly, and sometimes carelessly, used in efforts to understand disciplinary power in colonial societies. In both Mitchell's (1991) analysis of the British colonization of Egypt and Kaplan's (1995) study of colonial conditions in India, the panopticon model is applied to understand the distribution and the consequences of forms of disciplinary power produced by colonial regimes. Instead of abandoning panopticism and establishing more unique Foucauldian-based arguments, such as Stoler's (1995) examination of how colonial practices maintained, ordered, and displayed power relations by simultaneously drawing from discourses of sexuality, race, and class, both studies insist on adapting the panopticon as their main theoretical thrust. The most unique and fascinating aspect of Foucault's use of the panopticon is how one can exercise discipline on oneself. The self-policing element of the panopticon is captivating, but scholars must then establish how the disciplinary gaze is internalized. While it is attractive to use the various types of surveillance that are often present in many colonial societies to suggest that certain levels of discipline were prevalent, the use of panopticism is not very effective unless scholars can demonstrate this self-monitoring aspect.

At least a few scholars have used the panopticon in their interpretation of the surveillance systems on reserves that Indigenous peoples encountered during the nineteenth century. Greenwald's (2002) study is a systematic analysis of how government policies instituted levels of surveillance and spatial control on two reservations in the United States (Nez Perce in Idaho and Jicarilla Apache in New Mexico). Although it is a groundbreaking work, her examination of the panoptic gaze is not productive in some regards because it is difficult to provide evidence of the self-surveillance aspects in communities. In this case, Greenwald does not compellingly demonstrate how Indigenous peoples internalized the disciplinary gaze. It is clear that the colonial bureaucracy did establish several methods to increase surveillance as part of the reserve systems. However, as Foucault detailed, an extremely high level of discipline is required to internalize this gaze and ensure that individuals become the producers of their own subjection. Even when historical evidence is provided on how this gaze is internalized, I still find it unconvincing. In Furniss's (1999) comprehensive ethnographic study on colonial relations in Williams Lake, British Columbia, she uses church attendance records to suggest the power of assimilatory and disciplinary practices to take hold in communities. The problems with such archival materials is that they rarely capture the complexities of how colonial power is exercised on the ground. Participation in assimilatory institutions does not automatically negate the possibilities of jointly celebrating Indigenous cultural practices. For example, a Nakoda elder indicated that even though his family had rarely missed church services for decades, they simultaneously pursued their own cultural practices. Nakoda peoples quickly realized under a colonial regime that participating in the activities of the missionaries and Indian agents brought privilege to them and their families.[18] As Snow (2005) notes, at Morley individuals could have more rations and more leisure time if they gained the favour of members of the colonial bureaucracy. This second point is key because, as the elder suggested, this extra leisure time was sometimes spent pursuing Nakoda cultural practices, like the Sun Dance, away from the surveillance of missionaries, Indian agents, and the police. Alfred's work also supports this reading by suggesting that these supposed inconsistencies were in fact common responses to colonial influences in many Indigenous communities across the country. Through his in-depth consultation with elders, he shows how Mohawk peoples devoutly attended the local Catholic church and participated in other aspects of Christian ritual and faith while simultaneously pursuing traditional Mohawk values, cultural practices, and political systems of government (1995).

Despite these critiques of the panopticon, Smith (2009) does provide one productive discussion in the context of First Nations communities in Western Canada. By focusing on the panoptic gaze as a strategy for surveillance, he outlines the role of Indigenous men who took positions as scouts, farmers, mail carriers, interpreters, and stockmen. Some of these men also passed on information to the police and Indian agents regarding the behaviour of individuals and families on their reserves. Similarly to the Indian agent, these informants were recruited based on their ability to comply with government and missionary objectives. Using archival documents, Smith complicates our understandings of these relationships. He reveals that although arms of the colonial bureaucracy worked together to pursue assimilationist policies, they also kept tabs on each other. This adds an additional layer of observation and contributes to our interpretations of surveillance networks that evidently extended well beyond a simplistic unidirectional gaze from the colonial agents to Indigenous peoples.

The ambivalence of colonial rule and the complexities of interpreting it are also exemplified in Richardson's (1992) study on disciplinary power in colonial plantations in the Caribbean. He asserts that the horrendous journey of the Middle Passage, the terrible living conditions on slave plantations, and the high levels of surveillance did not automatically homogenize captured Africans into docile members of the plantation workforces. His study shows that even though disciplinary power constrained the agency of colonized peoples through violent forms of cultural oppression and exploitation, slaves continued to exercise autonomous action for survival and the pursuit of emancipation. Despite the brutal history of repression and assimilation principles that guided colonial policies and practices with regards to Indigenous peoples in North America, evidence of this level of visceral and internalized discipline was not found in Nakoda communities as most continued to refuse aspects of colonial discipline by pursuing opportunities to maintain their cultural practices. The colonial bureaucracy did indeed incorporate the technologies of both correct training and docility, but the extent of discipline required to ensure that Nakoda peoples embodied all the values of this discipline, fortunately, was never realized. This research at Morley demonstrates that some Nakoda peoples strategically navigated colonial relations to find spaces to continue their cultural and subsistence practices.

Knowing, Individualizing, and Assimilating Processes

It is important now to theorize the levels of discipline that were designed to repress the cultural practices of Indigenous peoples in the government's efforts to advance assimilation objectives. As Stoler contends, one group of disciplinary technologies does not cancel out another. Rather, disciplinary technologies act simultaneously, producing multiple levels or rungs of discipline (1995). As extensions of the levels of discipline exercised over the control of space, time, and the modalities of movement, technologies of correct training were also instituted as key components of the assimilation strategies initiated by the agents of the colonial bureaucracy. In the context of Indigenous peoples in the last quarter of the nineteenth century, the means of correct training are useful in examining the restrictions employed to repress the cultural practices of Nakoda peoples and eventually assimilate them into the broader Euro-Canadian society. As Foucault outlined, disciplinary technologies produce a set of knowledges that create demands to perform to various standards (1977). The collection of personal knowledge is a key disciplinary technology. Foucault suggests that the collection of personal knowledge has three critical aspects or instruments: "The success of disciplinary power derives no doubt from the use of simple instruments[:] hierarchical observation, normalizing judgement and their combination in a procedure that is specific to it, the examination" (170). The remainder of this chapter concentrates on how aspects of these three instruments were used by the colonial administration in Nakoda communities to collect personal knowledge and further implement technologies of discipline.

As an instrument to produce knowledge of a subject, hierarchical observation reflects the connection between visibility and power. "A visible body is a knowable body that can subsequently become subject to the workings of power" (Markula and Pringle, 2006: 41). As Foucault outlined in great detail, hierarchical observation often includes a rearrangement of space so that visibility can be optimized. In referring to how the design of many disciplinary institutions reoriented space to facilitate the exercise of disciplinary power, Foucault states: "The architecture would operate to transform individuals: to act on those it shelters, to provide a hold on their conduct, to carry the effects of power right to them, to make it possible to know them, to alter them" (1977: 172). Just as classrooms in French schools and the positioning of barracks in French military camps were reorganized for this purpose, the reserves that Indigenous peoples were limited to also underwent a series of changes to increase opportunities for observation and to structure visibility. In Nakoda communities, the reserve was organized so that the mission site, including the church and residential school, became the geographic centre of social life (Snow, 2005). This was an attempt to organize spaces on the reserve so that most community members were seen regularly by the missionaries and Indian agents. The government's intent of increasing the observation of community members aligned with the objective of locating Nakoda peoples in a fixed landscape and organizing that space accordingly.

Foucault suggested that the most effective disciplinary institutions had several sources of surveillance or calculated gazes (1977). In addition to Indian agents and missionaries, the mounted police also served an important disciplinary function during this period. While it was initially a positive relationship between the police and Indigenous groups involved in Treaty 7, within two decades of their 1874 arrival, these relations deteriorated as people became more aware of the role of the police as another arm of the government providing surveillance to constrain their land uses, restrict their movements, and erode their cultural practices. As noted earlier, by 1893 Indian agents and the police worked in conjunction to increase surveillance and identify those who were not present at various activities on the reserve. Similarly to the attendance records taken by missionaries in their schools and church services, this functioned as a roll call for Nakoda community members. Foucault specified that at schools, hospitals, workshops, and military exercises, "roll-calls were taken, from the list on the wall; the absentees were noted down in a register" (1977: 157). He identified roll calls as central to the exercise of discipline. As Deloria demonstrates, activities involving hunting and other cultural practices, such as Sun Dances, became a source of conflict between Indigenous peoples and administrators or missionaries. These types of activities were not only a fundamental contradiction to assimilation strategies attempting to discourage cultural practices, but they also drew Indigenous peoples out of, and away from, the visibility of church and government officials (2004). As early as 1938, the Indian agent at Morley, with the support of Indian Affairs, attempted to limit the number of Nakoda peoples who attended the Indian Days. While the justification that agricultural work was being neglected was put forward as the main reason for the restrictions, the opportunities that the Indian Days provided for individuals to travel away from the reserve, congregate, and celebrate their cultural practices were also concerns for members of the colonial administration.[19]

Foucault indicates that increasing observation and visibility are integrally linked to gaining or producing knowledge of subjects. At Morley, the Indian agents were encouraged to get to know the individuals on the reserve (Snow, 2005). This process of knowing individuals was not motivated by a desire to understand the personal needs or concerns of families undergoing abrupt changes to their lifestyles, but was intended to increase the amount of surveillance on communities to ensure that the reserve was converted into a productive space. As Snow explicates, "the agents were encouraged to become more thoroughly acquainted with them, as to their mode of life, character, etc, but the purpose of that interest was to promote 'greater progress'" (2005: 72). Following Treaty 7 and the attempt to fix Nakoda communities to the reserve lands, a series of methods were introduced to improve visibility on these newly constructed spaces and increase opportunities for colonial agents to observe the lifestyles and behaviour of Nakoda community members. This observation and visibility increased discipline and the "knowing" of local Nakoda peoples.

After the daily behaviour of community members was observed, it then became necessary to invent a system that promoted the repression and assimilation principles of the colonial administration. As Foucault suggested, normalizing judgment can involve a system of rewards and punishments where individuals are evaluated based on their ability or inability to replicate desired behaviour. The purpose of a punishment/reward system is to establish differences between individuals, attempt to close the gaps that exist, and consequently homogenize individuals and their experiences. "Disciplinary punishment has the function of reducing gaps. It must therefore be essentially *corrective*" (Foucault, 1977: 179). Ironically, it is critical to individuate in order to homogenize. Foucault explains: "In a sense, the power of normalization imposes homogeneity; but it individualizes by making it possible to measure gaps, to determine levels, to fix specialities and to render the differences useful by fitting them one to another" (1984: 196–7). While measuring and comparing individuals can establish norms and subsequently produce opportunities for individuality, normalizing judgment ultimately promotes homogeneity. A normalizing system involving both punishments and rewards was established for Nakoda communities at Morley in the late nineteenth century with comprehensible assimilation objectives.

In 1885 the enforcement of the pass system at Morley formed an aspect of this system as Nakoda peoples were severely punished for breaching the regulations that required them to seek approval from the Indian agent to leave the reserve. Individuals found off the reserve were fined or faced incarceration: "Any Indian person found off the reserve without a pass was treated as a vagrant and summoned to court ... A treaty Indian was ordered back to his reserve; the alternative was jail" (Snow, 2005: 73). Besides avoiding conflict with colonial agents, including the police, remaining on the reserve also had its benefits or rewards for Nakoda peoples. Localized Nakoda community members were more likely to receive their treaty payments and food rations. In addition, access to health facilities and education, although limited, were incentives for some to remain on the reserve and participate in activities supported by the Indian agent and missionaries, such as attending church or school and engaging in agricultural production (Dyck, 1991). This system allowed colonial agents to distinguish between those who remained on the reserve and those who left to continue their subsistence practices. The punishment/reward system "refers individual actions to a whole that is at once a field of comparison, a space of differentiation" (Foucault, 1977: 182). This field of comparison not only encouraged Nakoda community members to live year-round on the reserve and participate in activities designed to assimilate their cultures, but also singled out those who refused to adopt this new way of life. This field of identification and comparison allowed colonial agents to determine where and when more discipline was required. As a result, the normalizing judgments of colonial agents encouraged Nakoda peoples to assimilate Euro-Canadian lifestyles and cultural practices.

According to Foucault, the combination of hierarchical observations and normalizing judgments produce the examination, which he considered one of the most powerful tools for individualizing. The examination is an excellent example of how disciplinary societies make individuals and bodies the target and the effect of power relations. "The examination is at the centre of the procedures that constitute the individual as effect and object of power, as an effect and object of knowledge" (1977: 192). As described by Foucault in his analyses of French medical systems throughout the eighteenth century, documentation was a key aspect of the examination and the knowing of individuals and groups. The knowing of individuals also fostered processes of exercising discipline in communities. As he explains: "It is the individual as he may be described, judged, measured, compared with others, in his very individuality; and it is also the individual that has to be trained or corrected, classified, normalized, excluded" (191).

Although homogenization or assimilation were the colonial objectives, it was necessary to know individuals for this to occur. Individuation was a key step in the creation of sameness. Deloria (2004) refers to the process of "knowing Indians" on reservations throughout North America by highlighting how documentation facilitated the exercise of power. He explains these multifaceted procedures by describing how tribal rolls standardized names and replaced them with English monikers; church records collected demographic information about relations and dates of baptism, confirmation, and death; ration distribution records quantified the amount of food provided to individuals and families; Indian agents recorded infractions, property, character, education, and employment of individuals. As Snow notes, similar documentation processes occurred at Morley for many decades (2005). These records mapped individuals and families into spaces on reserve lands in a process that transformed personal knowledge into opportunities to discipline and exercise colonial power. To be recorded and known by name, relations, character, and physical location was to be intimately visible to the colonial bureaucracy. It made it possible and sometimes easy to locate individuals in time and space as well as determine when to intervene and the amount of discipline to implement. These processes made the acquisition of knowledge central to the exercise of power. The colonial bureaucracy achieved this by attempting to constrain Indigenous bodies and cultures in ways that furthered colonial assimilation strategies.

The instruments of correct training produced systems that observed, judged, documented, and differentiated with regards to the lives of Nakoda community members. The disciplinary technologies not only directed colonial assimilation objectives, but, in the process, they also circumscribed the boundaries of "Indian-ness." The production and recording of personal knowledge creates opportunities to determine how much difference there is between individuals and the norm, or the standard deviation from the norm. This is critical for colonial assimilation processes as one can evaluate how "civilized," progressive, religious, or Euro-Canadian an individual is based on the subjective judgments of colonial agents. The knowing, individuating, documenting, and homogenizing of Nakoda practices encouraged assimilation, and highlighted those who refused these methods. In reference to Indigenous groups in the Treaty 7 region, Smith describes how surveillance was linked to wider normalizing processes whereby outliers identify where discipline and further methods of assimilation were needed:

> The underlying impetus of all this observation and intelligence gathering was to provide a portrait of the progress of colonial rule. It identified individuals and groups that were adhering to state policies, and singled out those who were not for further remedial discipline ... This served to maintain and fortify the boundary between "Indian" and "non-Indian." (2009: 17)

These outliers were the individuals who did not yet meet the "standards" of Euro-Canadian society. The means of correct training were effective not only in furthering the government's assimilation intentions, but also in ascertaining where more discipline was required to achieve these objectives.

Conclusion

The conditions that led to the emergence of Canada's first national park and related regional developments clearly influenced the lives of local Nakoda communities. Limiting access to the region and actively encouraging Nakoda peoples to remain on the reserve, furthered the government's assimilation strategies. However, the exclusion of Nakoda peoples from park lands also had other profound impacts on their cultures. As Cruikshank (2005) demonstrates in her research with Tlingit peoples in Kluane National Park and Reserve in the Yukon Territory, when access to the region was limited, there were long-term cultural and socio-economic ramifications in their communities. When cultural knowledge was lost there was rupture in educational strategies, but spaces were also reorganized, reclassified, and bordered in ways that had devastating consequences for local peoples. Alfred (2005) identifies the loss of lands and access to sacred territories as some of the worst atrocities of colonial policies. In his analysis of the impacts in Mohawk societies, he poignantly demonstrates how these losses created disruptions or disconnections in physical, spiritual, and collective well-being. He found that colonization disconnected Mohawk individuals and communities from who they are, from each other and their sacred lands. For Nakoda peoples, one such impact was not having access to significant sites, such as the hot springs. This is an example of how these regulations formed barriers to the celebration of cultures which are so vitally connected to the landscapes the peoples occupied. As Poucette reiterates: "Our culture is about stories and all of our stories they come from the land ... It is through being on the land that we tell these stories ... This is to understand and later pass on who we are and where we come from."[20] Similarly to other Indigenous groups across Canada, the land and its resources are the lifeblood of Nakoda cultural practices. The creation of RMP severely altered the relationship between Nakoda peoples and the lands that were redefined as protected areas under the emblem of the parks system, but the coming decades would produce a unique set of opportunities to re-establish Nakoda cultural practices related to significant sites claimed by the Canadian government and safeguarded inside the boundaries of the national parks.

Chapter Four

Sporting and Tourism Festivals: Representations of Indigenous Peoples

From the 1880s until the middle of the twentieth century, the development of tourism economies in the Banff–Bow Valley initiated a dynamic period in the region's history. Local Indigenous peoples participated in the tourism industry and in various capacities contributed to the production of "naturalness" discourse, which was central to the marketing of Rocky Mountains Park and the Banff townsite. By selling certain images of the region while actively concealing others, tourism entrepreneurs promoted the Banff–Bow Valley as an international tourist destination. Nakoda First Nations community members influenced the production of this discourse through both their involvement in the tourism industry and the use of representations of their cultural practices in tourism advertisements. "Naturalness" discourse, which partly emerged through cultural and sporting festivals held for tourists, relied upon specific representations of precolonial Indigenous cultures that shaped tourists' perceptions of Nakoda peoples during this period.

Demystifying "Naturalness" Discourse

Before focusing on the development of the tourism industry in Banff, it is imperative to define the central concept of "naturalness." Over the last few decades, scholars from various disciplinary backgrounds have deconstructed the concept of "naturalness" in efforts to reveal that these discourses are formed by individual and collective human values, assumptions, interpretations, and inventions concerning the physical and social worlds humans occupy and produce. As Cronon (1996) argues, when environments or objects are produced as "natural" by individuals or groups, this discourse reflects as much about the orientations of the people as it does about what it attempts to identify. The problematic understandings of this discourse often stem from specific urban Eurocentric ways of explaining space and the tenuous and ambivalent relationships between humans and the environments they inhabit. Cruikshank explains: "Enlightenment categories, like nature and culture, were exported from Europe through the expansion of empire to places deemed to be at 'the verge of the world,' and these categories have become sedimented in contemporary practices" (2005: 245). Some urban Eurocentric perspectives position "natural" environments as essentially devoid of humans and their cultures (Colpitts, 1998). While many urban Europeans held values that supported binaries between "nature" and "culture," it must be recognized that similarly to North America, Europe comprises a diversity of peoples. Even though other European influences effected the production of "naturalness" in a Canadian context, "empire" in this case mainly refers to the colonial powers of England and France. It was particularly the urban perspectives in these nations that most impacted the production of "naturalness" in the colonies. Despite familiar binaries between "nature" and "culture," it is important to note that cultures produce the "naturalness" of any environment (MacEachern, 2001). As Nakoda elder Rollinmud succinctly expressed in reference to Rocky Mountains Park (RMP) and the relationships between First Nations and park lands: "You know that land is just a park there ... because there are no histories there without us. Without the people there is no life ... You know people made the nature?"[1] In direct contrast to common conceptions, it is difficult to conceive of any single environment that has not been substantially altered by human activity and culture. Notably, Williams (1980) contends that "natural" environments have always contained an extraordinary amount of human history. Cruikshank (2005) points out that as proliferating claims and counter-claims are made in the name of nature, areas deemed to be "natural" are (re)imagined as uncontaminated by humans. She demonstrates how through the creation and classification of parks and world heritage sites, when lands are defined as having exceptionally "natural" value, the "cultural" significance of the locations can be discounted. The idea that a "natural" world might be pried from its cultural moorings has become increasingly problematic in places where local understandings inform a different framework. As Said (1978) systematically exposed, the discursive conditions that produced Eurocentric cultural meanings were critical to Western imperialism in that they were used to justify colonial projects. Kaplan (1995) reminds us that "the making of the European self happens not in Europe alone, but in relation to real and imagined others in the world, in the experience and creation of difference" (94). These claims to "naturalness," and the discourse they support, act to exclude differing practices or understandings of place and thus can have major implications for Indigenous communities.

In addition to "naturalness" discourse that infers pristine or uninhabited landscapes, for the purposes of this book the use of "natural" also denotes a particular socio-cultural production propagated by tourism producers who relied on the exclusion of existing sites of labour and subsistence land-use practices. It is the production of "naturalness" that motivated tourism producers in Banff to actively forward certain representations of Indigenous peoples in a complex process involving both exclusion and inclusion principles. For the urban elite who travelled to national parks in North America beginning in the 1880s, the "natural" environment was not perceived as a site of productive labour or a permanent home, but rather as a place of recreation and consumption (Wilson, 1991). In the case of the Banff townsite and RMP, tourism entrepreneurs produced a variety of representations that contributed to "naturalness" discourse. This encouraged the active exclusion of sites of labour and subsistence land uses while simultaneously promoting and selling precolonial representations of Indigenous peoples. The production of "naturalness" had significant consequences for local peoples and it is important to assess the impacts it had in Nakoda communities.

The Origins of the Tourism Industry in Banff

Increasing significantly with the package travel business in the 1860s and the creation of the British travel firm Thomas Cook, Western elites toured mountain ranges like the European Alps and later more "exotic" destinations such as the Canadian Rockies. The touring of these environments emerged as these landscapes began to offer recreational experiences for elite tourists. Urban-elite conceptions of these environments also arrived with the affluent tourists and the flow of economic capital that facilitated the development of the tourism industry. Although it was established two decades after Thomas Cook, the CPR became one of the world's largest travel companies by the turn of the twentieth century.[2]

The 1887 formation of RMP was the beginning of tourism infrastructure development in the Canadian Rocky Mountains. As a joint venture between the Canadian federal government and the CPR, the national park was the first of its kind in Canada and was originally established as a means of generating railway tourism with few conservation or preservation objectives considered. As was the case for much of Canada's early history, and especially in the development of the west, public and private interests were strongly linked in the formation and development of RMP (Scace, 1970). The construction of the national railway and the building of a new nation brought about severe financial challenges. Through the creation of the park, the federal government and private corporations sought to develop the tourism industry to recover some of the mounting costs of completing the east-west railway that linked central Canada to the emergent west (Nicol, 1970).[3] As William Cornelius Van Horne, the president of the CPR, stated in 1888: "If we cannot export the scenery, we will import the tourists" (Hart, 1999: 114). The park solidified a symbiotic relationship between the CPR and the federal government that would prosper throughout much of the twentieth century. The park became a convenient way to establish a monopoly on transportation access to the region that effectively controlled development. The establishment of the national park designated governmental control of natural resource management and the leasing of property. Although this is a less glamorous account than some historians have put forward, few conservation principles shaped these decisions as the park was originally created to centralize control of the lands and restrict access to the region. Several key sources have argued that promoting mountain landscapes and the use of the railway to wealthy tourists were also primary motivations behind the creation of iconic national parks in the United States such as Yellowstone (Magoc, 1999), but especially Mt Rainier (Catton, 2006; Louter, 2006). Based on archival resources, Jacoby's research (2001) contradicts the grand narratives about US national parks emerging from an increasingly powerful environmental consciousness. Shadowing tourism development in or around parks and protected spaces in the United States, the formation of national parks in Canada were deeply shaped by American examples and experiences (Foster, 1978). Not only did public policy in the United States influence how Canadian processes unfolded, but the decisions that motivated Canadian leadership from the political and community side often mirrored what was occurring in the United States. Foster also shows that extensive relationships existed between American and Canadian policymakers and that they sometimes worked in conjunction by sharing resources to pursue conservation or preservation objectives.

MacLaren (2011) reveals that this relationship continued, as the 1930 National Parks Act in Canada paraphrases directly from the US Organic Act (1926) that was written just a few years earlier. As already shown, these close relationships between governments in the development of public policy concerning the establishment of national parks and related preservation movements had implications for Indigenous communities on both sides of the border.

While at least one researcher supports an argument that the Canadian National Parks Act also had important conservation principles to protect wildlife and preserve the region for the benefit of civil society, and this clearly was a factor (Locke, 2009), the majority of evidence suggests that even though the federal government did claim that it was securing land to be "set apart as a public park and pleasure ground for the benefit, advantage and enjoyment of the people of Canada,"[4] it was initially motivated by natural resource and tourism development opportunities. According to Sandlos (2011), during this early period in the Canadian west, it was local governments, recreational groups, and tourism entrepreneurs rather than conservationists that campaigned for the expansion of the national park system. It is apparent that the legislation actually endorsed the growth of the tourism industry and permitted, under government direction, the development of mining sites, timber interests, and grazing lands. As long as they did not "impair the usefulness of the park for the purposes of public enjoyment and recreation,"[5] these developments were encouraged and at times facilitated by the government. As Martin (2011) states: "[As] critics of both the Canadian and American national parks systems have often noted, an avowed commitment to wilderness preservation by government administrators has not always prevented intensive development and environmental modifications in the national parks" (274). This was most certainly the case in the first few decades of park policy in both the United States and Canada.

Returning to RMP, in the early 1880s, a small silver and copper mining town, referred to as Silver City, developed near Castle Mountain only thirty kilometres north of the Banff townsite. The formation of the park allowed the CPR and the government to shift the mining enterprise from a private operation into a public asset while also prohibiting the alcohol and gambling lifestyles of Silver City miners. There is little record of opposition to resource-extraction activities in the park during this period, and the federal policy of the Conservative government in the 1880s emphasized the desire to exploit natural resources in order to develop the national economy (McNamee, 1993). Dominion Parks' leadership also reflected the government's development intentions. Commissioner Harkin, in his annual report, stated that "nothing attracts tourists like National Parks. National Parks provide the chief means of bringing to Canada a stream of tourists and a stream of tourist gold" (Marty, 1984: 98).[6] If one reviews early government policy and practice, it is clear that tourism and natural resource development were the primary rationale in the formation of RMP. In addition, it is now apparent that Harkin used an economic argument, based on tourism development, in order to expand the national parks system after 1910 (MacEachern, 2011).[7]

In terms of tourism, the Banff townsite began as a spa destination for elite guests of considerable financial standing. The luxurious facilities built by the CPR, like the Banff Springs Hotel, completed in 1888, were designed to meet the needs of its affluent clientele and were some of the continent's most opulent accommodations during the period. As Canada's first prime minister, Sir John A. MacDonald, stated during the development of the townsite, "the doubtful classes of people will probably not find an overly gracious welcome at Banff" (Brown, 1970: 46). The MacDonald administration advocated developing the townsite in the style of an elite European resort community and only leasing the land to affluent individuals who could afford to erect buildings that would complement the local environment and reflect the government's vision of the townsite. The marketing of Banff also reflected the objective of attracting the urban elite of North America and Europe. Jessup's (2002) research recounts the processes that led to the CPR's hiring of members of Canada's famous Group of Seven artists to paint the Rocky Mountains and promote the region for tourism. Her study reveals how the CPR endeavoured to "establish the value of the region, not in the eyes of the traveller as such, but in the eyes of the urban elite that, like the artist it patronized, possessed the cultural capital necessary for discriminating between different landscapes" (150). While the initial promotional campaigns of the park concentrated on the wealthy clientele that had the leisure time to undertake an extended sojourn and the capital to facilitate it, tourism producers soon expanded the tourism market (see plates 3 and 4).

Access to the Banff townsite and RMP was rapidly increasing with the 1914 creation of the Calgary–Banff coach road and the proliferation of the automobile. After the road was completed, the CPR monopoly on

Figure 4.1 Banff Springs Hotel (1889). Set at the foot of Mount Rundle, at the time the Banff Springs was one of the most luxurious hotels in North America. Courtesy of the Glenbow Museum Archives. NA-1075–4. (Photographer: William Notman and Son Photography)

transportation access to the region ended and individual entrepreneurs began to expand the tourism market by providing cheaper accommodation and alternative forms of recreation. While access to the region was opening up, this did not signify the end of the CPR's dominant influence in Banff, as the company developed strategies to capitalize on new forms of automobile tourism (Bella, 1987). It was not until the 1920s, when several accommodation options were developed for middle-class visitors and the road became more frequently used, that access to the park was granted to a larger portion of society. By 1930, 88 per cent of the 188,000 tourists who arrived in Banff came by automobile (Hart, 2003). The park as a playground for more than society's elite began with the rise of the automobile and the subsequent expansion of road and highway infrastructure that provided greater access to the region (Manry, 2010).

With the democratization of tourism, local entrepreneurs began to shift marketing campaigns and subsequently changed the reputation of Banff. Hart (1983) contends that during this period, local tourism producers made efforts to convince the CPR that Banff did not have much of a future as a tourist destination if it continued to be marketed solely as an affluent spa or resort town similar to many elite European tourist locations throughout the Alps and the Pyrenees. These businessmen felt that Banff should be sold as a place that could offer all tourists outdoor recreational experiences. Entrepreneurs made convincing arguments for the expansion of the tourism industry to reach new markets, and as a consequence, the region began to be promoted as a destination that could provide outdoor leisure opportunities to tourists from diverse socio-economic backgrounds. Facilitated by transportation infrastructure and marketing campaigns, the attraction of middle-class tourists to Banff and the consequent expansion of accommodation and recreation opportunities to meet these visitors' needs led to a distinct shift in the orientation of the townsite. Although initially established as an elite tourist destination, with the introduction of the automobile, it was transformed into a place that also catered to middle-class tourists with an infrastructure that would accommodate the mass tourism of the coming decades.

The Production of "Naturalness" in Banff

In response to international travel trends of the late nineteenth century, "natural" environments were positioned as prime tourist destinations throughout the Western world. In an effort to explain the twentieth-century tourist's desire for spending time in remote mountainous environments like Banff, Schama (1996) asserts that the presumption was that in "natural" environments one could find the preservation of the world – it was out there awaiting discovery and it would be the antidote for the poisons of industrial society. Seizing upon the growth of interest in especially foreign travel to regions conceptualized as "natural," competing travel firms promoted the health benefits of visiting these locations. The tourists who travelled to places like the Canadian

Rocky Mountains were partly in pursuit of a healthy lifestyle. This is reflected in the tourism advertising campaigns that emphasize the health benefits of being surrounded by Banff's pristine mountain air and glacier-fed rivers (Williams, 1922). The healing and curative potential of visiting the hot springs were particularly promoted in marketing campaigns. In the 1880s, the CPR employed Dr Robert G. Brett to help establish and promote the healing values of the waters of the hot springs (Hart, 1999). The health benefits of the region made Banff an attractive place to visit for tourists of the period. Banff was sold as a location that provided not only curative properties, but also an escape from urban life. In this regard, "naturalness" discourse endorsed the region's tourism economies by marketing these features.

While the CPR and government sold Banff as a health destination, the rejuvenating value of mountains and rivers for the ills of industrial capitalism were as much a product of prevailing discourse as was the "naturalness" of the environments themselves. At the turn of the twentieth century, tourism materials suggest that Banff was advertised as a place that offered urban tourists an escape from the complexities of modernity as well as leisure opportunities that would rejuvenate the mind, body, and soul (Williams, 1922); however, this escape had to be carefully constructed by the producers. Motivated by capitalist objectives that facilitated the (re)imagining of the region to align with mass tourism markets, the federal government, the CPR, and local tourism entrepreneurs produced holiday experiences that sold Banff as an outdoor recreation paradise that had various health benefits while intentionally hiding the evidence of productive sites of labour and subsistence land-use practices. This often meant concealing the presence and history of the resource extraction industry, some technology such as hydro-electric power infrastructure, and local Indigenous and non-Indigenous communities as well as the work that sustained them, including mining, railway construction, hunting, trapping, gathering, and fishing.

With the creation of the park, access to the region for local Nakoda peoples was greatly reduced, as their subsistence land uses were redefined as intolerable or illegal. Wildlife, but especially large mammal populations, often served as a marker of the natural world. In Western Canada, "wild animals, too, helpfully defined the boundaries of this natural world against those of the civil one thousands of miles away. Even by the beginning of the twentieth century, back-to-nature adherents searched for wildlife so that the regions visited could be validated as truly natural" (Colpitts, 2002: 28). As a consequence, Nakoda communities were actively excluded from the park because their hunting, fishing, and gathering practices did not align with tourism entrepreneurs' production of the region. However, precolonial representations of Indigenous peoples were frequently used in tourism marketing campaigns to promote the Banff townsite and the park. This particular version of the "natural" not only included these representations, but relied upon them to reinforce the production of this discourse. Indigenous peoples were imagined by many tourists to be embedded within the "natural" environment and, as a result, a significant component of tourists' experiences. As Pratt (1992) reveals, early tourism promotion of "natural" locations was vital to producing a dichotomy between Europeans and all other peoples. In this regard, this imagery of the exotic colonial "Other" directly endorsed European superiority and justified colonial presence and expansion. This, in part, is the problem with the Noble Savage imagery that proliferated throughout much of the nineteenth century. It positioned Indigenous peoples in restrictive binaries as either the primitive, violent Native or the Noble Savage. Both of these representations were destructive, as they focused on, produced, and disseminated difference. As Stoler (1995) emphasizes, colonialism was not just about incorporation of cultural groups, but also about the distinction between colonizing and the colonized.

For the urban elite tourists who arrived from Europe and North America, conceptions of Indigenous peoples were heavily influenced by their exposure to Wild West literature, live performances, and film (Kasson, 2000). At the beginning of the nineteenth century, this imagery captured significant portions of popular culture markets. As Spence (1999) shows, the writings of Catharine Sedwick, Washington Irving, and James Fenimore Cooper romanticized the "Indian Wilderness" of the North American continent in the 1820s and 1830s. In the 1840s the market was flooded with "a long slew of stories and novels about life among the wild Indians" (13). The Wild West genre re-enacted colonial narratives and celebrated precolonial representations of Indigenous cultures (Deloria, 2004). Exemplified by the mass appeal of Buffalo Bill Cody's Wild West live theatre in the United States and Western Europe in the 1870s (Moses, 1996) and the incredible success of Karl Friedrich May's Wild West–themed novels in Germany in the 1890s (Bugmann, 2008), these precolonial representations were highly visible in Western culture before the turn of the twentieth century. Later, Wild West films, which were widespread by 1910, solidified the entrance of the Wild West genre into mainstream popular culture in both Europe and

North America. The genre proliferated precolonial images especially of North America's Plains peoples. The popularity of Wild West theatre dwindled by the 1930s and the film industry soon after began to orchestrate a variety of subplots that did not always reinforce precolonial imagery of Indigenous peoples (Deloria, 2004). However, the conceptions of Indigenous peoples that the Wild West genres helped manufacture greatly influenced the urban elite that travelled throughout Western Canada during this period.

Attracted by the Wild West imagery propagated in mainstream popular culture, tourists that ventured to national parks in the United States during this period had particular expectations of Indigenous peoples. In Yellowstone in the 1890s, there was a significant appeal for visiting tourists to encounter Indigenous peoples in the park. This is exemplified by the attempts to create a tourist display on Dot Island in Yellowstone Lake that featured a small herd of bison and a family of Crow peoples (Spence, 1999). Spence also notes, in the first few decades of the twentieth century, an increased interest in Indigenous cultures in Glacier National Park, where Blackfeet communities played significant roles in both tourism promotion and delivering services for tourists. Just as in Yellowstone and Glacier, the tourists who came to Yosemite National Park in California also expected to see Indians. By the turn of the century, Yosemite Indians had become an essential part of the tourist experience, not just in the cultural demonstrations they provided, but also in the labour and service jobs they performed in the park (ibid.).

The tourists who visited Banff from the formation of the park until the 1930s also arrived with specific expectations of Indigenous peoples that were linked to, and reinforced by, "naturalness" discourse that was supported by established tourism objectives. As a result, specific types of representations of Indigenous peoples were highly valued by tourism producers in Banff because they helped meet tourists' expectations by supporting the desired discourse and, importantly, did not depict the current lived realities of local communities. Analyses of marketing campaigns of the period and oral testimony both suggest that tourism producers were concerned with selling precolonial images of local Indigenous peoples while concealing the contemporary lives of Nakoda cultures on the nearby reserve at Morley. Through his work in the Yukon Territory, Neufeld argues that Euro-Canadians often "preferred to think of Aboriginal peoples as either untouched, invisible, and thus safely out of the way, or defiled by contact with modernity, visible, and therefore unwanted" (2011: 254). In the Banff–Bow Valley, this was the constant space that Nakoda peoples were asked to occupy – somewhere between presence and absence – depending on the fantasies, desires, and practices of tourists and the broader industry. In reference to the experiences of Yosemite Indians in the local tourism economies inside the national park, Spence found that if certain activities "contributed to the public's enjoyment of the park, then a native presence was strongly encouraged. As a general rule, however, park officials preferred to keep Indians outside the tourists' gaze" (1999: 119). In her research on the history of the Williams Lake stampede, which was established in 1919, Furniss (1999) reveals how a very similar process occurred in British Columbia. Although precolonial representations of Indigenous cultures that indulged tourists' Wild West imaginations were welcomed by tourism producers during the stampede each summer, local Indigenous peoples were largely excluded from social life.

Despite this selective presence in the tourism industry, official park policy in the United States and Canada attempted to increasingly restrict Indigenous use of park lands. Multiple sites of research that examine the histories of Indigenous involvement in the tourism industry around national parks in North America make it clear that Indigenous peoples often existed on the margins of tourists' experiences. However, perhaps a key point is missed in these assumptions. As will be explored in the following chapter, for Nakoda peoples, these experiences of limited inclusion in the tourism industry offered opportunities that were strategically exploited by participants in the tourism industry and especially by Nakoda leaders. Access to the park, building political relationships with the broader Canadian society, and financial resources are just some of the notable benefits witnessed in Nakoda communities. Nevertheless, the inequalities that structured the lives of local Indigenous peoples were often ignored, as they did not support the perceptions of cultures that were valued by tourism producers. At Banff, the quotidian lives of Nakoda peoples and their presence in the townsite and park were not the only elements that threatened the production of the "natural" environment.

While the 1887 Rocky Mountains Park Act specified that no permits would be issued to individuals or groups who might "impair the usefulness of the park,"[8] the region continued to support the development of resource extraction industries. This created an interesting paradoxical relationship, as it was the processes of industrialization and urbanization that generated tourists' interest in travelling to Banff and provided the transportation infrastructure that allowed access to the mountainous setting, while these very same influences threatened the production of "naturalness" and therefore had to be hidden from the tourist gaze. In her research on early tourism promotion in the Rocky Mountain national parks, Zezulka-Mailloux (2008) extends this point: "There is a paradox in the rhetoric that presented the tourist with the option not just to see the last wilderness, presumably a place that needs protection, but to penetrate its very core" (246). The Banff townsite and RMP, as with most locations in Canada, have been marked by productive sites of labour and subsistence land-use practices. Not only had local peoples lived and traded there for millennia before the European presence, but since the formation of RMP, the region had also been developed for hydro-electric power, mining, grazing, and timber interests for several decades.[9] The boundaries of the park were also altered on several occasions to facilitate these resource-extraction industries. Miners and other labourers, including those who worked in internment camps during the First and Second World Wars, were brought to the Banff–Bow Valley to develop transportation and mining infrastructure (Kordan and Melnycky, 1991).[10] The park was partly formed to safeguard CPR and government natural-resource interests and the multiple reorganizations of park boundaries offered further protection for these industries until conservation groups and the Canadian public eventually encouraged a rethinking of the orientations of national parks (Bella, 1987). In contrast to common conceptions, the "naturalness" of Banff and RMP were direct products of the discourse that was heavily influenced by tourism objectives.

In 1928, a survey of RMP recommended that the Kananaskis and Spray Lakes watersheds be removed from the park and secured for the province of Alberta to develop hydro-electric power as well as coal and timber extraction facilities (McNamee, 1993). On 30 May 1930, there was a fundamental shift in the direction of Canada's national park system with the establishment of the National Parks Act. Along with changing the official name to Banff National Park, the act settled the disputes between provincial development aspirations and protection of lands in national parks. Especially in the Rockies, the shifting of park boundaries removed lands with industrial potential and left them in trust to the provinces. In Banff, this included Canmore, Exshaw, the Spray Lakes, and the Kananaskis Valley (Bella, 1987). The act altered the park's administration and fundamental premise in declaring that parks were to be left "unimpaired for the enjoyment of future generations."[11] Even though the legislation did permit leases for grazing, small-scale mining, and timber and water rights for the purposes of replenishing park and railway supplies, a conservation ethic emerged that ended industrial resource extraction and restricted tourists' consumption and recreation practices. Rather than change the orientation of tourism markets, the National Parks Act only reinforced the intentions of tourism entrepreneurs to promulgate the perception of the parks as a "natural" wilderness area. The developing tourism industries would encourage not only the use of representations of Indigenous peoples in marketing the region, but also their employment in expanding tourism industries.

Nakoda Participation in Early Tourism Economies

After establishing how precolonial representations of Indigenous peoples aligned with the prevailing discourse and as a consequence tourism development objectives of the period, it is critical to provide tangible evidence of the ways in which Nakoda communities contributed to this discourse through their engagement in local tourism economies. While restrictions eventually reduced the number of Nakoda peoples who travelled inside the lands redefined as parks, there were individuals who formed unique relationships with entrepreneurs in the Banff region through the tourism industry. As a result of their extensive knowledge of the land and local ecosystems, Nakoda peoples often served as effective guides in the mountains. The history of Nakoda peoples as guides in the Rocky Mountains extends back to the first European explorers, who relied on Indigenous knowledge in their attempts to establish transportation and fur-trading routes (Colpitts, 2002). CPR employees also drew from the knowledge of local Indigenous peoples in their early surveys of the Rockies to denote the best mountain passes for railway construction (Hart, 1979). As Alfred (2009a) contends, the labour of First Nations peoples was key to early Canadian capitalist expansion through industry. This was particularly the case in the western and northern parts of the country. With park restrictions increasing the difficulty for Nakoda peoples to continue their subsistence practices, by the 1880s some community members began to pursue alternative types of employment in the tourism and development industries.

Nakoda man William Twin is a prime example of the adaptability that many Indigenous peoples exhibited during this period. Twin, who had previously worked for the Hudson's Bay Company, was employed by the CPR as a guide and labourer in the 1880s. In 1888, Twin began to work in the Banff townsite for the Brewster family, which was actively involved in the region's tourism industry. Although he was initially employed as a labourer in the family's dairy, in 1892 he began guiding trips throughout the park for the Brewster tourism ventures. Over the ensuing decades, Twin established long-lasting relationships with several members of the Brewster family (Bradford, 2005). He also worked with Tom Wilson, another notable tourism entrepreneur in the Banff–Bow Valley. After Edwin Hunter, a Nakoda man from Morley, took Wilson to *Ho-run-num-nay* (Lake of Little Fishes, later renamed Lake Louise) in 1882, Wilson began a small guiding operation based near the lake. Twin worked with Wilson guiding affluent tourists in the area throughout the 1880s and 1890s. In 1894, Twin and Tom Chiniquay, another Nakoda man from Morley, worked for the CPR maintaining trails around the CPR's chalet at the famed lake (Manry, 2010). Because of their skill set and experience in the mountains, some Nakoda peoples were offered employment by local tourism producers and, in some cases, unique opportunities to travel. In 1895, Twin ventured to New York City to participate in the CPR's exhibit in the New York Sportsman Show. With the approval of the local Indian agent, on the trip Twin represented a "real" grizzly bear hunter and promoted CPR railway tourism in the Canadian Rockies (Whyte, 1985).

While clearly there are examples of how some Nakoda men were able to participate in these developing economies associated with the tourism industry, in almost all cases, Euro-Canadian families owned these tourism productions and Nakoda men simply worked as labourers and guides in these profitable businesses. Even though personal relationships were established over the many years that Nakoda men, such as Twin, worked for the Brewster family, at least initially these relationships were formed because Twin and others possessed exceptional skill sets and knowledge that tourism entrepreneurs needed to facilitate their businesses. It must be stressed that these relationships, although unique during this period, cannot be considered outside the historical contexts in which they occurred. Thus, while it is important not to devalue the meaningful relationships that developed over many decades between Nakoda peoples and local tourism entrepreneurs, one also needs to interrogate how localized power dynamics and broader Indigenous–Euro-Canadian race relations informed this period of history.

In the United States, there are also examples of Indigenous peoples contributing to local tourism economies in national parks. From the mid-nineteenth century, Yosemite Indians found labour work in the developing tourism industries associated with the national park. They supplied tourists with wild game and fish as well as performing a variety of tasks related to the development of the park infrastructure (Spence, 1999). Similarly to what occurred in the United States, in addition to employment as labourers and guides, some Nakoda peoples also pursued their own opportunities to profit from the developing tourism economies as well as interact with tourists. Especially after the proliferation of the automobile, opportunities for Nakoda peoples to engage with tourists travelling from Calgary to the park greatly increased. Ralphine Locke, a Euro-Canadian woman whose family has lived in the Banff–Bow Valley for generations, recalls some of the ways that Nakoda peoples contributed to local tourism economies:

> Yes, a lot of the Stonies [Nakoda] had big horse businesses in those days and people would come out and go camping in the mountains with their horses and so they were employed through that as well as being guides and horsemen. So there was a lot of activity and exchange through tourism ... and quite a few relationships formed.[12]

Along with renting their horses to local guides and outfitters, some Nakoda peoples initiated their own small-scale tourism operations that catered to the needs of transient tourists. Several Nakoda peoples did participate in the early tourism economies, but for the most part access to the Banff–Bow Valley was greatly restricted for Nakoda communities and many individuals had difficulty consistently securing adequate employment. Furthermore, most of these opportunities were restricted to younger men, who were flexible enough to leave the reserve to pursue alternative occupations. While the tourism economies were growing at exponential rates in Banff and many entrepreneurs were subsequently prospering, during this same period Nakoda communities at Morley were facing difficult socio-economic conditions. Without their subsistence practices, many Nakoda peoples were struggling to adapt to an entirely new way of living.

The Banff Indian Days

While there are examples of a few Nakoda community members who were involved in Banff's tourism industry in various capacities, the Banff Indian Days were the primary instance of the mass participation of Nakoda peoples in local tourism economies. Subsequently, these events provide a case study of not only how Nakoda communities participated in producing "naturalness" through these festivals, but also how this discourse conversely came to shape perceptions of "Indigeneity." From the perspective of many Nakoda peoples, the antecedents of the Banff Indian Days precede the presence of Europeans in the Banff–Bow Valley. While later at the end of the nineteenth century more formalized events were established, most Nakoda peoples consider this event a continuation of earlier gatherings that occurred at the same location rather than something new. Nakoda elder Rollinmud explains:

> So, the Indian Days itself began way back … before the train lines, before Banff, before anything like that. It was a socializing of the First Nations. It really benefited a lot of relationships that gathered there as it became a trading area. It was a part of a meeting of the Shushwap [Secwepemc], Kootenay [Ktunaxa] and of course the Stoney [Nakoda] and even others. It was a gathering of the First Nations for exchanging and trading. So the Indian Days are just a continuing of what we always did anyway … the gathering that they always had.[13]

In addition to congregating at Banff for the purpose of establishing trading relationships, Indigenous peoples also used the area extensively for cultural purposes:

> This place [Banff townsite and proximal lands] was for a very long time an important place for the Stoney [Nakoda] and for other First Nations. My grandfather told me of the seasonal hunting camps that were held there for centuries. He remembers that the Kootenay [Ktunaxa], Shuswap [Secwepemc], and the Blackfoots [Siksika] participated with the Stoney in at least three Sun Dances in the eighteen hundreds at the same location prior to the Indian Days.[14]

What is critical to recognize from these perspectives is that many Nakoda peoples do not consider the Indian Days an event with a distinct starting point or as separate from previous gatherings and established cultural practices. In contrast to the few histories of the region that document the origins of the contemporary version of the Indian Days, many Nakoda peoples do not distinguish between the festival that began in the late nineteenth century and gatherings of First Nations that occurred at the same geographic locations in earlier periods.[15]

The modern version of the festival began when a significant spring flood washed out a section of the CPR railway lines, stranding a group of affluent tourists at the Banff Springs Hotel.[16] Wilson, a local guide and entrepreneur, travelled to Morley to try and convince some Nakoda peoples to come to Banff and put on cultural performances for the tourists. A Nakoda woman suggests that while other entrepreneurs were responsible for different aspects of the early organization of the event, Wilson played a vital role: "It was Tom Wilson who was really responsible for our [Nakoda] participation."[17] Under the leadership of Chief Hector Crawler, a group of Nakoda peoples were convinced, with appropriate monetary incentives, to travel to Banff on horseback, stage an event, and camp in the area.[18] With the typical patronizing tone imparted by newspapers of the period, an *Edmonton Journal* article that recounts the origins of the festival and explains Wilson's request to the Nakoda peoples to come to Banff and perform for tourists, stated: "The Indians, always delighted to play rather than work, were glad to fulfill the requests of local organizers and come to Banff."[19]

When one reviews the written historical accounts of the Indian Days, it is clear that they have difficulty determining an accurate date for when the modern version of the festival was established. Early in the twentieth century, the *Crag and Canyon* indicates that the first festival was in 1899.[20] Perhaps as a consequence, several historians have either noted the discrepancies or concluded that the first festival was held in this year.[21] Based on Department of Interior reports, Hart (1999) contends that it was in the summer of 1894 that a flood washed out the railway line and also resulted in an early closing of the Banff Springs Hotel. My analysis of the reports supports Hart's contention. As it was the only year the lines were not operational for a significant period, I deduced that it was in June of 1894 that Wilson made his journey down to Morley to negotiate with Crawler.[22]

After the Indian Days were established in 1894, however, newspaper analysis of the *Crag and Canyon* indicates that they were not held annually as an independent event until 1911.[23] While Nakoda peoples did gather in Banff on several occasions during this period, in conjunction with other gatherings, such as Dominion Day,[24] and they sometimes competed in horse races and other activities, 1911 is considered the inaugural year of the festival as an annual event.

The Banff Indian Days played an important role in the production of "naturalness" during this period. Although the festival began as a one-day affair, by 1912, as a consequence of its success as a tourist attraction, it was expanded to a two-day event. In 1928 it was extended to three days.[25] The festivals mainly exhibited the sporting and cultural practices of Indigenous peoples. In addition to an annual parade and musical and dance performances, the Indian Days also featured sporting competitions such as running races and rodeos. Even though they were sponsored by the CPR, the events were initially organized by local entrepreneurs Norman Luxton, Jim Brewster, Sam Armstrong, and Tom Wilson. As noted earlier, some of these men had established relationships with Nakoda peoples. In addition to the connections among Wilson, the Brewster family, and Nakoda individuals who worked in the tourism industry, Luxton also had extensive links with community members at Morley.[26] Locke, who was an ancestor of the McDougall family, explains Luxton's relationship with Nakoda peoples and his association with the family of early missionaries on the Morley reserve:

> Well, Norman took over David McDougall's trading post [on the reserve] for a while and started up a relationship there. That's where he met his wife of course, Georgina. You know he did quite a lot in trying to intercede a bit with the government on behalf of the Stoney [Nakoda]. And many of them speak very warmly of him.[27]

Rollinmud indicated the important relationship between Norman Luxton and some members of the community at Morley: "Every generation needs a good connector between the communities of Banff and Morley … During his time Luxton was that connection and at the Indian Days he was a great organizer."[28] Nakoda man Jackson Wesley expressed an appreciation for Luxton's role in their community: "It is like I owe him in my life, or at least I feel that way sometimes because he was really good to my people … He could be generous and he even saved them from bad circumstances on more than one occasion."[29] Although some Nakoda peoples did have issues with Luxton's influence in their communities (Snow, 2005), the Luxton family clearly had long-standing positive relationships with many Nakoda peoples. The established relations between Euro-Canadian entrepreneurs and local Nakoda peoples were critical in the early development of the Banff Indian Days.

Beginning with the 1914 completion of the Calgary–Banff coach road, Banff became a thriving mountain village capable of accommodating an increasing number of visitors. The Indian Days were very successful

Figure 4.2 From left: Georgina Luxton, Hector Crawler, Norman Luxton, Mrs Hector Crawler (1915). Although they at times had tumultuous relationships with some individuals at Morley, the Luxtons formed numerous close relationships with many families in the Nakoda community. Courtesy of the Whyte Museum of the Canadian Rockies. V263-na-3350. (Photographer: Byron Harmon)

at attracting tourists to the isolated community and park. Attendance peaked in 1922, when an incredible 71,540 tourists arrived to take part in the festivities and 600 Indigenous people participated.[30] The festival became a massive event that was an important economic generator for the CPR, tourism entrepreneurs, and the local Indigenous peoples. A substantial body of research demonstrates how cultural festivals that embody considerable financial benefits to host communities can be particularly influential in shaping perceptions of place through producing influential representational images.[31] As one of the region's largest tourist draws, the Indian Days was a prominent aspect of international marketing campaigns promoting the Banff townsite and RMP national park.

Along with having significant economic impacts on the region, the festivals also sold Banff as a "natural" tourist destination (Mason, 2008). Precolonial representations of Indigenous peoples had a mass appeal to Western tourists as they were perceived as an important characteristic of the "natural" setting. As a consequence, tourism producers went to great lengths to preserve the "naturalness" of various representations of Indigenous cultures. For example, in the 1950s and 1960s, when numerous Nakoda families transported themselves to and from the Indian Days by automobile, tourism producers emphasized that cars and trucks must be hidden behind the campgrounds so that precolonial images of Indigenous peoples were not disrupted by their use of modern technology.[32] The media coverage of the Indian Days also helped explicitly establish connections between Indigenous peoples and "naturalness" discourse. Particularly in reference to Indigenous music and dance performances, these links were evident. In 1938, a description of a Nakoda performance suggested that "their songs and dances come from nature itself."[33] Later in 1956, this type of reference also appears in newspaper accounts. A review of one musical performance suggested that the "singing of the Indians was just as it was intended in nature."[34] Precolonial representations in media and tourism promotions were also aspects of marketing the festival and the region to tourists. These promotions contributed to prevailing discourse by shaping the expectations of tourists and solidifying the region's reputation as a uniquely "natural" environment (see plate 5).

Considering that some productive sites of labour and subsistence land-use practices were removed from RMP and the Banff townsite to support productions of the region as a "natural" environment, why were Indigenous peoples included in advertising campaigns while other working-class peoples remained on the margins? Whereas Indigenous peoples were a pre-eminent part of marketing, including tourism posters, local and regional newspaper advertisements, and formal CPR publications,[35] labourers were not represented in any form in the materials consulted. One must assume that the presence of precolonial Indigenous peoples was an important aspect of promoting RMP and Banff. As Meijer-Drees (1993) contends, these precolonial representations were symbols of how "natural" the Rocky Mountains were, and as a result their presence aligned with current tourism markets. In direct contrast, the labourers who worked in mines or built transportation and accommodation infrastructure that met tourists' needs and allowed access to the region served no purpose in Banff once their work was complete and they were subsequently excluded from the public imagery. In comparison to these labourers, the presence of Indigenous peoples supported prevailing discourse and the vested interests of government and private enterprise as long as they continued to sell valuable images of the town that were evidently in high demand.

Even though the tourism industry was democratizing with the improved access to the region, until the late 1920s, the majority of the tourists were from affluent and upper-middle-class backgrounds. Arriving from urban centres throughout North America and Europe, tourists were not necessarily familiar with the local environment. As a result, nature was often interpreted for them. Everything – animal populations, mountain weather, glaciers, and especially local Indigenous peoples – required explanations (Meijer-Drees, 1991). As indicated by Wilson (1991), throughout North America at the beginning of the twentieth century, nature had to be explained to tourists. In 1915, park rangers at Banff began a process of institutionalizing nature by creating an interpretive trail, the first of thousands that soon developed all over the continent.[36] Influential entrepreneurs capitalized on the desire for interpretation and the growth of the mass tourism industry. Tourism producers benefited, as they were able to position themselves as the local experts on all things "natural."

Luxton's tourist souvenir shop, the Sign of the Goat Curio Store, became a lucrative source of revenue as it featured impressive specimens of taxidermy and the craft work of Nakoda peoples (Meijer-Drees, 1991). During this period the success of Luxton's shop exemplifies tourists' consumption of all that was considered "natural." Tourism producers acted as the master interpreters for the activities during the Banff Indian Days by translating their cultural significance for the crowds. Luxton and other entrepreneurs would often provide a running commentary for tourists while participants competed in the sporting and cultural events. As a *Calgary Herald* article states: "Luxton was a longtime friend of the Indian and he was able to interpret the red man to the white at the Indian Days."[37] His tourist shop and the cultural festival he helped organize and initiate are two examples of how he and other business elite marketed Banff as a "natural" place, produced this "naturalness" in various forms, interpreted it for the public, and fostered its mass consumption.

Figure 4.3 Spectators at the Banff Indian Days sporting grounds (1915). This photograph demonstrates the class orientation of some of the tourists who attended the festival in its early stages. Courtesy of the Whyte Museum of the Canadian Rockies. V465-pd3–012. (Photographer: Underwood Fonds)

Problematizing Representations of Indigenous Peoples

The precolonial representations of Indigenous peoples disseminated in promotion of the Indian Days were problematic in several respects. As Kirshenblatt-Gimblett asserts (1998), festivals organized by agents or institutions that control some aspects of cultural representations may share a performance discourse that often stands in opposition to the ways communities may stage themselves. From his work with the Maasai in Kenya, Bruner (2001) contends that when tourist productions are consumed predominantly by one cultural group and that same group also controls some of the means of production, representations of Indigenous peoples can often reinforce racist stereotypes as they are in some ways designed to simulate consumers' expectations of Indigenous groups and meet market demands to satisfy the tourism industry. Analogously to Bruner's findings, the representations of Indigenous peoples produced through the Banff Indian Days were at least partly determined by tourism producers and were designed to satisfy non-Indigenous stereotypical conceptions of "Indigeneity." However, an *Edmonton Journal* article that traces the changes in events and prizes throughout the festival's history indicates that Indigenous peoples did have some control over the events they participated in, their scheduling, and the negotiation of the prizes that were given to top finishers.[38] Parker (1990) and Meijer-Drees (1993) both suggest that Nakoda leaders did negotiate with organizers in Banff to determine various components of the event. Oral accounts indicate that many aspects of the festival, including the appropriate remuneration for Nakoda participation, were constantly discussed as Nakoda leaders interacted with organizing groups.[39] Nakoda peoples had some leverage over control of their representations at the Indian Days – including their ceremonial attire, their horses, and their own embodied labour.[40] Conversely, tourism producers exercised considerable power in the production of the cultural representations by controlling the spaces the festivals were celebrated in and tourists' access to the events. Access to spaces and the spaces themselves are powerful mechanisms of controlling representation at any tourism production. The tourism producers who organized and profited from the Banff Indian Days exercised influence on representations at the festival by controlling access and space. This influence encouraged the use of precolonial representations, which supported the production of discourse that sold Banff as a "natural" environment.

Through an analysis of the CPR tourism promotional posters circulated for the event, local and regional print media coverage, and Nakoda accounts of the festival, it is clear that the Banff Indian Days homogenized Indigenous peoples, as they were all represented under a generic term and presented as one single cultural group. None of the sources reviewed suggest that the diverse Indigenous peoples who participated in the festival were represented as anything other than "Indians." Over the many decades the events were held, Nakoda leaders and organizers of the event invited numerous Indigenous groups to participate.[41] In addition to the three Nakoda bands, the Cree from Hobbema, the Ktunaxa (Kootenay), Tsuu T'ina (Sarcee), Pikunni (Peigan), Siksika (Blackfoot), and Kainai (Blood) were all regular participants and invited performers at the festival.[42] While Nakoda peoples were certainly the lifeblood of the event, oral and newspaper accounts establish that various local Indigenous groups did regularly participate. On special occasions, other Indigenous groups from different parts of North America also attended.[43] Even though diverse groups of peoples participated in the festival over the many decades it was held, the marketing images overtly homogenized participants, as they are represented under the generic term "Indians" and presented as one cultural group (see plate 6).

As Sioux anthropologist Beatrice Medicine argues (2001), a lack of sensitivity and perception has been the main tragedy of understanding Indigenous cultures throughout the twentieth century. Homogeneous labels can support offensive and even racist stereotypes regarding Indigenous peoples by glossing over the diversity of their languages and cultures. While homogeneous labels were applied to the participants at the Indian Days, it is critical to consider how these labels at times had productive meanings for Indigenous participants. As Hertzberg's (1971) work has shown, in other regions of North America during the early decades of the twentieth century, while Indigenous peoples did resist homogeneous categorization, they also unified themselves according to it and established intertribal networks to secure specific social, political, and economic objectives. Arndt's (2005) research indicates that intertribal identities were also formed during this period to extend cultural networks around powwow celebrations. My discussions with an elder revealed that the Nakoda community strategically adapted various labels throughout the twentieth century. Specifically, reference was made to how this occurred in the community: "We've been called Indians, Natives and sometimes people thought we were Blackfoot or Cree ... so we did not always object ... but we've always been Stoney [Nakoda] ... because that is who we are to ourselves."[44] In what can be considered a form of strategic essentialism, some Nakoda presented a unified front as a productive way of exercising power in their relations with Euro-North American groups and institutions. Spivak (1988) contends that ethnic, minority, or marginalized groups can form solidarity for the purpose of social action by accepting essentialist subjectivities. While major differences exist between members of these heterogeneous groups, at key moments it can be advantageous for them to temporarily essentialize themselves to assert a unified group identity in pursuit of significant goals. Brah (1992) reveals that it can be particularly productive for groups when they are conscious of the values and consequences of adopting essentialized subjectivities. In the case of Nakoda communities, calculated steps to unify local peoples were welcomed when tangible socio-economic, political, or cultural advantages resulted. Furniss suggests that these unifying practices "should be considered a form of political action through which symbols of Indianness are deliberately and carefully mobilized to bring about specific political effects" (1999: 165). Nakoda elder Poucette referred to how the mixing of groups during the Banff Indian Days unified the distinct cultures and identities of the Indigenous peoples who participated:

> It wouldn't matter if it was Stoney [Nakoda] there, or Kootenay [Ktunaxa] or Cree or whoever, they [tourists and organizers] would just say the "Indians" and that sort of thing. Today that might be pretty offensive because obviously we have different languages and different cultures. You know from what I remember the Stoneys invited the other Native groups when it was going good ... because when there was no hardship, there was no competing. Everybody enjoyed themselves and all the groups lived amongst each other. The days were such a mixture of the different groups, you camp someplace and there would be Cree, Kootenay, or Bloods [Kainai] right beside you. It was a real uniting thing to be intermixed like that and it also was good to share stories and some of the similarities between all of our cultures.[45]

The Banff Indian Days offered a unique opportunity to local Indigenous groups to gather, socialize, and celebrate some of their cultural practices. From 1894, when the festival began, throughout the first few decades of the twentieth century, these types of opportunities were infrequent for many communities. As federal-government assimilation strategies were strictly enforced by the agents of the colonial bureaucracy, Indigenous peoples had difficulty finding spaces and opportunities to celebrate their cultural practices and interact with other groups. This was certainly the case for the Nakoda communities during this period, as any occasion to leave the reserve was meticulously scrutinized by the acting Indian agents. Cultural gatherings where Nakoda peoples could interact with other Indigenous communities were particularly viewed with suspicion and at times they were strongly discouraged or prohibited.[46] In this manner, the opportunities facilitated through the

Indian Days to leave the reserve, gather with other groups and engage with broader society were highly valued by many Nakoda community members.[47]

Foucauldian Power Relations and Colonial Societies

Foucault's understandings of micro power relations can reveal why forms of strategic essentialism were used during this period by Indigenous individuals and communities. In the example of homogeneous labels at the Banff Indian Days, Foucault's (1980) theories of how power is exercised in a capillary-like nature suggests ways that cultural labels could have been strategically or ironically taken up in various contexts. Through their interpersonal interactions with tourism entrepreneurs, spectators, and even with each other, participants strategically essentialized themselves to exercise power in processes that had potential to enact political and cultural change. Understanding how homogeneous labels were productive for Indigenous participants demonstrates why Foucault's conceptions of power relations are so effective. Foucault summarizes his notion of productive power: "In fact, power produces; it produces reality; it produces domains of objects and rituals of truth. The individual and the knowledge that may be gained of him belong to this production" (1977: 194). In contrast to Marxist-oriented paradigms, his perspective rejects binary oppositions and refuses to see power as an oppressive tool that is only held by dominant groups. He explains further: "What makes power hold good, what makes it accepted ... is simply the fact that it doesn't weigh on us as a force that says no, but that it traverses and produces things, it induces pleasure, forms of knowledge, produces discourse" (Foucault, 1980: 119). In *The History of Sexuality Volume I: An Introduction* (1978), Foucault rejects the repressive hypothesis as he demonstrates the actions of productive power by revealing how the attempts to control and monitor sexuality led to an explosion of discourses of sexuality. By viewing power as productive, it is easier to more fully appreciate the complexities of colonial relations, as this perspective investigates the enabling possibilities in constraints, not just their limitations (Shogan, 2002). In the case of the Indian Days, the use of homogeneous labels for Indigenous participants cannot be isolated from the complex systems of colonial power that they existed in and helped reinforce. These labels were reproduced in Canadian society as part of government assimilation objectives, whereby not recognizing differences in the diversity of Indigenous cultures was tactically encouraged. However, homogeneous labels were also a productive force for local Indigenous peoples as they consciously unified themselves according to these one-dimensional racial and linguistic categories when it furthered the various political, cultural, or socio-economic intentions of their communities.

Foucault's conceptualizations of power are useful for understanding relations in the context of colonial politics in Alberta throughout the twentieth century. His theorizing of power relations accounts for complexities of discursive formations by focusing on the fragmentation and the indeterminacy of these articulations. Foucault's theories challenge analyses that would reduce the intricacy of colonial power to dichotomies between state apparatuses and Indigenous peoples, or dominant and subordinate subject positions (Wakeham, 2008). For Foucault, power is not possessed or centralized in single individuals or groups, but is part of all human relationships as it radiates and penetrates throughout all of society (1987). This does not suggest that Foucault thought that power was exercised equitably in any society. While his relational perspectives of power have been interpreted as pluralism, his view of power relations in fact argues that power is continually renegotiated under asymmetrical organized structures (Markula and Pringle, 2006).

Following Foucault's theorizing of power relations, one would recognize that Indigenous peoples are members of diverse groups who hold perspectives that may or may not have similar objectives, motivations, and actions. As Bracken (1997) asserts in reference to power relations in Indigenous communities, it is "patronizing to assume that they did not hold a diversity of views or opinions – or that they did not often disagree when it came to deciding how to best manage their own lives" (79). For example, key Indigenous organizers or leaders had more to gain through their interactions with entrepreneurs involved with the Indian Days in comparison to the many performers who participated. Similarly, the business community in Banff had more at stake in the success of the event compared to Euro-Canadian spectators or international tourists. Struggles involving Indigenous peoples cannot be reduced to simple conflicts between European colonizers and the colonized, as it is sometimes difficult to draw clear distinctions between government initiatives and the multiple objectives of Indigenous communities. Foucault's studies illustrate how individuals are constituted through discursively produced power relations within specific socio-historical contexts. His works offer researchers a nuanced model of how power is exercised in relational, productive, and not necessarily hierarchical processes that can escape limiting binaries that, in some cases, predetermine and overdetermine power relations. When considering the experiences of Indigenous peoples at the Banff Indian Days, it is vital to comprehend that for Nakoda participants, these opportunities had important enabling, as well as limiting, implications.

Conclusion

In order to challenge research that reduces the complexities of representational images of marginalized groups, it is imperative to avoid simplifying cultural representations and consequently the possibilities within their display. This is key when examining the intricate web of power relationships that often characterize colonial societies. It is particularly important for studies in colonial contexts, as the theorizing of these relations have predominantly been viewed from Marxist-oriented postcolonial perspectives. As Loomba (2005) notes in her critique of Said and other postcolonial scholars who focused on representations of colonized peoples: "[They] … concentrated too much on imperialist discourses and their positioning of colonial peoples, neglecting the way in which these people received, contributed to, modified, or challenged such discourses" (193). Scholars can avoid predetermining power relations by adopting theoretical lenses that open up spaces for the intricacies of colonial power to be unravelled. Post-structural theories and specifically Foucault's productive, relational, and omnipresent perspectives on how power is exercised present researchers with models that can escape predetermined binaries and demonstrate the complexities and possibilities in representational processes. However, Wetherell and Potter (1992) argue that post-structural discourse analysis has generally concentrated more on texts of representational images than on everyday discourse, which can include discussions, interactions, and personal accounts. This book contributes to a growing body of research that contests claims that scholars using post-structural theoretical and methodological approaches focus too intently on the images of display and subsequently ignore, or uncritically account for, the material conditions underpinning the production of representations.[48] This analysis of the Indian Days emphasizes that cultural representations which are situated within colonial power relations require scholars to adopt in-depth approaches that adequately interrogate the complexities and possibilities that they often embody.

Oral accounts of the Banff Indian Days indicate that they offered unique opportunities for Nakoda peoples to contest, produce, and assert representations of their cultural practices. In spite of this, precolonial representations of Indigenous peoples and cultures contributed to "naturalness" discourse throughout the history of the event. While this discourse was heavily influenced by the objectives of the region's developing tourism economies, as they were produced and consumed through the tourism industry, Nakoda peoples also pursued opportunities to strategically manipulate these representations and (re)interpret them for their own socio-economic, political, and cultural purposes.

Chapter Five

Rethinking the Banff Indian Days as Critical Spaces of Cultural Exchange

The production of "Indigeneity" in the Banff–Bow Valley from 1911 to 1980 was informed by the regional development of tourism economies. The participation of Nakoda peoples in the Banff Indian Days cultural and sporting festivals was a significant part of these processes as they offered unique socio-economic, political, and cultural opportunities. Clearly, the exclusion of Indigenous peoples from the lands and resources inside RMP, which were fundamental to their cultural practices, had significant impacts on their communities. The Indian Days facilitated a process whereby Nakoda peoples returned to important sites within the park boundaries and reasserted their cultural links to these landscapes. While the prevailing discourse that was circulated during this period is the focus here, this chapter is also concerned with how Nakoda peoples responded to the expectations that were created in the production of "Indigeneity" through their engagement in the tourism industry. Nakoda peoples sometimes pushed the limits of what was possible by playing with the very boundaries that constrained their lives as they refused structures and defied limiting definitions of their cultural practices. Through the Indian Days, Nakoda peoples created critical spaces of interaction and identity-making possibilities.

Precolonial Representations of Indigenous Peoples

Over the many decades the festivals were celebrated, the Indian Days became one of the most influential cultural events in the history of the Banff–Bow Valley. The festivals originally involved only Nakoda peoples, but by the 1920s, several other Indigenous groups also participated. The majority of Nakoda peoples did regularly attend, and with the support of other participating groups, some years there were over 1000 Indigenous participants, with a record high of 1500 in 1927.[1] Although the audiences were predominately Euro–North Americans and Europeans for the first three decades of the twentieth century, in the 1950s and 1960s they were quite diverse. Some years, all American states and Canadian provinces were represented in the audiences and over thirty nationalities were noted in attendance.[2] Along with their considerable economic impact, the festivals were also events that shaped regional, national, and international perceptions of Banff and the surrounding area.

The Indian Days consisted of numerous activities that profiled the sporting and cultural practices of local Indigenous peoples as well as other events that featured Indigenous participants. At the turn of the twentieth century, very few Indigenous peoples lived in the Banff townsite and they were not permitted to live in the surrounding national park. As a consequence of the marginalization facilitated by the reserve system, there were few spaces during this period where Indigenous peoples simultaneously interacted with broader Canadian society and international tourists. The Indian Days festivals not only became an essential space for audiences to learn about Indigenous cultures, but were also an influential part of the processes that informed the production of "Indigeneity." There were many different factors that impacted the production of "Indigeneity" through the Indian Days, and thus it would be impossible to assess all these influences. As a result, the focus here is on how the prevailing discourse endorsed precolonial images that exoticized and temporalized local cultures. Importantly, how some Nakoda peoples responded to the prevailing discourse and positioned themselves within these processes is also considered.

An article from the *Crag and Canyon* indicates that throughout the history of the event a "typical Indian village" was erected at the "Indian campgrounds" and sporting competitions became the main forms of entertainment.[3] While the location of the campgrounds did change on several occasions, the tipi village was always an aspect of the gathering. The campgrounds not only provided a space for participants to gather, socialize, sleep, and eat during the festival, but they were also a main tourist attraction. Promotional materials for tourists circulated by the CPR described the tipi village in the following manner: "The braves mounted on their gaily decorated ponies wearing magnificent bonnets of eagle feathers is a sight to be remembered … Visitors are welcome at their camp where good-natured squaws [Indigenous women] sit at the doors of the tepees and watch their brown babies sprawling at their feet."[4] A description from a regional newspaper that promoted the Indian Days also centres on exoticized aspects as it itemizes the contents of the tipi village: "Beating tom-toms, ki-yiing Indians, madly galloping cayuses [horses], gaudily painted braves and squaws, papooses [Indigenous children], dogs, a hundred tepees and everything that belongs to the Indian village."[5] These statements highlight some of the exotic elements of the camp, its subsequent appeal to the Western tourist gaze, and the potential intimacy of some of these encounters. Time slots were allotted for visitors to tour the campgrounds, examine the tipis, and interact with participants.[6] As Nakoda woman Snow indicates: "Especially the tourists from Europe liked the village. They would say that it was an Indian camp and would come to take pictures. It was the centre of attraction."[7]

Nakoda peoples did open their camps to be toured by visitors, but some community members expressed a concern over the tours of the campgrounds because of what can be characterized as their invasive aspects.[8] Other Nakoda individuals welcomed the campground tours and viewed them as opportunities to display and sell their art, bead and quill work.[9] Despite differing perspectives, visiting the tipi village was an occasion for tourists to be exposed to and learn from Indigenous cultures. The tourists' desire to tour the campgrounds was partly driven by their interest in Wild West depictions, which re-enacted colonial narratives and primarily circulated precolonial representations. These powerful genres shaped Western tourists' expectations of "Indigeneity."

The Indian Days consisted of diverse activities, but a crowd favourite was always the annual parade, where participants were expected to dress in "Indian" attire and be judged for the most colourful and decorative costumes. As early as 1911, it is noted that it was "the barbaric splendour of their costumes" that attracted most spectators to the parade.[10] In 1921, one newspaper account summarized a scene at the parade: "The braves mounted upon Indian ponies, resplendent in buckskin beadwork, feathers and war paint make a showing which can be witnessed nowhere else upon the American continent."[11] As demonstrated in the following description from 1925, regional newspaper reports of the parade emphasize its exotic elements: "Painted with brilliant red and yellow from the old Indian ochre beds at Marble Canyon, the costumed Indians drew large crowds of tourists to view them in the glimmer of their ancient glory. Many of the tourists had never seen Indians before."[12] Some Nakoda peoples expressed that they were

Figure 5.1 Banff Indian Days Campground underneath Cascade Mountain (1920). Courtesy of the Whyte Museum of the Canadian Rockies. V263-na-3229. (Photographer: Byron Harmon)

uncomfortable with the attention they received during the parade. One elder recollects his experiences: "As a young kid in the parade, all of these tourists were taking pictures of us and you know holding our hands … and taking more pictures. They [tourists] wanted to be around you and they liked coming. For them … I'm not too sure, but to us Native peoples it was a way of living, not a onetime show."[13]

The Indian Days parade was a feature event that was a main tourist attraction. Tourists lined the streets of Banff Avenue to take pictures of and interact with the participants, who were usually paid for posing in photographs.[14] Prizes were given to the "best dressed" in the parade and the judges were most often notable residents of the Banff townsite. From analyses of descriptions of Nakoda participants, it is clear that

Figure 5.2 The Banff Indian Days parade (1941). In full regalia, including elaborate headdresses and decorated horses, Indigenous peoples pass by the Banff Springs Hotel during the parade. Nakoda men George McLean on foot at right and Job Sleven on foot at left. Courtesy of the Glenbow Museum Archives. NA-1241-753. (Photographer: F. Gully)

awards were predominantly given to the men, women, and children whose attire most accurately met Western tourists' expectations of "Indigeneity,"[15] which as discussed earlier were generally based on precolonial perceptions promulgated in the Wild West depictions of film, literature, and theatre.

Sporting competitions were also a component of the Indian Days and by 1915 they constituted the majority of the program. An article from the *Calgary Herald* recounting the history of sporting events specifies that foot and horse races along with Indian wrestling, a unique competition which took place on horseback, were part of the Indian Days from the very beginning.[16] Other competitions involving horses, such as barrel jumps, bare and saddle bucks, calf roping, steer riding, and relay and carriage races, were some of the rodeo-oriented events that formed the festival's sporting schedule in the 1920s.[17] Nakoda elder Rollinmud reflects on the rodeo events at the Indian Days:

> Ah … and then there were the rodeo events. Back then there were no fancy suits and equipment, like the rodeos today. You just hold on to the horse, sometimes without a saddle or anything. As far as I can remember, back then you just got on. You'd bring your fastest horse and if you won you would have one-year of bragging rights [*laughs aloud*].[18]

Tipi pitching, pie eating, and tug-of-war competitions were also eventually added to the itinerary in the 1930s.[19] According to an article from the *Calgary Herald*, archery competitions clearly had the most appeal for the crowd.[20] As outside of these annual contests they rarely ever used bows and arrows by the 1930s, local Indigenous peoples should not have been expected to display very much proficiency in archery competitions. The fascination of the archery competitions for tourists was at least partly related to the fact that archery reinforced and celebrated precolonial perceptions of "Indigeneity."

Although in the early stages of the Indian Days, non-Indigenous and Indigenous competitors participated together in many athletic events, as the festival became more established in the 1920s, interracial events were abandoned in favour of all-Indigenous contests.[21] Kirshenblatt-Gimblett (1998) maintains that festivals that re-enact activities in a discrete performance setting designed for the consumption of spectators can objectify participants by clearly separating the performers from the observers based on ethnicity. Especially when Indigenous peoples are involved, this is inherently problematic as these spectacles can highlight exoticizing and marginalizing aspects. Sporting events at the Indian Days became a significant component of the festival. Along with entertaining spectators and at times displaying precolonial representations, participants were positioned and positioned themselves within the Western tourist gaze during the athletic competitions.

Figure 5.3 Indigenous contestants in the men's foot race at the Banff Indian Days (1925). Courtesy of the Whyte Museum of the Canadian Rockies. V263-na-3327. (Photographer: Byron Harmon)

Figure 5.4 Indigenous competitors in the men's horse race at the Banff Indian Days (1925). Courtesy of the Whyte Museum of the Canadian Rockies. V263-na-3323. (Photographer: Byron Harmon)

Figure 5.5 Indigenous participants in the archery competition at the Banff Indian Days (1939). Courtesy of the Glenbow Museum and Archives. NA-1241–563. (Photographer unknown)

During this period, a parallel event profiling Indigenous cultures was being attended by tourists in Yosemite National Park. In 1914, an Indian village was created for tourists in the park and in 1916 the Indian Field Days tourism festival was established. Running annually between 1916 and 1929, the event included an Indian parade, rodeo demonstrations, horse races, and an Indian baby show where local Yosemite Indian participants were paid for their time and efforts. As Spence (1999) notes, tourists were entertained by local performers and would also visit their camp to view "native" life. With the popularity of Kodak cameras, photographing Indigenous peoples became another tourist highlight at the event. Similar to what was witnessed at Banff, the Indian Field Days mostly presented Plains Indian culture, which conformed to popular Euro-American conceptions of how "Indians" were supposed to look. Stereotypical representations were common that exoticized and homogenized Indigenous peoples. The commercialized festival was discontinued in 1929 due to the crash in the US stock market, which limited the number of tourists who travelled to California from the larger urban centres in the Northeast (Spence, 1999).

One aspect not directly addressed in Spence's research on the history of Indigenous experiences of the tourism industry inside national parks in the United States is the specific participation of Indigenous women in these local tourism economies. Although rarely mentioned by newspaper accounts, Indigenous women played fundamental roles at the Banff Indian Days. In contrast to most sporting and physical-activity spaces in other regions throughout Canada at the beginning of the twentieth century, where women were often excluded or marginalized (Hall, 2009), Indigenous women were active participants in the Indian Days in several respects. Nakoda women were key organizers of the events by facilitating their family's participation. While the tasks of preparing meals, organizing the campgrounds, and taking care of children supported men's participation in the festival, Nakoda women also actively engaged in many of the sporting and cultural events.[22] Although men led most of the pre-festival negotiations with tourism producers and more often represented their communities through the various public ceremonies, Nakoda women were the backbone of the events' organization.[23]

Not surprisingly, Indigenous women were participants in the cultural performances that often highlighted the Indian Days' schedule. In addition to the annual parade, of which women were directors and organizers, the music and dance performances relied upon women's participation. In the earlier versions of the Indian Days, the women's sporting events consisted mainly of foot races and horse races wherein, similarly to the men, they demonstrated their endurance and skill in competitions for monetary prizes.[24] Nakoda women also participated in some rodeo contests.[25] Kelm's (2011) research on the history of rodeo in Western Canada suggests that although women competed at a few rodeos early in the twentieth century, the rise of professional organizations sidelined them for several decades until they formed their own associations. In alignment with women's rights movements, new spaces in rodeo contests and performances were not created until the second half of the twentieth century. Wall's (2012) research on the social history of sport in Alberta highlights not only the limited participation of Indigenous women in rodeo during this period, but also how all women were marginalized from mainstream sporting life in the province. She notes that women were strongly discouraged from participation in sports that involved risk or more direct physical contact. While some Euro-Canadian women were at times supported to engage in tennis and golf, Indigenous women were also marginalized and excluded from these spaces because of the direct associations with particular class and Christian values. As Indigenous women actively participated in rodeo and other sporting events at the Indian Days throughout the first five decades of the twentieth century, this is an interesting example of the inclusion of women that contradicts not only most rodeo forums in Western Canada during this period, but also women's sport and leisure participation in general throughout the province.

By the 1930s, women-specific events, including travois races, tug-of-war, tipi pitching, and nail-driving competitions, were also added to the program.[26] In 1954, an Indigenous women's fashion show was scheduled into the festival.[27] Even though the number of events and participants in the women's competitions were significantly fewer than in the men's, the scale of participation of women in the sporting competitions remains quite remarkable considering their extensive contributions as organizers and facilitators in other aspects of the festival. Moreover, when one acknowledges the limited and severely restricted involvement of women as competitors in international sporting events during this period, such as the Commonwealth or Olympic Games, the extent of participation of Indigenous women during the Indian Days remains quite exceptional (Hall, 2012). This is especially notable when considering the struggles that Indigenous women continue to encounter as both participants as well as organizers and leaders in sporting institutions and structures in the twenty-first-century Canadian context (Paraschak, 2000; Giles, 2008, 2012; Paraschak and Forsyth, 2010).

Moving beyond a focus on gendered participation in the event to an examination of the cultural representations during the Indian Days, it is clear that the festival temporalized Indigenous peoples as a part of a bygone era – as a stagnant or unchanged aspect of Alberta's past, not an active component of the historical present. In 1923, newspaper accounts that promoted the events sold the Indian Days as the last chance for tourists to witness a "vanishing culture that was quickly disappearing."[28] In a *Calgary Herald* article entitled "Redskins Invade Mountain Resort," the author describes a scene from the parade: "Medicine men with their girdled loins and painted bodies dressed in their feathered finery and beaded costumes, others in simple Buffalo hides, paraded through the crowded streets of Banff to their teepee village at the foot

Figure 5.6 Banff Indian Days campgrounds (1923). Several woman organizers preparing to set off to participate in the parade. From left: Mrs Hector Crawler, Mrs Enos Hunter, Enos Hunter, unidentified Nakoda woman and an unidentified child. Courtesy of the Whyte Museum of the Canadian Rockies. V263-na-3257. (Photographer: Byron Harmon)

Figure 5.7 Indigenous women participants in the Banff Indian Days (1941). Indigenous women race around the track during the travois race as a component of the rodeo events. Courtesy of the Glenbow Museum and Archives. NA-1241-699. (Photographer: F. Gully)

of Cascade Mountain."[29] A 1955 article projects a similar tone in describing the event: "It is the day that time rolls back, and the Stoney [Nakoda] Indian tribe members present themselves as they were 100 years ago, in their soft skin suits made of elk, deer and other hides, the braves with eagle feather head dresses and brightly beaded gloves and suits."[30] These descriptions of the clothing worn by some of the individuals who participated in the parade and the spaces they occupied indicates some of the ways precolonial representations were displayed at the festival. During the parade and cultural events, participants and performers were encouraged to endorse representations which supported particular conceptions of "Indigeneity" (see plate 7).

Although attempts to fracture precolonial images were made by some Nakoda peoples, they were often rejected by tourism producers. As early as 1913, organizers prohibited any participants who chose to wear modern attire from marching in the parade.[31] Later, during cultural performances, a similar code of dress was reinforced. It is important to indicate that the ceremonial dress of Nakoda peoples should not only be characterized as disciplinary. Throughout the history of the Indian Days many Nakoda participants took a great deal of pride in displaying their forms of ceremonial dress.[32] What is notable regarding the exchanges between Nakoda participants and Euro-Canadian organizers over appropriate attire is the amount of control that tourism producers attempted to exercise over what Indigenous peoples wore. How certain participants responded to these attempts in ways that either supported or contradicted tourists' expectations of "Indigeneity" is also of interest. Participation in the events alone can be considered a disruption of a temporalizing discourse. In referring to Indigenous participation in rodeo events during this period, Kelm argues that "riding in parades, setting up Indian villages, or dancing before dignitaries forcefully demonstrated to both spectators and Aboriginal people themselves that they were not just remnants of the past but very much had a place in a modernizing Canada" (2011: 11).

However, from an analysis of tourism materials, photographs, newspapers, and oral accounts, it is clear that understandings of how Indigenous peoples managed introduced European influences or the current state of their communities were absent from any of the cultural interpretations or representations at the Indian Days. Because tourism producers sought to maintain precolonial representations to align with tourists' expectations, the complexities, histories, and contemporary lives of local Indigenous peoples were not overtly part of the festival and its marketing campaigns. As Rudin's (2009) nuanced history proves, this is a powerful strategy. He documents how Acadians were marginalized and First Nations excluded through processes that redefined spaces and the public memory on Canada's east coast. His research demonstrates how celebratory historical monuments and tourism ventures were devised in ways that not only reflected dominant socio-cultural forms, but marginalized communities, depoliticized their cultural representations, and attempted to erase contemporary issues or struggles.

In their influential study on photographic representations, Lutz and Collins (1993) contend that colour, pose, framing, and vantage point can be used to produce precolonial representations that position Indigenous peoples in earlier stages of progress while simultaneously celebrating Western ideals and modernity. Wakeham (2008) asserts that precolonial representations can racialize Indigenous bodies and relegate them to static spaces of primitive nature uninfluenced by history and the progressive temporality of Western culture. Temporalizing and exoticizing Indigenous peoples at the Indian Days was problematic because non-Indigenous consumers, who always constituted the majority, were left with simplistic understandings of Indigenous cultures and histories. As Moses reveals with his study on Wild West shows, which occurred throughout North America and Europe from 1883 to 1933: "The most popular Indian shows and performances appeared to be those that exhibited old-time habits and pagan ways which placed Indians in a false light" (1996: 258). Similarly to Wild West theatre, the cultural performances at the Indian Days were more focused on celebrating precolonial aspects of Indigenous cultures. With no attempt to foreground Indigenous peoples in their contemporary realities, the representations reinforced understandings of "Indigeneity" that were based on stereotypes or urban Western perceptions. Misleading representations left consumers at the Indian Days with inaccurate impressions of the contemporary lives of Nakoda peoples in the Banff–Bow Valley. Even in the twenty-first century, representations of Indigenous peoples are still challenged by discourses that situate them in a primitive past (Mason, 2009). By juxtaposing precolonial representations with Indigenous accounts that highlighted their lived experiences, the Indian Days could have potentially located cultures in spaces that would have fragmented the perception of Indigenous peoples in an idealized past. This would have forced consumers to acknowledge Indigenous peoples as a component of contemporary Canadian cultural life.

The Indian Days as Socio-economic, Political, and Cultural Opportunities

While the Indian Days did popularize precolonial representations, it is imperative not to discount the roles that local Nakoda peoples played in these festivals and the significance of these gatherings. As researchers in sport studies have continued to argue, events celebrating physical, sporting, and cultural practices can be influential arenas where North America's Indigenous peoples can exercise agency, be self-determining, create opportunities, and challenge or assert representations (Heine, 1991; Paraschak, 1996, 1997; Springwood, 2001; Robidoux, 2004; Forsyth and Wamsley, 2006; Giles, 2012; Mason and Koehli, 2012). The histories of the Indian Days support this research, as they offered Nakoda communities considerable socio-economic, political, and cultural opportunities. Becoming increasingly relevant throughout the first few decades of the twentieth century, the festivals presented limited financial assistance for Nakoda peoples in a period when supplementary income was in some cases necessary for survival. Although many communities on reserves in southern Alberta experienced poor living conditions throughout the first half of the twentieth century, it was during the depression (1929–39) that some reserves became desperate for governmental support. As a 1935 article in the *Calgary Herald* indicates, Nakoda peoples at the Morley reserve relied upon the food rations and supplementary income that was intended to compensate them for their participation at the Indian Days during these difficult times.[33] Heavy cattle losses and the construction of the Banff Highway through their reserve, which resulted in poor hunting conditions, made Nakoda leaders petition the federal government in 1935 to reinstitute the Treaty 7 rations system that had been discontinued in 1904. Although local peoples began to rely heavily on the Indian Days as early as 1920, during the Depression the remuneration for participating in the festival became a major source of subsistence.

Beginning in the 1940s, the high-profile Indian Days were ideal for Nakoda peoples to hold inductee ceremonies and introduce honorary members of their nation. These individuals, mostly prominent men and women from Calgary's business and political communities, were singled out for their dedication to improving the lives of Nakoda peoples.[34] In some cases, famous celebrities and members of royalty were also given honorary status.[35] From 1940 until the 1970s, Nakoda leaders, using their own cultural capital, took advantage of the media exposure of the Indian Days to build and publicly solidify connections with influential persons in broader urban Euro-Canadian communities and internationally. Greenstein (1995) notes that despite the focus of colonial histories on dichotomies between the powerful and the powerless, colonial relationships also presented opportunities for alliances across colonial divides and institutions. This aligns with related research in Western Canada showing that even though Indigenous peoples seldom controlled the staging of public celebrations, they did use them to communicate directly with visiting dignitaries and politicians about their concerns, which included treaty rights and access to resources. Kelm (2011) states: "Aboriginal people used these moments of encounter to raise awareness of their cultures, their histories, and their current concerns" (7). The Indian Days were used to strategically build political bridges between Nakoda peoples and individuals in powerful positions. If one was made an honorary member it was indicative of a past interest in helping Nakoda communities, but it also established a responsibility to do so in the future. In this capacity, the festivals were key political networking opportunities.

Along with socio-economic and political benefits, the festivals also offered cultural opportunities for Indigenous peoples during a period when legitimate spaces for representation were uncommon. As Moses (1996) asserts, these types of events were among the few places in North American society where Indigenous peoples had some measure of control over material aspects of their lives. The 1877 Treaty 7 Agreement and subsequent policies attempted to assimilate Indigenous peoples, but resulted in advancing the socio-economic, political, and cultural exclusion of communities from many aspects of Euro-Canadian society. For much of the first half of the twentieth century, this isolation limited interactions between Indigenous and non-Indigenous peoples. In many cases, events like the Indian Days were one of the main opportunities for international tourists and Euro-Canadians alike to learn from and engage with Indigenous peoples. This was a valued aspect of the gatherings, as Nakoda communities had opportunities to share their cultures with interested participants. As one Nakoda man, who spoke about the Indian Days in a positive light, emphasized: "The people [Nakoda community members] enjoyed coming to Banff to interact and perform for tourists because we liked helping them learn about Native cultures."[36] This sharing of cultures was recognized by Nakoda elder Poucette, who clearly depicted the Indian Days as honouring their people: "They [tourists and Banff residents] didn't want to make a mockery of us and they weren't bad people. Back then it was more about honour. They came because they wanted to understand us and honour our cultures."[37] Nakoda peoples had few chances to interact with broader Euro-Canadian communities during this period. Especially earlier in the twentieth century, the Indian Days were critical sites of cultural exchange. In contrast to other spaces where Nakoda interacted with non-Indigenous peoples in the province of Alberta, the festivals not only provided viable financial support for participants, but also offered periodic cultural opportunities for Nakoda peoples, tourists, and some residents of the Banff townsite.

While some of the representations offered through the Indian Days did temporalize and exoticize Indigenous peoples in ways that negatively contributed to perceptions by reinforcing the expectations of tourists, the festivals also presented several unique cultural possibilities to the Nakoda. There were numerous music and dance performances that were staged for tourists throughout the Indian Days gatherings. The fact that these performances were primarily held as tourist events does not negate the significant meanings Nakoda peoples generated from their involvement. Because of their interactions with tourists, local entrepreneurs, and other Indigenous groups, Nakoda peoples valued these performances as critical spaces of exchange.[38] It is important not to construe the tourist performances at the Indian Days as insignificant to the participants. Oral accounts indicate that Nakoda participants relished opportunities to engage with both international audiences and local Banff residents. Poucette refers to the value community members placed on these types of interactions at the Indian Days:

> We enjoyed meeting all the different people. We would mingle and ... you know Native people we like to talk to people, laugh and bring humour ... At the same time that was a gathering place to visit relatives and new friends and that was the only certain time that they could see one another as some of them live in different areas and they couldn't get together very much.[39]

In addition to the music and dance performances, both Nakoda and Euro-Canadian participants frequently created theatre productions for the Indian Days that re-enacted aspects of Indigenous histories and cultures. Some years, these plays were entirely organized by Nakoda participants. These productions allowed Nakoda directors and performers a great deal of licence to represent their cultures in the ways they desired.[40] It is crucial to recognize that there were few spaces throughout most of the twentieth century where communities could interact with broader society on such mass scale of participation. Annually for over seven decades, the Indian Days provided these types of extended periods of interaction.

In addition to the performances staged for tourists, Indigenous participants held their own cultural events in conjunction with the gatherings, which included powwow ceremonies and Indigenous games or sporting contests.[41] Often in the evenings after participants had returned to their campgrounds, they continued to engage in activities away from the gaze of tourists and non-Indigenous organizers. These evenings for participants, which were enthusiastically anticipated by community members, were regularly referenced in oral accounts as the most significant aspect of the festivals. Poucette passionately explains the central rationale behind the evening components of the gatherings in his descriptions of how the elders would share their stories around the campfire:

> What we [Nakoda community members] appreciated the most about coming down to Banff was the telling of stories of how life is and at the same time to express to all the young people what life is all about. Events may happen during the day ... games and sports, but it was during the night that the elders had time to sit down with the young people and talk to them. You see, a family member can tell her kids a story and then another family comes over and tells them their version in a different way. All of them may be different, but when you listen to these stories together, you'll understand who we are and where we came from. It was a great learning time ... how to take care of a horse or how to present yourself to others. They would teach us how to listen with respect and that's why the gatherings were so important.[42]

These experiences were viewed as valuable spaces for younger generations to celebrate and learn about their cultures. In addition to providing an understanding of the histories that shaped Nakoda cultural life in the past, these learning sessions, articulated through stories, also facilitated discussions about many of the contemporary issues facing their communities. The following statement by an elder highlights this point:

> This was not just a celebration. It was about the long learning process of survival ... life moving from the traditional towards the contemporary. There are so many stories that I heard there [Indian Days campgrounds]. The stories were about what we should do in the future and what not to do ... They told us who our relatives were and taught us to respect them as well as Mother Earth. All this and more ... I learned there.[43]

Oral accounts suggest that Nakoda peoples considered the Indian Days important sites of cultural exchange through their public interactions and private gatherings. Although these experiences took place in both public and private spaces, they both cultivated the processes of the production and transmission of cultural knowledge for Indigenous and non-Indigenous participants.

In order to understand the cultural importance of these gatherings for Nakoda peoples, the colonial contexts in which the Indian Days occurred must be considered. It was not until 1951 that the federal government revised its policies prohibiting Indigenous cultural practices (Hildebrandt et al., 1996). The Indian Days presented the opportunity for Nakoda peoples not only to celebrate their cultures among themselves, but also to interact and share with other participating groups. Particularly during the decades when legislation banning their cultural practices was harshly enforced, festivals like the Indian Days served as critical gathering locations. This was also witnessed in British Columbia, where annual tourist festivals were considered the most significant annual gathering for Indigenous groups (Furniss, 1999). When one takes into account the colonial policies of assimilation which continued to severely repress forms of cultural celebrations in Indigenous communities throughout most of the history of the Indian Days, it is easy to understand why these opportunities were coveted by Nakoda peoples.

In any effort to appreciate the Indian Days as opportunities to celebrate Indigenous cultural practices it is crucial to connect the Banff–Bow Valley as a pivotal location for Nakoda peoples. The restricted access to these areas not only greatly influenced their subsistence land uses, but also limited the celebration of their cultural practices, which were anchored in the places they had travelled through and lived in for centuries. Over the last two decades, there has been an increase in scholarly investigations into the fundamental links between landscapes and cultures (Wilson, 1991; Cronon, 1996). Schama (1996) metaphorically refers to landscapes as "a work of the mind. Its scenery is built up as much from strata of memory as from layers of rock" (5). As humans inhabit specific locations, land formations become repositories for memories, as they always contain the cultures of the peoples who occupy them. This is particularly relevant for oral cultures, such as those of Canada's Indigenous peoples, whose histories are often stored in the many geological features that frame their lives (Palmer, 2005). Cruikshank (2005) suggests that there is a growing body of research on social memory that portrays landscapes as critical sites of remembrance where culturally significant landforms provide archives that store the memories and related histories that are held within them. Early European explorers in the Canadian Rocky Mountains viewed the region's rivers, mountains, and glaciers as considerable but conquerable obstacles to progress. Conversely, for Indigenous peoples these land formations evoked individual and collective memories, marked their histories, and embodied their cultural practices.

For Nakoda peoples, the Banff–Bow Valley, particularly the proximal lands surrounding the townsite, contains their histories. Many specific sites also have close associations with aspects of their cultural practices.[44] In one interview, Nakoda man Jackson Wesley eloquently emphasizes the role that mountains play in the storing of valuable knowledge and culture: "We keep our secrets secret ... We are very quiet people who don't like to share stories with outsiders."[45] Even though we sat in a small room with a low ceiling, he made a circular motion with his extended finger, pointed to the sky, and continued: "You see these mountains around us? All of our secrets are in these mountains ... Millions of our secrets are held in these mountains and they are not meant to be shared."[46] Despite the fact that we were indoors at the time, he knew that I would realize his meaning. He was referring to the collection of peaks that dominated the horizon – towering above the Banff townsite. In reference to the importance of the Rocky Mountains and the land encompassing the national parks to Nakoda peoples, Chief Snow writes:

> The Rocky Mountains are sacred to us. We know every trail and mountain pass in this area. We had special ceremonies and religious areas in the mountains. These mountains are our temples, our sanctuaries, and our resting places. They are a place of hope, a place of vision, a place of refuge, a very special and holy place where the Great Sprit speaks with us. *Therefore, these mountains are our sacred places.* (2005: 19)

After decades of being excluded from RMP, the Indian Days were viewed by the Nakoda peoples as periods for their communities to reassert their physical and cultural links with the region. In the following statement, Rollinmud discusses why access to the lands around the Banff townsite is integrally connected to his community's culture: "In the mountains around there the spirits are all around. You feel them … That is the place where we will never be forgotten. It is what we are and it preserves us … because we protected this land."[47] A Nakoda woman succinctly reinforces this point: "It [the Banff townsite and surrounding region] is a healing place … When you are there … your mind is really calm as you have moments in time with nature.[48]

For some Nakoda peoples the Indian Days represented a type of homecoming.[49] In reference to the exclusion of Indigenous peoples from park lands and their eventual return to the region, which was facilitated by the gatherings, a Nakoda elder explains: "Well in that way the Indian Days have always been a bit about forgiveness … as we could return to use the lands that were important to our cultures for so long."[50] For many participants, the Indian Days were considered a holiday or a rejuvenation period. The festivals were regarded widely by Nakoda peoples as something to look forward to and a period to celebrate their cultures away from the constraints of life on reserves. Rollinmud explains this perspective: "Boredom on the reserve has always been a great problem. The Indian Days was always important as a way to break away from the social life on the reserve. We would leave Morley to head to Banff and leave it behind to enjoy life for awhile."[51] For Nakoda communities the Indian Days were widely viewed as chances not only to leave their reserves and interact with other Indigenous groups and tourists, but also to establish or maintain relationships with Banff residents. However, perhaps the most significant aspect of the festivals for Nakoda communities was regaining access to the lands and sacred places that over centuries had become fundamental to their cultures. This access reasserted the links with the lands that had shaped their practices and connected Nakoda communities to the places that hold their cultural secrets, knowledge, and histories.

Identity Making

The Indian Days festivals also presented identity-making possibilities for Nakoda peoples. Before one examines the production of Indigenous subjectivities through the Indian Days, it is essential to deconstruct "Indigenous" racial categories. Like all individuals and cultures, Nakoda peoples are not homogeneous. As Poucette reveals in a discussion of his family's history or ethnic background: "I'm part Kootenay [Ktunaxa]! Yeah on my late dad's side, you know his great-grandparents were part Kootenay. At the same time … I don't know how this works, but I'm also part Cree. So you could say that I am represented by the meeting of all those peoples at the Indian Days [laughs aloud]."[52] Even though prevailing discourses and related disciplinary technologies shape what is possible to understand in society about racial subject positions, this does not devalue the significant meanings that are formed through and around the production of any subjectivity. Biolsi (2004: 400) succinctly explains: "One of the central challenges in understanding race and racism is to grasp simultaneously the utter *social constructedness* of 'race' (the fictional nature of race) and the *social fact of race* (the inescapable human consequences of race for the individual in a racist society)." The ways power relations are exercised in society have direct implications for individuals and communities in relation to the subject categories they occupy. In other words, discursively produced identities are no less lived or experienced as "real" and "natural." While some researchers feel threatened by knowing that race as a category is discursively produced or that discourse and disciplinary technologies shape what experiences are possible, it is necessary to indicate that these conceptualizations of identity-making processes do not in any way deny the material experiences of individuals or communities. As will be demonstrated in the following examples, when interrogating the production of marginal identities, whether they are racial or otherwise, one must acknowledge that the maintenance of these categories does have tangible consequences.

Foucault's treatment of discourse suggests the importance of understanding the practices of subjectivity. Foucault considered how historically and culturally located practices of power/knowledge produce subjects and their worlds. He indicated his concentration on discursively produced subjectivities:

> I am interested in the way the subject constitutes himself in an active fashion, by practices of the self[;] these practices are nevertheless not something that the individual invents by himself. They are patterns that he finds in his culture and which are proposed, suggested and imposed on him by his culture, his society, and his social group. (1987: 11)

Accordingly, a Foucauldian is interested in which discourses define an individual's identity and how discourse becomes prevailing in current power relations. Using a Foucauldian understanding of discourse and privileging the perspectives of Sioux peoples, Biolsi (2004) reveals that the central question is not what race is, but how race is exercised in broader power relations. The key to comprehending race making is to centre on the micro-practices used by actors in historical situations with particular attention to how individuals turn her/himself into themselves. These processes require insight into how an individual is caught in a network of historical power relations in which they constitute themselves as a subject acting on others.

Examples of how Nakoda peoples played with the very cultural forms they were articulating to broad audiences reveal much about the diverse representations they were performing at the Banff Indian Days and how these representations, within a network of power relations, impacted the production of "Indigeneity" and Nakoda subjectivities. However, Nakoda peoples were not the only ones playing with cultural forms. Instances of playing with Indigenous cultural insignia, whether it be for the purpose of entertainment or to co-opt Indigenous identities and cultures, have been well documented internationally (Scanlon, 1990; Moses, 1996; Nesper, 2003). Particularly in sport and tourism forums, "playing Indian" became especially prevalent in North American popular culture in the later decades of the nineteenth century (Springwood, 2001; Biolsi, 2004). In addition to encouraging exoticized and temporalized representations, Euro-Canadians did play with representations of Indigenous cultures at the Indian Days. A prime example of this comes from the 1950s, when a visitor, Shaman Chief Kitpou, arrived to participate in the festival. Claiming he was part of a First Nations group in British Columbia, Kitpou stayed in the tipi village and took part in cultural performances along with his son and Euro-Canadian wife. Kitpou wore a hide of a wolf with deer antlers adorning each side of his head, beads, and a loin cloth. In addition to refusing to change out of his exotic regalia, which many people had difficulty placing or understanding, he spun a mixture of exaggerated narratives and lies that resulted in the questioning of his ancestry and knowledge of Indigenous cultural practices. The inconsistencies in the stories of his past led at least one account to suggest that he was "more of an imitation than the genuine article" (Parker, 1990: 141). A considerable amount of scepticism regarding Kitpou circulated among the participating Indigenous groups and he was notified that he would not be welcome to attend the following year. The level of "authenticity" in Kitpou's Indigenous ancestry is irrelevant for this analysis. However, this peculiar occurrence in the history of the Indian Days can be paralleled with numerous other examples where Euro–North Americans took great pleasure in mimicking or mocking Indigenous cultural forms in ways that often reinforced the precolonial imagery and discourse that informed the production of "Indigeneity."

With a few notable exceptions (Deloria, 1998; Robidoux, 2006), what is less prevalent in the scholarly literature is how Indigenous peoples also employed these strategies through representations of their own cultures. Loomba (2005) indicates that this is because postcolonial representational works often ignore the self-representations of the colonized and focus too much on the imposition of colonial power rather than the responses to it. The result is more of a static model of colonial relations where colonial power is possessed by the colonizer with little space for negotiation or change. As noted earlier with other examples, this is another situation where a Foucauldian lens of relational and omnipresent perspectives of power can be revealing. Deloria's (2004) examination of the histories of notable Indigenous athletes, performers, and leaders in the United States demonstrates how Indigenous actors produce diverse representations and meanings around their cultures and their identities – subverting, impacting, and asserting discourse that inform the production of "Indigeneity." In his research on Kahnawake Mohawk political systems and their engagement with multiple levels of government, Alfred (1995) complicates our knowledge of the production of Mohawk identities. He demonstrates that while colonial structures of power impacted the production of localized and traditional practices, including associated linguistic and cultural identities, ultimately Mohawk responses to these influences are what shaped identities within their communities.

Although Nakoda peoples did occasionally play with cultural forms in the performance of their own identities at the Indian Days, it is more difficult to locate evidence of these processes. Through their interactions with tourists, entrepreneurs, and other Indigenous groups, Nakoda peoples actively sought out opportunities to challenge prevailing discourse and the related representations of their cultures. Numerous studies indicate that performers are particularly well situated to challenge stereotypical representations of their cultures (Kasson, 2000; Kirshenblatt-Gimblett, 1998). As Furniss (1999) argues, Indigenous peoples do "use performance to express distinct cultural meanings and identities, but also to subvert and challenge dominant colonial stereotypes" (172). Hokowhitu (2013) reminds us "that discourse cannot be simply referred to as oppressive or emancipatory. All knowledge formations have the possibility to do both" (227). Oral accounts of Nakoda performers indicate that even though many of the representations of their cultures were produced to align with tourists' expectations, participants also played with these expectations in ways that disrupted their reception.[53] One example comes from Chief Tatanga Mani (Walking Buffalo), who was extensively involved with organizing the Indian Days for many years, beginning in 1920 when he was elected chief of the Nakoda First Nations until his death in 1967. As well as a strong and committed leader, Tatanga Mani was well known for his great sense of humour and his insistence on the acceptance of Indigenous peoples as an important part of Canadian society.[54] He regularly played with aspects of his own identity and those of tourists or Banff residents. He was known to refer to Euro-Canadians as "white savages." In one instance in 1946 at the ceremonial Indian Days address following the parade, he used the "white savages" reference to "confuse and delight the large crowd."[55] Tatanga Mani also added that he noticed how the "white savage women wore more paint on their faces than the Indians."[56] Chiefs not only had more opportunities to play with representations and performances of their identities, but also had greater potential to draw attention to cultural stereotypes, as their positions as leaders afforded higher-profile interactions.

By performing "Indigeneity" in ways that played with representations of their cultures, Nakoda participants, and sometimes Euro-Canadians, did confuse conceptions of race. As Butler (1993) asserts in her examination of the discursive production of subjectivities related to sexuality, identities are stabilized by repetitions of stylized acts of certain behaviour performances in preference to others. It is because identities are repeated performances of acts that they can be contested or refused. As a consequence, if one were to change the patterns of these repetitions, identities could be destabilized in ways that could subvert perceptions of them. One way in which this is accomplished is through using forms of parody to play with identities. However, representations can be read in a multitude of ways and as a result only some readings have the potential to create alternative understandings or critiques. If the parody of a representation is lost in its consumption because the consumer lacks the necessary resources to reinterpret it, the readings can actually support damaging stereotypes of racial subjectivities. Unfortunately, there are no ways to ensure that practices of parody will reach their intended audience (Robidoux, 2004; Brayton

Figure 5.8 Playing with identities (1935). The tourism industry became an interesting space to fracture one-dimensional imagery of Indigenous peoples. This picture was taken during the Indian Days for a postcard promoting tourism in Banff. It depicts several Nakoda leaders and one young woman golfing at the Banff Springs Hotel course as tourism entrepreneurs caddy for the group. Courtesy of the Whyte Museum of the Canadian Rockies. V263-na-3284. (Photographer: Byron Harmon)

and Alexander, 2007). Accordingly, the subversive value of any parody entirely depends upon the contexts and receptions in which the disruptions occur. For example, when Indigenous participants exaggerated exotic regalia in the Indian Days parade or played with stereotypes in their interactions with tourists, if their performance of identity aligned with expectations around their identities, instead of subverting stereotypical perceptions, it could serve to strengthen them within the audience.

As critical studies in sport and physical activity reveal (Shogan, 1999; Pringle and Markula, 2005), discipline can take control of individuals by filling in gaps in space, time, and movement. Organizations of these modalities constitute the technologies or constraints of docility that were used by agents of the colonial bureaucracy in attempts to assimilate Indigenous peoples by closing gaps of behaviour and culture. Despite the relentless influence of disciplinary technologies, Nakoda peoples did not become homogeneous because of the breaks or interruptions in identity production that are omnipresent. Technologies of discipline are not absolute in the ways they impact individuals or implicate the processes of identity production, a point Foucault (1977) emphasizes: "Instead of bending all of its subjects into a single uniform mass, it separates, analyses, differentiates" (170). Just as Foucault's technologies of the self do not guarantee a weakening of disciplinary processes or changes in the discourse that produce power relations, disciplinary technologies do not ensure the production of homogeneous subjects.

While Foucault conceptualized disciplinary technologies as producing homogeneous and eventually docile bodies, the fact that discipline implicates individuals differently is exemplified in the production of hybrid identities in colonial societies. Hybrid identities are produced by the multiple and competing subject positions that individuals simultaneously occupy as well as the influence of disciplinary technologies (Young, 1995). Bhabha (1994) contends that it is the ambivalence of colonial rule that enables hybrid identities the capacity for resistance. In the case of the Nakoda peoples participating in the Indian Days, individuals had different levels of privilege at stake in the continuation of relationships with tourism entrepreneurs and in the performance of "Indigeneity." Both newspaper and oral accounts indicate that convincing Nakoda youth to participate in the parade was always a difficult task, as few were willing to wear the elaborate regalia and dress of the generations before them.[57] By the late 1930s, young Nakoda men in particular were interested in showcasing the "cowboy" attire that more accurately reflected their quotidian lives, as many were active participants in rodeo events throughout the spring and summer seasons.[58] Although proper attire was noted as an issue as early as the 1930s, it became a problem in the 1960s for the Indian Days organizing committee chairman, Claude Brewster, who stated that "no one will be allowed in the parade unless they are wearing full Indian regalia."[59] In 1965, a *Crag and Canyon* article states that the younger generations had become consumed by cowboy attire and were no longer "interested in being Indian."[60] Even though participants' appearance in precolonial dress when in the public spotlight or tourist gaze was strongly encouraged by tourism entrepreneurs, Nakoda youth defied one-dimensional representations of their cultures by disrupting these images and insisting on dressing like "cowboys" throughout the festival.[61] These representations of Nakoda peoples, which included chaps, cowboy hats, and boots, not only conflicted with the discourse that promoted precolonial imagery, they also signified the hybrid aspects of the identities of young Nakoda men. While some youth dressed like cowboys especially during the parade, they also wore traditional dress in other celebrations associated with the festival, including the evening powwows held away from the gaze of tourists.[62] In this case, the presence of hybridity is evidence of the different ways that some Nakoda youth were implicated by discipline and responded to the technologies that were designed to simplify, or in some cases assimilate, their cultures. In discussing the emergence of the "Indian cowboy" in Western Canada during this period, Kelm (2011) emphasizes what is significant in the performance of these hybrid identities in this arena: "What is important to remember, in all of this, is not that some version of authenticity was either staged or negated, a tradition invented or commodified, but rather that new authenticities, identities, and relationships arose in the contact zone where audiences and performers interacted" (12).

Just as Nakoda youth were reproved for their lack of compliance with dress codes established by tourism producers, representations of Indigenous peoples that do not align with tourists' expectations are often discouraged by agents of the tourism industry (Bruner, 2005; Sweet, 2004; Johnston, 2006). Responding to prevailing discourses that endorse, exoticize, and temporalize aspects of their cultures, Indigenous peoples who successfully and creatively adapt to changing conditions are rarely conceived as cultural strategists, but more often portrayed as peoples who have lost their cultures. This should be considered one of the catch-22 situations that Indigenous youth regularly encounter, and is particularly relevant as Indigenous peoples try to represent their cultures in forms that assert their contemporary realties but also meet tourists' expectations. Butler (1990) argues that it is when individuals are required to satisfy the demands of competing disciplines that they can "necessarily fail." The disciplinary demands of subjectivities eventually open gaps for individuals to make decisions about how they will participate in various disciplines. Conflicts most often occur as individuals are managing the technologies of docility of one discipline and cannot meet the requirements of another. Shogan (1999) notes that it is when participants realize some dissonance from the demands of other disciplines to which they are committed that they might choose to engage in the technologies of the self and refuse aspects of their identity. Although they often have limited resources to draw upon, and as a consequence have fewer opportunities to alter prevailing discourses in comparison to adults, youth are sometimes less invested in the disciplines they engage with and subsequently have more potential to refuse them (Dallaire, 2003, 2006). It is when refusals occur that opportunities are created to produce new understandings of "Indigeneity." These understandings have the potential to open up spaces for alternative ways of participating in discourse. As Sivaramakrishnan (2004) reminds us, hybridity was a weapon for colonized peoples as "they invoked the ideas of Western societies not only to hold them true to their own beliefs, but also to claim a hybrid for the colonized that was a product of foreign and Indigenous values" (367). As Loomba (2005) contends, hybrid identities have enormous influence in the construction of anti-colonial narratives, as individuals exposed to colonial discipline are themselves complicated products of diverse colonial histories. Hybrid identities become the result of a complex interplay wherein colonized peoples negotiate the cracks of colonial discourse in a multitude of ways.

Disciplinary Technologies and Refusals in Colonial Contexts

Foucault (1978) argued that in power relations there is always the possibility of resistance. He stated that "where there is power, there is resistance, and yet, or rather consequently, this resistance is never in a position of exteriority in relation to power" (95). In his theorizing it is necessary to recognize that disciplinary practices continue to function when there is resistance. He asserts in describing the role of resistance in power relationships: "Their existence depends on a multiplicity of points of resistance: these play the role of adversary, target, support, or handle in power relations. These points of resistance are present everywhere in the power network" (ibid.). As noted by Loomba (2005), Hall made significant critiques of Foucault's diffusive conception of resistance. Hall (1996) argues that Foucault only understood the process as a disorganized affair, where exercising power and responses to it are so diffuse that they cannot be challenged. Hartsock (1990) adds to this by describing the Foucauldian model: "Power, being everywhere, is ultimately nowhere" (170). While I agree with this aspect of these critiques in response to Foucault's early archaeologies, I do not think that they take into account Foucault's later works, where he addresses these issues by specifying the types of resistance available to individuals and groups. While Foucault spent less of his career examining how specific individuals responded to disciplinary technologies and prevailing sets of discourses, this was the focus of his later works. Foucault's technologies of the self (1985) and practices of freedom (1986, 1987) provided a sophisticated map of how individuals managed these structures to actively engage in processes of self-negotiation. These works give not only examples of responses to disciplinary technologies, but also strategies that individuals can employ to contribute to the production of their own subjectivities as well as problematize discourse with the intent of transforming it.

Despite the significant changes to Nakoda ways of life that were instigated by the disciplinary technologies that they were exposed to in the creation of the reserve system, many community members continued to pursue their long-established subsistence land uses. The regime of disciplinary power that Nakoda communities encountered before the turn of the twentieth century was extended into the ensuing decades through a multitude of technologies. Many of the aspects of the Indian Days festival itself can be considered disciplinary, but once again Nakoda participants at times refused certain disciplinary practices while engaging in others. As Foucault (1980) recognized, when disciplinary techniques fail, it does not signify the dwindling influence of power, but rather that it requires a specific reorganization. From this perspective, resistance is not an indication that power is loosening its grip, but rather is demonstrating that it is being exercised at a particular point. Resistance simply symbolizes the need for power to be exercised in new ways, as it actually works as a catalyst to create new strategies of exercising power and consequently strengthens its positions in society (Markula and Pringle, 2006).

In referring to the complexity of theorizing the resistance of marginalized peoples in colonial contexts, Loomba (2005) suggests that "subaltern agency, whether at the individual level or collective, cannot be idealized as pure opposition to the order it opposes; it both works within the order and displays its own contradictions" (198). Butchart's (1998) research on colonial systems of medicine in South Africa provides an example of how Foucault's (1980) concept of strategic elaboration works on the ground in colonial contexts. In his study of how disciplinary power gave rise to specific socio-medical technologies, methods of surveillance, and social controls that produced knowledge about African bodies and peoples, Butchart reveals how forms of resistance created new opportunities to exercise power and produce subjectivities. As one of the few historians to adopt a Foucauldian approach in the study of racial discourse, he uses archival evidence to indicate how a marketing campaign produced by Western doctors to educate Indigenous peoples about pressing health issues was rejected by local populations because it used European actors and did not include Indigenous perspectives of health. In contrast to Marxist-based analysis, which celebrated the protest by local populations over the campaign as the height of resistance against Western medical practices and the British colonial administration, Butchart argues that the response to the protests instituted changes to the health campaign that further entrenched colonial systems of discipline. By adopting some aspects of Indigenous medicine, the campaigns had more appeal to local populations, but Indigenous health practices were co-opted in processes that clearly situated them as supplementary and secondary alternatives to Western medicine. This had devastating implications for local traditional knowledge and Indigenous medicinal practices as they supported the health apparatus that was deeply invested in the philosophies of Western medicine.

Another example of how resistance produces new corridors for the exercise of colonial power can be seen in the history of the Indian Days. Whether one considers local and regional newspaper coverage or oral accounts, the majority of perspectives present a positive image of the event and very little direct public resistance to the festivals has been recorded.[63] However, in 1970, members of the American Indian Movement (AIM) arrived to investigate the involvement of Indigenous peoples in the festivals. Responding to racial-based oppression in the United States, pan-Indian political movements like the AIM mobilized in the late 1960s in support of growing continental Red Power campaigns (Ross, 1998). After some initial meetings with leadership, the AIM convinced some Nakoda participants to demand complete control over the event and exclude any outside influence in making representational decisions. The idea was raised by some Nakoda participants to shift the location of the festival to the Nakoda reserve at Morley to further facilitate this process. In addition to some negative media coverage on the Indian Days, AIM's influence forced a reconsideration of the roles Nakoda participants played in the organization of the event, which opened up discussions for representational changes and negotiations on compensation. While this resistance can be viewed as creating better conditions for Nakoda participants at the Indian Days, it fuelled an internal debate within Nakoda communities which led to a boycott of the Indian Days the following summer, 1971.[64] As a result of the Nakoda boycott, other Indigenous groups, including the Cree, Ktunaxa (Kootenay), Tsuu T'ina (Sarcee), Pikunni (Peigan), Siksika (Blackfoot), and Kainai (Blood), were asked to fill the void at the Indian Days, and due to their participation, the event ran quite smoothly. Consequently, Nakoda peoples temporarily lost their position and status as the majority group, which over many decades had afforded them a unique position of influence compared to the other Indigenous participants who were considered guests of the Nakoda. The 1971 festival clearly demonstrated that the Nakoda contributions to the Indian Days were replaceable by those of other groups and left them in a somewhat vulnerable position. Disapproval of the direction of the Indian Days and the desire of Nakoda leaders to exercise more power over key decisions was certainly the intent of the boycott. However, this expression of resistance facilitated a shifting of the balance of power in ways that reinforced the authority of Euro-Canadian tourism producers to run the events in ways that did not relinquish control to participating groups. In this manner, resistance encouraged the formation of new and strategic currents of disciplinary power that allowed Nakoda peoples to participate in the Indian Days as long as tourism producers maintained the degree of organizational and representational control that they had become accustomed to over several decades of running the events. These examples demonstrate some of the complexities in the ways power relations are exercised in colonial contexts. This analysis also reveals the need for interpretive frameworks that account for the intricacies of these interactions by acknowledging the resistive strategies employed by groups and also how these points of resistance fit into broader processes of colonial power relations.

Conclusion

The disciplinary practices that were introduced as part of the colonial administration's objectives to control and assimilate Indigenous peoples cannot be viewed from only one perspective. It requires a multifaceted approach to capture the heterogeneity, disjuncture, and fragmented nature of the historical conditions that shape subjectivities and discursive realities in periods of colonial rule. Bhabha (1994) encouraged further interpretations of colonialism as dynamic processes that were more than something frozen in earlier temporal periods, but entities that continually inform the present by demanding that we transform our understandings of cross-cultural relations. Spivak (1988) reminds us that all that was considered precolonial was continually reproduced through the history of colonialism. Subsequently it is not easy to discern pristine forms that are neatly separated from colonial histories. She suggests that scholars need to interpret colonialism as an interruption to extensive and complex histories. This will ensure that localized practices, histories, and related knowledges do not become overshadowed by colonialism, making it their defining feature.

In regard to the Indian Days, this requires a rethinking of the historical conditions which the festivals contributed to and existed within. To comprehensively examine the impact of the festivals within a broader historical context, one must understand how they not only exoticized and temporalized Indigenous peoples in the processes of reinforcing precolonial conceptions of their cultures, but also provided atypical socio-economic, political, and cultural opportunities for Nakoda individuals and communities. As Kasson (2000) argues, relationships between Indigenous performers, entrepreneurs, and audiences were filled with complexity and contradiction. Similarly, through the Indian Days, questions of representation and derived meanings for Nakoda performers were varied and complicated as each individual produced many layers of understanding on how they were represented by others and how they represented themselves through the performance of their cultures in response to tourists' expectations. Oral accounts with Nakoda peoples reflect the great diversity of experiences that were embodied by generations of participation in the Indian Days. Despite the presence of varied perceptions and interpretations of the event, Indigenous peoples who participated in the festivals were never passive victims of the colonial policies that marginalized and disadvantaged their communities. Sporting and tourist festivals during colonial periods have often been characterized too simply as hegemonic or disciplinary. This overlooks the capacities of Indigenous actors to navigate the terrain of colonial structures and policies. In direct contrast to imagining colonial power relations as only disciplinary, the history of the Indian Days demonstrates that, in response to the constraints that affected their lives, Nakoda peoples constantly negotiated with Euro-Canadian tourism producers, made decisions that best served their communities' interests, and pursued any potential opportunities to celebrate their cultural practices and reassert their links to significant spaces.

Chapter Six

Looking Back and Pushing Ahead

The Awakening (August 2009)

It was a summer evening and I was travelling east on the 1A highway through the Nakoda reserve near Morley. The sun was shining with brilliance and I had just turned away from the sparkling Bow River, heading into the shadow of Mount Yamnuska, a summit that has particular significance for Nakoda peoples as a location for cultural ceremonies. I was on my way to a sweat lodge at the home of Lenny Poucette, an elder I had met through volunteering.[1] I felt honoured each time I was invited to such an intimate cultural experience by a respected elder and medicine man. I had moved to Banff earlier that year to be closer to the people I was working with, and had enjoyed a productive summer interacting with community members as a volunteer. Most of the projects I was involved with centred on developing cultural and youth programs to help manage some of the pressing health and social issues facing the growing under-twenty-five population on the reserve. I was always hopeful that my research and volunteering would be part of positive developments in this community, but now the specifics of how these small, but meaningful, contributions would impact the lives of some community members were starting to emerge.

Unfortunately, before I arrived at the sweat lodge, I was involved in a significant car accident with a local Nakoda woman who was later charged with driving under the influence of alcohol. Over the next few weeks my time was filled with accident reports, insurance forms, and self-reflection. I had a series of interactions with insurance adjustors, RCMP officers, a medical examiner, a tow-truck driver, and numerous others over the details of the accident. Through these exchanges, I was awakened to all the different forms of institutionalized racism that were expressed in these processes. At times overt racial tropes were evoked regarding the "natives" and also more subtle comments that linked my accident to broader issues facing Nakoda communities. Through these discussions, individuals reaffirmed their knowledge of and experience with Indigenous peoples and contributed to discourse that informed the production of "Indigeneity." For me, these experiences not only emphasized the relevance of my research, but also demonstrated the forms of colonial violence that were continually being constituted through diverse discursive fields.

Cherokee author Thomas King states that "the truth about stories is that that's all we are" (2003: 32). Similarly to the personal narrative that opened this book, this account of the accident aligns with many of the experiences of the Nakoda peoples who contributed to this research in that it represents only a few of the many possible stories that could or should be shared. While this book is primarily about the histories of Nakoda peoples, my own subjectivity as a researcher is also a part of this story, especially in how the experiences of Nakoda peoples have been shared, interpreted, and presented in the context of this written text. For several years I have tried to understand my own position as a Euro-Canadian, male, researcher working with Indigenous peoples. This issue first surfaced early in my graduate studies as I spent time reflecting on some of the key works in standpoint theory,[2] which outline the strengths and pitfalls of adhering to standpoint positions in research with marginalized peoples. I appreciated several aspects of the standpoint approach, including the concentration on the experiences of marginalized peoples and the privileging of their knowledges. However, I was uncomfortable with the binaries maintained by some standpoint positions. I felt that when epistemic perspectives were tied too closely to social or material locations, possibilities for political action were severely limited. Years later, while on a break between intense rounds at a sweat lodge on the Morley reserve, an important conversation with a Nakoda elder expanded my thinking on this topic. Through the telling of a story, he expressed his opinion that the best political work is accomplished by individuals who share similar objectives, though not necessarily cultures. To him, the collective values that guide political work are far more important than the specific social locations from which researchers arrive at such work.[3] This aligns with Butler's (1992) point of view that argues against showing one's "identity card" at the door before being granted access to come inside and work on political issues. She suggests that politics needs to get done by people coming together through issues they are committed to rather than their having to identify with specific groups. Alfred (2009b) offers a similar point: "It is not a matter of red versus white, but of right versus wrong, considered within the broad framework of values we all share: freedom, justice and peace" (16). He continues, specifically referring to strategies to build productive relations that demand social justice:

> In our relations with others, we need to engage society as a whole in an argument about justice that will bring about real changes in political practice. We need to convince others to join us in challenging the state's oppression of Indigenous peoples. This will require a broad-based intellectual and political movement away from prevailing beliefs and structures. (180–1)

While always critically aware of how my own subjectivity impacted my research, whether it was in how I behaved or how my behaviour was evaluated when working in communities, I was reassured by affirmations that my research mattered to community members, that it served community interests and that it was generally welcomed by leaders and elders. The accident itself, and its aftermath, encouraged a deeper level of self-awareness that forced me to reconsider the ways that I was connected to the peoples and stories that informed this book.

The relationships I established through this research were due in part to my commitment to privilege Indigenous perspectives in the histories I was listening to, learning about, recording, and later interpreting. Rooted in the theoretical and methodological choices that guided this research, this work makes an explicit call for scholars working with Indigenous communities to establish collaborative relationships and privilege their perspectives. There is an increasing body of scholarship in anthropology, tourism, sport, and Indigenous studies which is concerned with the inequalities that face Indigenous communities internationally (Paraschak, 2000; Bruner, 2001; Harkin, 2003; Sweet, 2004; King, 2005; Stewart-Harawira, 2005; Butler and Hinch, 2007; Forsyth and Heine, 2008). Unfortunately, of the extensive amount of research that examines the disparities in quality of life that exist between Indigenous and non-Indigenous communities, only a small portion consults Indigenous perspectives. In the sport and tourism disciplines, these studies are predominantly focused on representational issues. As both Said (1978) and Bhabha (1994) contend, examining representations in colonial contexts is decisive because the motivations behind and sources of Western compulsions to colonize are due in large part to Western representations of foreign cultures. In this regard, all critical examinations of representations of Indigenous cultures are important, but the epistemological basis of these studies also needs to be reconsidered periodically.

I encourage researchers to move beyond deconstructions of representations that leave underpinning historical and material aspects uncritically examined. Scholars can avoid these epistemological issues by selecting methods that consult with those who produce and consume representations. Especially when Indigenous peoples are involved, a lack of consultation is considered a major oversight (Battiste and Youngblood Henderson, 2000). Therefore, it is essential to identify with the experiences of the individuals who have the most at stake in these representations – Indigenous peoples and communities. By incorporating their perspectives, scholars can commit to conducting research that privileges Indigenous knowledges, voices, and ways of interpreting. Māori education scholar Bishop (2005) argues that to evade reifying colonial discourses, scholars must form extensive collaborations with communities in any types of research that involve Indigenous peoples. Indigenous methodologies (Battiste and Youngblood Henderson, 2000; Wilson, 2001; Weber-Pillwax, 2004; Tuhiwai Smith, 1999, 2005; Alfred, 2005; Kovach, 2009) do provide helpful guidelines for researchers to build research designs that are culturally sensitive, that collaborate with communities and directly serve their interests. While these frameworks do offer a map for approaches to ethical research, what matters most is what researchers actually do in communities with community members, not what is written in the methodology and ethics sections of publications and grant submissions. In recognition of the limitations of the research that informed this book, I acknowledge that this work does not meet the high expectations of exemplary collaborative ethnographies emerging from anthropology (Cruikshank, 2005; Palmer, 2005; Field, 2008). As Field suggests, collaborative ethnographies are not simply interesting experimental enterprises, but serve broader epistemological, theoretical, and political goals. Field's point is that while scholars may initiate research, it must focus on the issues of importance in the community and voice multiple perspectives from the community. These consultation and collaboration procedures connect Indigenous representations and histories with the present material conditions of their lives. I hope that this study encourages other scholars, both

Indigenous and non-Indigenous, to privilege these perspectives by collaborating with the communities that enable their research.

One key collaboration that researchers can support in Canada is the co-management of parks and protected areas. This requires fundamental understandings of the histories that inform and at times inhibit these relationships. Spence (1999) argues that the histories of parks are relevant because parks serve as a microcosm for the history of conflict and exploitation that has characterized the unequal relations between the nation state and Indigenous peoples. This is exemplified in the displacement of Indigenous communities from national parks throughout the continent and the repression of their subsistence and cultural practices. It is critical to recognize that these types of displacements and repressions were not limited to the first half of the twentieth century. As Martin (2011) confirms with his work on the formation of protected areas in northern Canada, parks were founded as new recreational frontiers that "were tailored to the expectations of southern visitors and presaged for local Aboriginal peoples the sort of dispossession and disruption that had accompanied the creation of Banff and other national parks decades earlier" (274). While co-management strategies have been touted as new ways forward for productive relationships between government representatives and local Indigenous peoples in the formation of new parks, researchers who are familiar with the histories of exclusion and cultural repression are typically quite pessimistic about any contemporary co-management of parks. MacLaren (2011) refers to the "merciless binaries" created between conflicting groups of humans inside national parks. He states: "Protected landscapes are heralded for the species they protect but are seldom examined for the ideologies or cultural values that they protect and project" (340). He sees no panacea in co-management strategies, as for him co-management is more about ideas in boardrooms and less about practices on the land. Nadasdy (2003) concurs with MacLaren's perspective, as he feels that co-management relationships are often based on European understandings of knowledge, land, and conservation, which are not always reconcilable with Indigenous perspectives. Sandlos (2007) asserts that even in the twenty-first century, Indigenous peoples feel distanced "from a system that demands they conform to Euro-Canadian bureaucratic norms and contribute traditional ecological knowledge in a manner consistent with scientific models of understanding wildlife" (244).

While I share some of this healthy scepticism, I am more optimistic about the possibilities. National parks offer opportunities to mend broken relationships and reintegrate or extend the influence of Indigenous peoples in key ecosystems. As Martin's (2011) work profiles, in northern Yukon, the 1984 formation of Ivvavik National Park has provided a productive model for future co-management relationships. The Inuvialuit were aware of the previous experiences of Indigenous peoples across the country and were wary of engaging with the National Parks Branch. However, they used this knowledge to strategically navigate the bureaucracies of conservation organizations and governments to ensure that their interests were protected and honoured in the agreement. This provided an alternative model that respected evolving Inuvialuit perspectives of conservation. Co-management meant equal representation on committees and the accommodation of Inuvialuit interests and cultural values. Further agreements solidified in the formation of Torngat Mountains National Park (Newfoundland and Labrador, 2005, with Inuit) and Nááts'ihch'oh National Park Reserve (Northwest Territories, 2012, with Dene and Métis) may provide more opportunities for communities to assert their cultural rights or control development on their lands. As MacLaren (2011) insists, forms of Indigenous "presence remain worthy of consideration and adoption: biodiversity includes a human presence – and not just the presence of privileged recreationalists and other tourists – as well as the commemoration of cultural values and practices that the historical oral and written records justify" (355).

These collaborative relationships will be of increasing importance in a Canadian context where Indigenous lands face mounting pressure from natural-resource development industries and leaders continue to make difficult decisions about the futures of their communities. These are critical decisions because some types of natural-resource development can directly constrain local subsistence and cultural practices. As Alfred (2009a) convincingly argues, natural-resource development can stand in opposition to the health and sustainability of Indigenous communities. He sees the connections to Indigenous lands, which are fostered through subsistence and cultural practices, as essential to not only community control of their resources, but also support for cultural continuities throughout forthcoming generations.

Returning to the context of Banff National Park, there are also productive relationships being established in the oldest of the parks in the national network. Since 2005, a small group of Nakoda have been returning to their traditional camping grounds underneath Cascade Mountain near the Banff townsite. Led by elder Rollinmud, but also supported by Parks Canada, Nakoda peoples have been invited into the park to camp and spend time on their ancestral lands, where they now have harvesting rights for some traditional plants and medicines.[4] Over the last five years the ecological knowledge of Nakoda and Sisika communities has been recruited by Parks Canada to contribute to management plans dealing with increases in wildlife-human conflicts and the culling of elk populations around the Banff townsite.[5] Recently, Indigenous perspectives have been privileged in the renovated Cave and Basin interpretation site, which reopened in the spring of 2013.[6] This is only the beginning of reintegrating local communities into the cultures and ecosystems of the national parks in the Canadian Rocky Mountains, but if these types of small, but meaningful, changes can be instituted in the oldest portions of the national parks system, there is significant potential for change throughout the country.

Co-management of parks and protected areas is only one manner in which bridges can be built to establish relationships whereby Indigenous leaders and local knowledges can direct policy and practice. The forms of institutionalized racism alluded to above demonstrate why it is critical for broader Canadian society to foster relationships where non-Indigenous peoples can learn from and with Indigenous peoples. Both my teaching and research experiences have offered reminders that most forms of intolerance are fundamentally based on a lack of understanding of a particular subject. In a Canadian context, projects that privilege the experiences of Indigenous peoples can certainly make key contributions to informing all Canadians about the distinct challenges that many communities encounter. Exploring aspects of Indigenous cultural histories, practices, and identities is a necessary step in building relationships wherein their viewpoints can be shared in ways that encourage appreciation, tolerance, and respect. Cruikshank (1994) argues that listening to the experiences of Indigenous peoples will promote respect for the human diversity of North America and produce innovative solutions to many of the problems our societies currently face. For example, as the Canadian federal Conservative government continues to promote short-sighted economic development at the cost of polluting the air we breathe and the water we drink, diverse Indigenous perspectives of subsistence land uses and environmental sustainability could help preserve ecosystems and attend to the complex environmental challenges that all Canadians confront.

This book offers new understandings of the cultural histories of the Banff–Bow Valley, as it centres on the experiences of Nakoda peoples in their interactions with the colonial bureaucracy and later with tourism industries. The intent of this research was not to outline the diverse meanings generated around racism for Nakoda peoples, but to highlight the specific constraints and barriers that operated in ways that had distinct consequences for the individuals who contributed to this research and their respective communities. While examining how the technologies of discipline that the colonial regime systemically instituted have altered the lives of Nakoda peoples, this work is also concerned with how individuals and groups reacted to these limitations to generate meanings from their lived experiences. An analysis of the discursive conditions that led to the formation of the national parks and the development of tourism economies makes it clear that local Indigenous peoples played a significant role in the production of discourse that positioned their cultures as part of an emerging multicultural Canada. Consequently, this research contributes to our understandings of the experiences of Nakoda peoples and the discourse that informed the production of "Indigeneity" during this dynamic period in the history of Western Canada.

As with the personal account that opened this discussion, in many ways new experiences and knowledges can engender more complex readings. By reflecting on the experiences associated with conducting this research, it is clear to me that this work has produced more questions than it has actually addressed. A plethora of relevant areas of inquiry surfaced in the processes of completing this book, including: what other types of experiences opened up spaces, or presented limitations, for Indigenous actors to pursue socio-economic, political, and cultural opportunities in the Banff–Bow Valley?; how do more flexible perspectives on power relations offer new understandings of the diverse intentions, interactions, and meanings that produced colonial relationships?; and how do acts of colonial violence endure in contemporary Canadian societies in ways that form significant barriers for Indigenous peoples? The knowledge I have gained through this research into the cultural histories of the region has not provided answers to these multifaceted questions, but I pose them because they demand the attention of critical scholars.

By anchoring this work in the experiences and knowledges that are situated on the margins, I have tried to recognize the ways that discourse is enabled and, as a consequence, reveal opportunities for both the production of alternative discourse and the refusal of prevailing discourse. Jiwani (2006) argues that it is through disturbing complacencies that we get a glimpse at alternatives. The first step in this process begins with an investigation of the discourse that produces perceptions of racial identities. Determining which discourses are prevailing and how they implicate the lives of marginalized peoples can open up possible sites of intervention. She directs her attention to sites of intervention or places where such power relations can be challenged, transformed, or diverted in the interests of privileging subjugated knowledges. Wetherell and Potter (1992) claim that it is important to identify the forms that legitimation takes and then chart the fragmented and dilemmatic nature of discourse, as it is at these points of fracture and contradiction that there is scope for transformations. Offering alternative stories to the ones that are usually told is integral to these processes. After the prevailing discourse is identified, it then becomes necessary to refuse it, in an attempt to generate alternatives. Although sites of refusal may be tenuous and only available at particular moments, they are crucial for formalizing changes to the lives we live and the practices that shape them. It is when these brief possibilities arise that the practices that produce discourse and related representations or identities can be subverted (Hutcheon, 2002). Shogan (1999) asserts that it is through questioning discursive codes, then refusing to passively engage with their standards, that opportunities to push the limits of subjectivity are formulated. By identifying discourse and how it has impacted the lives of Nakoda peoples, this research serves as a springboard for social change as sites of intervention or refusal, and the possibilities within them, are subsequently exposed.

Histories of colonial exploitation and violence cannot be partitioned from the contemporary realities of racial discourse, identity making, and power relations. In Mackey's (1999) influential work she demonstrated how representations of marginalized peoples throughout Canadian history informed the production of racial discourse that excluded Indigenous peoples while simultaneously redefining the nation as, essentially, Euro-Canadian. Francis (2011) extends this analysis by revealing how racial discourse produced narratives that misrepresented the historical encounters between Euro-Canadians and Indigenous peoples. The brutal histories of conquest, conflict, and cultural repression upon which Canada was founded were de-emphasized, or in some cases erased. These narratives, which espoused myths of equality and social responsibility, point to the inherent contradictions of the Canadian nation state and federal government policy. Francis refers to the most obvious contradictions shaping Canadian identity: "Namely, our history as a country founded on a commitment to democratic forms of order and good government for some, while, at the same time, endorsing devastating forms of legal exclusion, forced assimilation, and mass death for others" (2011: 9). Warry (2007) also refers to these contradictions: "The irony of our society is that the values of tolerance and multicultural diversity are accepted and heralded as part of a national ethic even as Aboriginal peoples are marginalized and their cultures denigrated" (13). Jiwani (2006) effectively connects the historical underpinnings of racial discourse to the significant consequences they have in contemporary multicultural Canada. She contends that discourses of racism are systematically denied by Canadians in ways that contribute to the trivialization or dismissal of racism as a form of violence and a remnant of colonial histories.

How do these contradictions in imagining Canada's colonial history inform current race relations and the government's treatment of Indigenous peoples? The federal government's 2008 apology for its institution of Indigenous education through residential schools and its 2010 decision to sign the United Nations Declaration on the Rights of Indigenous Peoples suggest that a progressive approach may be adopted that could begin to address the considerable inequities that exist in Canada. However, the refusal to recognize health issues in Indigenous communities downstream from Tar Sands developments on the Athabasca River and attempts to circumvent and undermine Indigenous governments in the Enbridge Northern Gateway Pipelines Project, as well as other strategies of natural resource extraction, more clearly expose the government's intentions. The "Idle No More" political protest movement, which began in November 2012 and was led by Indigenous leaders and activists, expressed considerable opposition to the federal government's plans to weaken environmental-protection mechanisms to facilitate the work of natural-resource extraction industries.[7] This powerful statement by united groups of Indigenous communities across the country may signify a new era of organization and commitment to asserting Indigenous rights in Canada. Injustices persist as a consequence of the government's failure to address the concerns of Indigenous leaders and communities, including pressing health and education issues. Sadly, over two decades after the Oka crisis, an event that was highlighted at the beginning of this book, profound challenges related to Indigenous rights remain at the heart of the relationships between Indigenous peoples and the Canadian nation state.

Gilroy (2005) contends that we must pursue ownership of our own pasts in order to properly contextualize these histories in ways that account for the current processes of decolonization, multiculturalism, identity making, and social justice. It must be stressed that these histories of colonial violence cannot be erased from our collective memory. Ultimately, it is my hope that this book will contribute to our knowledge and understanding of the histories of colonial oppression in Canadian society and of the discursive conditions that shaped the experiences of Indigenous peoples. Acknowledging these experiences is a critical aspect of appreciating our collective pasts; however, it is also a necessary mechanism for pushing ahead, as these processes allow us to strategically navigate political corridors, build relationships, and enact meaningful changes.

Appendix

Research Notes on Historical Sources

Newspapers

(Calgary Herald, Edmonton Journal, Crag and Canyon, Stoney Country)

Newspaper accounts represent valuable mass-communication documents for research on the cultural history of the Banff–Bow Valley. Due to the broad temporal scope of the historical research involved here, it would be almost impossible to review all the content of several publications. As a result, there are several delimitations that I placed on the newspaper data collection. I selected one local weekly newspaper: the *Crag and Canyon*, which was first published in 1900. In conjunction with the years where coverage of the Banff Indian Days festivals was identified, the *Crag and Canyon* was reviewed for the years 1906–1980. In addition to using a search engine to find relevant articles, I reviewed them based on specific times of the year that were of particular relevance. For example, the Banff Indian Days were annually held in July, so all the months of July were analysed. Important events that occurred were also investigated. The *Crag and Canyon* became the *Banff Crag and Canyon* in June 1958, but for the purposes of clarity the newspaper is only referred to as the *Crag and Canyon*. The *Crag and Canyon* is available on microfiche from the Whyte Museum of the Canadian Rockies Archives in Banff. Also the articles can be read on the Alberta Heritage Digitalization Project site "Our Future Our Past."

To gain a broader regional perspective, I also examined the province of Alberta's two largest regional daily papers. The *Calgary Herald* and *Edmonton Journal* were reviewed using an electronic search index. Keywords and significant dates were effective in locating relevant materials. In contrast to the weekly *Crag and Canyon*, where the focus is on local events, a much broader approach was adapted for the provincial dailies. The search engine was used to investigate issues concerning Indigenous peoples and government policies, as well as information about the Banff Indian Days and Rocky Mountains national parks. While the provincial-dailies data collection was also fruitful, as one might predict, the scope was much broader and, as a consequence, so was the evidence that was collected. While the *Calgary Herald* covered the Banff Indian Days and related topics consistently throughout the period under investigation, the *Edmonton Journal* only had regular coverage of the festival in the 1950s and 1960s. The *Calgary Herald* and *Edmonton Journal* were available on microfiche from the University of Alberta's Leddy Library in Edmonton. Both newspapers were investigated from 1920 to 1971. It is important to acknowledge that two undergraduate students (Jayn Villetard and Leslie LeMoal) participated in various aspects of my newspaper data collection as a component of the Senior Research Experience course that I directed. I thank them for their individual contributions to this study.

Although only analysed from 1970 to 1979, one local Nakoda publication was reviewed. For information regarding the later period of the Banff Indian Days, I reviewed *Stoney Country* using a search engine. This data collection offered the only mass-communication documents written by Nakoda community members. This paper was available from the University of Alberta's Leddy Library.

Archival Analyses

(Glenbow Museum, Whyte Museum of the Canadian Rockies, CPR Archives, Library and Archives Canada)

Formal documents concerning park policy, including national parks acts, park warden reports, and municipal, provincial, and federal government policies were included as a component of this research. An analysis of these documents offered insights into how policies and laws affected Indigenous peoples and contributed to circulating discourse. These types of official documents were primarily obtained from Library and Archives Canada in Ottawa and the Whyte Museum of the Canadian Rockies archives in Banff.

Personal collections are another group of documents examined. This includes the collections of tourism entrepreneurs and guides who had extensive relations with Nakoda peoples. These collections contain important correspondence between tourism producers and Nakoda peoples in regard to various tourism ventures over the twentieth century. They also feature the correspondence of the Banff Indian Days Committee, with which Norman Luxton was involved for decades. The Norman Luxton File at the Glenbow Museum and Archives and the Norman Luxton Papers at the Whyte Museum of the Canadian Rockies archives were productive in this regard. I also investigated other collections of families who were involved in the tourism industry, including the Brewster and Whyte families. In addition, some collections also contained extensive photographic images that provide a unique and valuable window into less-publicized historical events. Although one personal collection was housed at the Glenbow Museum Archives in Calgary (F. Gully), most of the relevant collections for this study are at the Whyte Museum of the Canadian Rockies in Banff. The Notman, Underwood, and especially the Harmon collections were of most value.

I analysed all CPR images concerning travel in the Canadian Rocky Mountains over an eighty-three-year period (1897–1980). Produced in Canada and distributed internationally to major markets in Europe, Asia, and the United States, the images offered important perspectives on how the Canadian Rockies, but also Canada as a whole, was marketed through advertising campaigns and sold to audiences. This provided a unique window into discourses of travel that focused on selling certain aspects of the cultures, landscapes, and technological infrastructures of the Canadian Rockies. These marketing campaigns not only shaped tourists' expectations of Canada and the Rocky Mountains, but also impacted the processes whereby Canadian governments, tourism companies, and local entrepreneurs met these expectations in the Banff townsite and surrounding national park. All images were examined using the CPR online archives.

Oral History Interviews and Participant Observation

Oral accounts complement archival evidence by introducing first-hand perspectives that in some cases are completely absent from documents and cannot be obtained through any archive. Semi-structured oral-history interviews give the researcher a broader knowledge base for an individual's life, rather than just the interviewee's specific perspective on a certain topic. Interviews were conducted with twelve individuals who were identified by the communities as having extensive knowledge of regional history. The group consisted of individuals from both Nakoda (11) and Euro-Canadian (1) backgrounds. All interviews were tape-recorded and transcribed in their entirety. The total time recorded per individual varied from forty-five minutes in a single session to five hours and forty-eight minutes over multiple sessions. Five interviews were conducted with women and seven with men. As Hart (1995) contends, this method is an appropriate means of engaging with Indigenous peoples because it encourages listening by the researcher, long segments of speech without interruption, and overall cultural sensitivity. It is critical to recognize that elders especially have different speech patterns, methods of communicating, manners of listening, and ways of knowing (Battiste and Youngblood Henderson, 2000). I strongly encourage all researchers to seek out diverse Indigenous perspectives when pursuing information on Indigenous histories of the Banff–Bow Valley. As a consequence of privileging evidence obtained from these important contributions, oral histories were a seminal source in this research.

The band council, elders, and I had to ensure that information sensitive to the community was protected and that individual participants were protected. This is particularly important for Nakoda communities as they have several ongoing land claims. The evidence obtained from the interviewees could be grouped into three different categories of information resulting from both my evaluation of the sensitivity of the material and how an individual requested the information be treated. These categories broke down material as (1) unusable because of its cultural sensitivity, (2) usable, but the source is to remain anonymous, or (3) usable and linked to the contributor. The overall objective of these filtering and consultation procedures was to privilege these perspectives throughout the research and writing process by working with community members to ensure that the historical, and at times personal, materials collected were only used in appropriate manners. All contributors were asked to review the transcripts from the interviews to confirm their accuracy and to highlight any statements or parts of the discussions they wished to have removed or not be associated with their names. Even though some contributors did not offer any feedback on the transcripts, others provided detailed comments that resulted in the reconsideration of some information. In only a few circumstances where individuals did not want their named associated with sensitive information, but insisted that it be included, a general reference to a

"Nakoda elder" was automatically applied in the text. In most cases contributors wanted their names linked to the information they provided in the interviews.

Participant observation informed this study in several manners. However, it must be clearly stated that while I was at times an "observing participant" through some of the activities with which I was involved in the Morley community, none of the information acquired from these experiences was included as evidence. Experiences working in a community necessarily facilitate aspects of research, and by reflecting on how our work is informed by what we know and the relationships we build, we can learn from others, become more culturally sensitive, and develop relationships. In some respects these experiences did inform and facilitate my research.

Methodological Approaches

It is critical to include a brief description of methodology to indicate how my theoretical perspectives align with the methodological approaches that directed this research. A form of discourse analysis was used to identify the ways that discourse is structured, organized, and produced. There are of course many ways that scholars apply different kinds of discourse analysis in their own work. This research used a variety of discourse analyses informed by the methods of Foucault to interpret the collected texts. Foucauldian-based analyses aim to identify the discourse operating in a certain area of life and to examine the implications for subjectivity, practice, and power relations. Foucauldian-informed discourse analyses (FIDA) are concerned with what Foucault has termed archaeologies (1970, 1972, 1988, 1994). His method determines how the historical development of discourse influences how power can be exercised. These approaches aim to distinguish the power relations embedded in and being produced by a prevailing discourse, which also includes how discourse may be refused and transformed in various human interactions. In contrast to critical discourse analysis, which is a top-down, linear, hierarchical approach that is interested in classifying dominant–subordinate relations and determining how ideologies are manifested in a text, FIDA is not hierarchical, as it stems from Foucault's productive and relational conceptions of power relations. The objective is not to challenge the hegemony of a certain group, but to map how power is used through discourse to produce and define practices in certain fields. While conceptual tools to guide the application of FIDA are not common, there are a few scholars who have created in-depth models. Willig's (2001) method is particularly helpful when applied to texts in a well-organized data set. In sport studies, Liao and Markula (2009) and Barker-Ruchti (2009) both offer models of Foucauldian-based analyses that define the process even further.

It must be recognized that all forms of discourse analyses are interpretive tasks that involve selection processes that privilege, frame, and edit. While some questions are useful in elucidating the operating power relations, researchers still need to decide which discourses will be examined. I take this into account by including direct quotations and large portions of dialogue from the texts produced as examples of the discourse identified. Despite careful attention to include directly quoted texts as much as possible, it must be clear that these are mediated interpretations and should not be presented or considered in any other manner.

Ethical Obligations

Most of the individuals who participated in my research had several suggestions about how to give back to the community. In their minds, being culturally sensitive and adhering to high ethical standards were the minimum requirements for conducting research with community members. Participants emphasized that the results of the study should be made available to the community in a condensed and accessible form. After numerous discussions with elders, it was decided that it was of interest to community members to have a condensed written summary of what occurred annually at the Banff Indian Days festivals over the history of the event (1894–1978). Completing this document and making it available for all community members at the Nakada Institute and Archives was important for several elders.

I feel that my responsibility to give back to community members has been expressed for the most part through volunteering. At the beginning of my research, I was fortunate to meet several welcoming and generous individuals who shaped the remainder of my experiences in the community (most notably Roland Rollinmud and Margaret Snow). My initial interest was in volunteering at the Banff Indian Days gatherings held annually near the Banff townsite. These experiences provided opportunities to meet and interact with community members. A few years later, I was invited to join the organizing committee of the Stoney Park Aboriginal Cultural Society, a group that facilitates cultural opportunities for Nakoda youth, mainly in the form of Indigenous music gatherings. In September 2009, I was named to the board of directors, which entailed a new level of engagement and responsibility. In October 2009, I was asked to be part of the foundation of an Indigenous-owned and -operated cultural and ecotourism organization in Morley. The organization is a tourism venture that supports Nakoda perspectives of spirituality and subsistence land uses. I take all these opportunities and responsibilities seriously and am encouraged by the possibility that my time and skill set can make a contribution to these specific organizations and the broader community.

As a result of developing relationships through these interactions over the years, I began to be invited to both community events and private cultural practices. I am honoured by these types of invitations and attend as often as I can. During the period that this research was conducted, I have been fortunate enough to attend numerous rodeos, powwows, and other community functions. I also regularly participated in sweats at the private lodge of elder Lenny Poucette. All these experiences have allowed me to get to know community members and develop meaningful relationships that extend beyond research interests into the realm of my personal life.

Notes

Introduction

1 Roland Rollinmud, personal interview, 1 Nov. 2008.

2 The Bow Valley gets its name from a Nakoda translation of *mun-uh-cha-ban*, meaning the place of bows. This refers to the strong withes of the Douglas Fir trees that were found along the river's banks. Nakoda hunters used them to make bows before the arrival of Europeans to the region (Hart, 1999: 8).

3 Currently in Canada, "Indigenous" has become a more useful term to collectively refer to First Nations, Métis and Inuit peoples. For this reason, throughout this book I have chosen the term "Indigenous" when describing general Canadian contexts. As Alfred (2005) recognizes, the term "Indigenous" represents an experience that is shaped by a politicized colonial past and present. However, it is critical to invoke an individual nation's own self-appellation whenever possible and I do this throughout referring to Nakoda peoples. Attention to such terminological specificity prevents a homogenization of distinct cultures and recognizes the heterogeneity and diversity of Indigenous languages and cultural groups in Canada.

4 The individuals from Nakoda First Nations (NFN) communities who participated in this research refer to themselves, and are referred to, by several appellations. Nakoda First Nations is the contemporary appellation that many individuals use in formal references. The word Nakoda means "the people." The name Nakoda peoples has mostly replaced the older reference to Stoney Peoples, although Stoney is still widely used by many individuals in informal settings and exclusively by some elders. I have chosen to use NFN, but will also at times refer to Nakoda peoples depending on the context of use. The name Stoney is derived from a Euro-Canadian

reference based on their unique practice of boiling water by placing large heated rocks or stones into water-filled pits that were lined with bison stomachs (Snow, 2005).

5 Diverse topics of Euro-Canadian histories of the Banff–Bow Valley examined by historians include transportation infrastructure (Williams, 1948; Hart, 1983; Marty, 1984); the development of the Banff townsite and national park (Williams, 1922; Brown, 1970; Scace, 1970; Robinson, 1973; Bella, 1987; Colpitts, 2002; Hart, 1999, 2003, 2009); miners and labourers (Gadd, 1989; Kordan and Melnycky, 1991; Waiser, 1995); outdoor recreation guides and their organizations (Williams, 1936; Hart, 1979; Reichwein, 1996; Scott, 2000, 2005, 2009); park wardens (Marty, 1978; Peyto, 2002, 2004); high culture and the arts (Jessup, 2002; Reichwein, 2005); and tourism promotion and cultural festivals (Yeo, 1990; Henderson, 1995; Colpitts, 1998; Robinson, 2007).

6 These works include Luxton, 1974; Whyte, 1985; Parker, 1990; Meijer-Drees, 1991, 1993; Dempsey, 1997, 1998; Hart, 1999; Bradford, 2005; and Binnema and Niemi, 2006.

7 Either directed by First Nations authors or in collaboration with local First Nations, research on the following topics has been undertaken: the life of Nakoda Chief Frank Kaquitts (Jonker, 1988); Indigenous participation in sporting festivals and the tourism industry (Mason, 2009, 2010); oral accounts of specific cultural practices of the diverse groups who lived in the Canadian Rockies (Hungry Wolf and Hungry Wolf, 1989); histories of towns and transportation infrastructure in the Banff–Bow Valley (Alexander, 2010; Manry, 2010); the Bow River (Armstrong, Evenden, and Nelles, 2009); institutional representations of the cultural practices of Nakoda peoples (Mason, 2009, 2012); the finer details of the Treaty 7 agreement (Hildebrandt et al., 1996); and the political and cultural basis for Nakoda land claims (Snow, 2005).

8 For much more information on some of the volunteer work and related ethical considerations that informed this research, please see "Ethical Obligations" in the appendix.

9 Although weekly issues of the *Crag and Canyon* and *Stoney Country* were examined, the daily issues of the *Calgary Herald* and the *Edmonton Journal* were reviewed using an index for the month of July in each specified year. Special attention was allocated to this month because the Indian Days were normally held during the middle of July. For a much more detailed account of the historical research processes, including specifics of each resource base, please see "Research Notes on Historical Sources" in the appendix.

Chapter 1: Theorizing Power Relations in Colonial Histories

1 Many colonized individuals and groups still live with the repressive structures that were instituted during the colonial era. As Loomba (2005) argues, the race relations produced during colonialism survive long after many of the economic structures underlying them have changed. Racial stereotypes still circulate and contemporary global imbalances are built upon the inequities that were formed during the colonial era. She states: "A complex amalgam of economic and racial factors operates in anchoring the present to the colonial past" (111). In Canada, the inequalities stemming from the colonial period have not been erased, and as a result it is difficult to imagine a postcolonial space. Therefore, when I reference postcolonialism in this book, I am referring generally to the Marxist-derived genre of social theory that examines the legacies of colonialism, not a temporal postcolonial context or space.

2 Even though Foucault defined discourse in several capacities over his career, in this study my uses of Foucauldian discourse stem from his explanations of discourses as ways of knowing that are circulated as "truths." These ways of knowing are deeply informed by social practices. Foucault suggests that discourses control the production, circulation, and consumption of statements and related understandings of realities. He viewed discourses as more than merely bodies of ideas or ideologies, but also as attitudes, modes of address, terms of reference, and actions that are reflected in social practices (Foucault, 1972).

3 Post-structural conceptualizations of identities argue against totalizing models that paint identities as sustained, coherent, static, reliable, and homogeneous. In contrast, they consider identities heterogeneous, fluid, unstable, contested, and discursively produced (Tierney, 2003). Post-structuralism is particularly valuable in disrupting the artificially produced and unified subject that many social scientists have relied upon for decades in their theorizing of social relations. Hall (1996) argues that identities are points of temporary attachment to the subject positions which discursive practices construct for us. From diverse disciplinary perspectives, a number of scholars have examined what is at stake in these temporary attachments: Anzaldua, 1987; Robins, 1996; Frith, 1996; Zhan, 2005; Sen, 2006.

4 Some scholars have effectively demonstrated how post-structural theoretical perspectives can complement postcolonial and community-driven methodological approaches. For examples see Cameron and Gibson, 2005; and Wetherell and Potter, 1992.

5 Post-structuralism in general, and specifically the works of Foucault, have not been incorporated nearly as often as critical or Marxist paradigms of social theory in the literature examining the phenomena of tourism (Wearing and McDonald, 2002). Subsequently, much of this scholarship reinforces binaries between racial groups and predetermines or over-determines power relations (Bruner, 2005). Although a few scholars have used Foucault in their research on tourism and parks, these have been limited to only some aspects of his broad range of concepts. Most research centres on interpreting power relations in tourism productions (Rojek, 1985, 1992; Hollinshead, 1999; Cheong and Miller, 2000, 2004), but some other aspects in tourism research, including the "tourist gaze" (Urry, 1990; Hollinshead, 1994), the body (Veijola and Jokinen, 1994) and resistance (Wearing, 1995), also borrow from Foucault. There is a large and extensive body of work that examines tourism, parks, and Indigenous peoples (Blundell, 1993; Butler and Hinch, 1996, 2007; Nesper, 2003; Harkin, 2003; Bruner, 2005; Mason, 2004; Sweet, 2004), but very few scholars overtly take up Foucault in their research (Bruner, 2001; Winter, 2007) and there are even fewer who adopt a Foucauldian-based methodological approach (Wearing and McDonald, 2002; Mason, 2009). When it comes to analyses of racial discourse in tourism and parks-oriented research, there is a clear gap in scholarship. This book does draw from material in tourism studies for examples of Foucauldian-based analyses to address this substantial gap by using Foucauldian-centred methodological and theoretical approaches in research that involves tourism and parks in an examination of racial discourse.

6 Over the last decade there has been a significant increase in the number of sport and physical-activity scholars that effectively employ some of Foucault's various tools. Some of the better examples, include Andrews, 2000; Johns and Johns, 2000; Shogan, 2002; Markula, 2003, 2004; Pringle, 2005; Pringle and Markula, 2005; Markula and Pringle, 2006; Jette, 2006; Thorpe, 2008; Liao and Markula, 2009; and Barker-Ruchti, 2009. The majority of this research uses Foucault to interpret and problematize sexuality, and sometimes gender, discourse related to specific sport, exercise, and activity topics of inquiry. Despite the growing number of scholars using Foucault's theories in physical activity and sport studies, Foucauldian-based research on racial discourse has rarely surfaced. There is a small group of scholars who have used Foucault's tools in their interpretation of racial discourse, but this body of work remains severely limited. See Cole, 1996; Cole et al., 2004; Sloop, 1997; Grieveson, 1998; Dallaire, 2003; Hokowhitu, 2003, 2004, 2005, 2013; Farnell, 2004; Giles, 2005; and Mason 2009, 2010, 2012. Only a few of these researchers explicitly use Foucault in their theoretical

perspectives or methodological approaches (Cole, 1996; Sloop, 1997) and even fewer do this in a colonial context (Farnell, 2004; Hokowhitu, 2004, 2013; Giles, 2005; Mason, 2010, 2012).

Chapter 2: Colonial Encounters

1 This region only includes the upper stretches of the Bow River, which runs 587 kilometres from Bow Lake to where it joins the South Saskatchewan River in southern Alberta. For more detail and an excellent history of the Bow River see Armstrong, Evenden, and Nelles, 2009.
2 Roland Rollinmud, personal interview, 1 Nov. 2008. Among Nakoda peoples, elder is a respected title given only to some members of the community. Elder is not necessarily a gender or age category. Elders are considered educators about cultural practices and life in general. Because of their unique experiences and knowledge base, their values and wisdom make them highly regarded as decision makers.
3 Lenny Poucette, personal interview, 9 Oct. 2009.
4 Ibid.
5 For example, John McDougall especially lobbied the government on several occasions to increase reserve lands and improve Nakoda access to resources. That being said, some Nakoda elders seriously question how often he put their concerns ahead of his own personal objectives. For examples of this, see Snow, 2005: 100–1; and Hildebrandt et al., 1996: 262–9.
6 The Red River Rebellion was a dispute between the established Métis settlement along the Red River and the newly formed Canadian government. In addition to a conflict over control of land and resources, the rebellion was fundamentally about Indigenous and French cultural and linguistic rights. The rebellion was quelled with the Manitoba Act of 1870, which brought the province into Canadian Confederation. Although Métis leader Louis Riel went into hiding in the United States in 1870, he remained a significant voice in furthering the rights of Indigenous and Métis peoples until he was executed by the Canadian government in 1885 for his role in the North-West Rebellion. For more see Pannekoek, 1996.
7 For a good analysis of some of the consequences of the illegal whisky trade for some Indigenous communities in the west see Allen, 1983: 229–46.
8 While the Indian Act of 1876 did precede the Treaty 7 agreement, it dealt with some of the issues that affected Indigenous communities in a generalized form and did not address the individual concerns of specific Indigenous groups. The Indian Act did not really have any immediate implications for Indigenous peoples of western Canada as they were

excluded from most sections. The groups in the west were not considered to be "civilized" by the superintendent general of Indian Affairs (Tobias, 1983). Although the Indian Act did specify the qualifications for "Indian status," directly promoted assimilation policies, and repressed cultural practices, the individual treaties were designed to manage the particular definition of lands and resources for specific groups. For more on the 1876 Indian Act and the earlier regulations see Bartlett, 1980.

9 Nakoda elder, personal interview, October 2009.

10 Poucette, interview, 9 Oct. 2009.

11 Ibid.

12 It is critical to acknowledge that while the assimilationist aspects of the Dominion of Canada policies concerning Indigenous peoples were developed in the 1870s, these were merely extensions of the imperial governments' approaches that can be traced to the middle of the eighteenth century.

13 While there are current land claims that have yet to be resolved over the size of and access to Nakoda lands, the Nakoda raised the Kootenay Plains issue in 1934 through the newly formed League of Indians of Canada. It was not until 1946 that a 5000-acre ranch on the Highwood River was turned into the Eden Valley reserve (Reserve 216). In 1948, another 5000-acre reserve was formed on the Kootenay Plains (Bighorn Reserve 144A) by agreement between the province and the federal government. For more on this see Snow, 2005: 89–104; Hildebrandt et al., 1996: 139–41; and Smith, 2009: 200.

14 Poucette, interview, 9 Oct. 2009.

15 Rollinmud, interview, 1 Nov. 2008.

16 Nakoda elder, personal interview, December 2009.

17 The question of how to define the ethnicity of community members in order to determine who has access to reserve lands and resources remains a heated issue in the twenty-first century for some Indigenous communities. On 9 February 2010, on the Kahnawake Mohawk reserve in Quebec, the band council evicted non-Mohawks who were in common-law relationships with local band members. As a result of conflicts over the use of resources, the band has established a strict review process to determine the "Mohawk-ness" of community members and subsequently their access to these resources. For more on this specific issue, see *Globe and Mail*, 15 February 2010, 18. Tracey Deer's 2008 documentary film entitled *Club Native*, overviews some of the fundamental principles that surround these complex issues in Indigenous communities.

18 Nakoda elder, interview, December 2009.

19 Rollinmud, interview, 1 Nov. 2008.
20 Poucette, interview, 9 Oct. 2009.
21 Nakoda elder, interview, December 2009.
22 Nakoda elder, interview, December 2008.

Chapter 3: The Repression of Indigenous Subsistence Practices in Rocky Mountains Park

1 Lenny Poucette, personal interview, 9 Oct. 2009.
2 Margaret Snow, personal interview, 14 Nov. 2008.
3 Roland Rollinmud, personal interview, 1 Nov. 2008.
4 Ibid.
5 Rocky Mountains National Park Act, 23 June 1887 (Statutes of Canada, 50–51 Victoria, chapter 32).
6 As sourced in Binnema and Niemi, 2006: 729.
7 Poucette, interview, 9 Oct. 2009.
8 There is a significant body of literature that covers the history of the expulsion of residents inside national parks in Canada. E.g., Prince Albert National Park, Saskatchewan (Waiser, 2011); La Maurice National Park, Québec (Craig-Dupont, 2011); Point Pelee National Park, Ontario (Sandlos, 2005). Specifically in reference to Indigenous peoples, see the expulsion of Métis from Kouchibouguac National Park, Manitoba (Rudin, 2011); Kluane First Nations and Tinglet peoples from Kluane National Park, Yukon (Neufeld, 2011; Cruikshank, 2005); Ojibway from Riding Mountain National Park, Manitoba (Sandlos, 2008); Ojibway from Georgian Bay Islands National Park, Ontario (Sandlos, 2005); Métis from Jasper National Park, Alberta (Murphy, 2008; MacLaren, 2011); Nakoda from Banff National Park, Alberta (Snow, 2005; Mason, 2008; Binnema and Niemi, 2006).
9 Rollinmud, interview, 1 Nov. 2008.
10 Howard Sibbald to Frank Pedley, 23 Dec. 1903. Howard Sibbald, Indian Agent's Annual Report, Annual Report of the Department of Indian Affairs, 1903, 192.
11 Well-researched examples include the displacement of Blackfeet in Glacier National Park, Montana (Urion, 1999; Spence, 1999; Burnham, 2000); Crow, Shoshone, Sheep Eater, and Bannock peoples in Yellowstone National Park, Wyoming (Spence, 1999; Keller and Turek, 1999; Jacoby, 2001); Ahwahneechee or Yosemite Indians in Yosemite National Park, California (Spence, 1999; Keller and Turek, 1999); Seminoles in Everglades National Park, Florida (Keller and Turek, 1999); Lakota in Badlands National Park, South Dakota (Burnham, 2000); Havasupai Indians in Grand Canyon

National Park, Arizona (Burnham, 2000; Jacoby, 2001); Puebloan or Anasazi peoples in Mesa Verde National Park, Colorado (Burnham, 2000); Tinglet peoples in Glacier Bay National Park, Alaska (Cruikshank, 2005); and Timbisha or Shoshone peoples in Death Valley National Park, California and Nevada (Burnham, 2000).

12 Sadly, the prohibiting of Indigenous cultural practices remained a component of Canadian government policy until 1951.

13 Rollinmud, interview, 1 Nov. 2008.

14 Poucette, interview, 9 Oct. 2009.

15 Ibid.

16 By 1945, the Canadian public was beginning to demand that the government address the issues surrounding the rights of Indigenous peoples. In 1969, the "White Paper," a government policy document was introduced by Prime Minister Pierre Trudeau and Minister of Indian Affairs Jean Chrétien. The policy attempted to absolve the government of the responsibility of managing Indian affairs by essentially withdrawing the special status granted to Indigenous peoples. This document drew massive protests from communities across the nation. It was not until 1981, and the adoption of the Declaration of First Nations by the chiefs across the country, that Indigenous peoples' sovereign rights to self-government was achieved. For more, see Tester et al., 1999.

17 Alfred makes a strong argument for understanding these destructive consequences historically in Indigenous communities. He also contends that reinstating traditional forms of government should be a priority for communities in the twenty-first century. "Traditional government is the antidote to the colonial disease and its corruptions and abuses of power, and to the disempowerment of our people and communities" (2009b: 5).

18 Nakoda elder, personal interview, December 2009.

19 *Crag and Canyon*, 1 July 1938, 4.

20 Poucette, interview, 9 Oct. 2009.

Chapter 4: Sporting and Tourism Festivals

1 Roland Rollinmud, personal interview, 1 Nov. 2008.

2 The CPR was formed in 1881 with the intention of building a railway that would unite central Canada to British Columbia and the Pacific coast, a task they completed in 1885. From the 1880s until the beginning of the Second World War, the CPR diversified into tourism ventures, including hotel and infrastructure construction, in addition to numerous other profitable businesses. For more see Choko and Jones, 2004.

3 Although the railway was completed at Craigellachie, British Columbia, on 7 November 1885, it did not become officially operational until June of 1886. The completion of the railway fulfilled the 1871 commitment of the Canadian federal government to connect British Columbia to central Canada. The promise of a transcontinental railway was a significant factor in securing the western province in Canadian Confederation (Nicol, 1970: 23–5).

4 Rocky Mountains Park Act, 23 June 1887 (Statutes of Canada, 50–51 Victoria, chapter 32).

5 Ibid.

6 For an excellent resource on J.B. Harkin and his role in the development of the Rocky Mountain national parks see Hart, 2009.

7 MacEachern (2011) argues that Mabel Williams played a key role in convincing commissioner Harkin of the value of tourism in parks. It was her idea to market tourism as an incentive to create national parks and she delivered the important financial documents to encourage Harkin's agenda to expand the national park system. Part of the evidence that supported this economic argument was Williams's creative calculation that suggested that wheat fields were worth $4.91 an acre while scenery was valued at $13.88. Her calculation was even quoted at length in the US congress discussion about creating a national park service in 1916. For more see MacEachern, 2011: 33.

8 Rocky Mountains Park Act.

9 Although there were already hydro-electric power developments inside RMP, opposition to power dams did occur between 1910 and 1930. This opposition was led by the Alpine Club of Canada (ACC), which was formed in 1907. In 1923 a conservation organization related to the ACC, the Canadian National Parks Association, would organize to protect national parks from commercial development and exploitation. One of their first priorities was to oppose the creation of a hydro dam on the Spray River near the current town of Canmore, Alberta. For more on the issues and controversies that surrounded the development of hydro-electric power in or near park lands, see Bella, 1987; McNamee, 1993; and Reichwein, 1996. Hydro-electric dam developments also occurred just outside the park on the Nakoda reserve at Morley between 1914 and 1920. These developments had significant implications for local peoples, as the flooding of portions of the reserve and the increase in human activity in the vicinity, including heavy machinery, greatly reduced the presence of large mammal populations on and around the reserve. For more see Snow, 2005.

10 In what remains a dark shadow in the history of the Rocky Mountain parks, prisoners of war were forced to labour in internment camps in both Banff and Jasper National Parks. Hungarians, Germans, Austrians, and especially Ukrainians worked at the Castle Mountain internment camp during the First World War and Japanese and Mennonite prisoners worked in Banff and Jasper during the Second World War. For excellent sources on internment camps in the Rocky Mountain parks see Kordan and Melnycky, 1991 and Waiser, 1995. From more of a national context see Kordan, 2002.
11 The National Parks Act, 30 May 1930 (Statutes of Canada, 20–21 George V, chapter 33).
12 Ralphine Locke, personal interview, 18 July 2009.
13 Rollinmud, interview, 1 Nov. 2008.
14 Roland Rollinmud, personal interview, 14 Nov. 2008.
15 See Whyte, 1985; Parker, 1990; Meijer-Drees, 1991; Dempsey, 1998; and Hart, 1999.
16 *Crag and Canyon*, 26 July 1913, 2; *Calgary Herald*, 20 July 1921, 14.
17 Margaret Snow, personal interview, 14 Nov. 2008.
18 *Crag and Canyon*, 11 July 1914, 1.
19 *Edmonton Journal*, 14 July 1956, 7.
20 *Crag and Canyon*, 14 June 1913, 2.
21 Noted discrepancies: Meijer-Drees, 1991, 1993. Contending that the inaugural festival was in 1899: Whyte, 1985; Parker, 1990; Dempsey, 1998.
22 I must acknowledge E.J. (Ted) Hart for sharing his resource base and pointing me in the proper direction to make this assessment. See Department of the Interior Report, 1894, part 5, *Report of the Superintendent of Rocky Mountains Park*.
23 *Crag and Canyon*, 22 July 1911, 1.
24 Dominion Day is the name of the holiday that commemorated the confederation of Canada on 1 July 1867. The holiday was renamed Canada Day in 1982. For a description of a Dominion Day event in Banff, see *Crag and Canyon*, 7 July 1906, 1–2.
25 *Crag and Canyon*, 20 July 1912, 8 (for a description of two-day event expansion) and *Crag and Canyon*, 6 July 1928, 1 (for a description of three-day event expansion).
26 *Calgary Herald*, 18 July 1953, 1.
27 Ralphine Locke, personal interview, 18 July 2009.
28 Rollinmud, interview, 1 Nov. 2008.
29 Jackson Wesley, personal interview, 3 Dec. 2007.
30 *Crag and Canyon*, 22 July 1922, 1.

31 See Urry, 1990; McKay, 1994; Hughes, 1995; Greenwood, 2004; and Mason, 2008.
32 *Crag and Canyon*, 30 July 1980, 4.
33 *Edmonton Journal*, 24 July 1956, 13.
34 *Crag and Canyon*, 16 July 1938, 23.
35 For examples of these print media advertisements, see: *Crag and Canyon*, 14 June 1913, 2; *Crag and Canyon*, 5 July 1913, 4; *Crag and Canyon*, 1 July 1916, 4.
36 The trails and the interpreters themselves are simply one example of how early-twentieth-century visitors to national parks were spoon-fed a version of nature that simultaneously expanded tourists' experiences of the "natural" world while often supporting capitalist objectives. By the post-war years, the institutionalization of nature interpretation was in full bloom as directors of parks created positions for interpreters and built visitor centres and gift shops. The process of fostering the consumption and institutionalization of nature through interpretation is perhaps best exemplified in a post-war Parks Canada memorandum stating that "parks will now be explained and interpreted as living museums of nature, where people can observe and appreciate the beauty that surrounds them." The figurative and literal construction of "living museums" encouraged the active consumption of nature and its products. These centres of interpretation led to successful park programs that facilitated expansions to accommodate more visitors. Ironically, the increases in public use and the expansion of infrastructure to meet the visitors' demands also had detrimental effects on the very same aesthetic resources that were the objects of consumption, interpretation, and conservation. For more see Wilson, 1991: 52–8.
37 *Calgary Herald*, 7 July 1950, 9.
38 *Edmonton Journal*, 14 July 1958, 11.
39 Rollinmud, interview, 14 Nov. 2008.
40 Ibid.
41 Lenny Poucette, personal interview, 9 Oct. 2009.
42 The Ktunaxa (Kootenay) and Tsuu T'ina (Sarcee) first participated in 1914 and soon after attended regularly, as reported in the *Crag and Canyon*, 18 July 1914, 1. While oral accounts suggest that the Cree from Hobbema and members of the Blackfoot Confederacy may have participated with the Kootenay, Tsuu T'ina, and the Nakoda earlier, newspaper accounts first acknowledge Cree and Blackfoot participation in the 1930s. See *Calgary Herald*, 6 July 1931, 15.
43 Numerous Indigenous groups did attend over the decades the event was held. The 1962 festival was a particularly inclusive year, as in addition to

the Nakoda (Stoney), Cree, Tsuu T'ina (Sarcee), and members of the Blackfoot Confederacy, Cree from Manitoba, Saskatchewan, and other regions of Alberta participated in the events, as did Umatilla from Oregon, Peigan from Montana, and Yukamis from Washington State. In total, over 820 Indigenous peoples were in attendance in 1962. See *Calgary Herald*, 19 July 1962, 27.

44 Nakoda elder, personal interview, December 2009.
45 Poucette, interview, 9 Oct. 2009.
46 Nakoda elder, personal interview, December 2008.
47 Margaret Snow, interview, 14 Nov. 2008; Merisha Snow, personal interview, 14 Nov. 2008.
48 For examples see Butchart, 1998; Deloria, 2004; Wakeham, 2008; and Mason, 2009.

Chapter 5: Rethinking the Banff Indian Days as Critical Spaces of Cultural Exchange

1 *Crag and Canyon*, 29 July 1927, 13. It is also worth noting that 1200 Aboriginal participants were recorded in the late 1950s. See *Calgary Herald*, 15 July 1959, 49.
2 *Calgary Herald*, 20 July 1956, 2; *Calgary Herald*, 20 July 1963, 15.
3 *Crag and Canyon*, 19 July 1958, 11.
4 See Williams, 1922: 34.
5 *Calgary Herald*, 19 July 1926, 5. Although not deconstructed in the text, it is important to state that the references to "squaws" and "braves" used in 1926 became part of the racist terminology of ethnic slurs referring to Indigenous peoples later in the century.
6 *Calgary Herald*, 18 July 1929, 18.
7 Margaret Snow, personal interview, 14 Nov. 2008.
8 *Calgary Herald*, 17 July 1947, 1.
9 Roland Rollinmud, personal interview, 14 Nov. 2008.
10 *Crag and Canyon*, 22 July 1911, 12.
11 *Calgary Herald*, 20 July 1921, 1.
12 *Calgary Herald*, 22 July 1925, 8.
13 Rollinmud, interview, 14 Nov. 2008.
14 Snow, interview, 14 Nov. 2008.
15 For early period see *Crag and Canyon*, 24 July 1925, 1; *Crag and Canyon*, 17 July 1931, 10.
16 Rollinmud, interview, 14 Nov. 2008; also supported by *Calgary Herald*, 20 July 1921.

17 *Crag and Canyon*, 12 July 1936, 7. Also supported by Snow, interview, 14 Nov. 2008.
18 Rollinmud, interview, 14 Nov. 2008.
19 *Calgary Herald*, 21 July 1955, 13; *Edmonton Journal*, 16 July 1957, 12.
20 *Calgary Herald*, 19 July 1958, 14.
21 *Edmonton Journal*, 16 July 1957, 12.
22 *Calgary Herald*, 24 July 1936, 9.
23 Snow, interview, 14 Nov. 2008; Rollinmud, interview, 14 Nov. 2008.
24 *Calgary Herald*, 19 July 1926, 2.
25 Snow, interview, 14 Nov. 2008.
26 *Crag and Canyon*, 16 June 1939, 1. A travois, which is a V-shaped frame of poles, is a method of carrying loads behind a horse in rough terrain. They were often used by Plains peoples to carry children. Margaret Snow, interview, 14 Nov. 2008; Merisha Snow, personal interview, 14 Nov. 2008.
27 *Crag and Canyon*, 15 July 1954, 1.
28 *Calgary Herald*, 18 July 1923, 7.
29 *Calgary Herald*, 22 July 1925, 7.
30 *Calgary Herald*, 21 July 1955, 3.
31 *Crag and Canyon*, 11 July 1913, 2.
32 Rollinmud, interview, 14 Nov. 2008.
33 *Calgary Herald*, 12 July 1935, 15.
34 For an example of some of the individuals, see *Crag and Canyon*, 25 July 1941, 1.
35 Helen Keller (*Crag and Canyon*, 28 July 1939, 1) and British princess Margaret Rose (*Crag and Canyon*, 18 July 1958, 7) are examples of some of the more famous honorary Nakoda First Nations members.
36 Jackson Wesley, personal interview, 3 Dec. 2007.
37 Lenny Poucette, personal interview, 9 Oct. 2009.
38 *Calgary Herald*, 4 Aug. 1927, 6.
39 Poucette, interview, 9 Oct. 2009.
40 For descriptions of these theatre performances, see *Crag and Canyon*, 19 July 1929, 1; *Calgary Herald*, 18 July 1941, 1.
41 Poucette, interview, 9 Oct. 2009.
42 Ibid.
43 Ibid.
44 Roland Rollinmud, interview, 1 Nov. 2008.
45 Wesley, interview, 3 Dec. 2007.
46 Ibid.
47 Rollinmud, interview, 14 Nov. 2008.
48 Margaret Snow, interview, 14 Nov. 2008.

49 *Calgary Herald*, 11 June 1943, 4.
50 Rollinmud, interview, 1 Nov. 2008.
51 Ibid.
52 Poucette, interview, 9 Oct. 2009.
53 Rollinmud, interview, 14 Nov. 2008.
54 Ibid. Also supported by *Calgary Herald*, 21 July 1956, 1.
55 *Calgary Herald*, 20 July 1946, 1.
56 Ibid.
57 *Crag and Canyon*, 19 July 1931, 9.
58 Poucette, interview, 9 Oct. 2009. Also supported by *Calgary Herald*, 11 July 1936, 17.
59 *Crag and Canyon*, 19 July 1961, 2.
60 *Crag and Canyon*, 17 Aug. 1965, 1.
61 Ibid.
62 Nakoda elder, personal interview, December 2008.
63 The Banff Indian Days were last celebrated in 1978 because of changing attitudes and organizational problems. Beginning in 1971, disputes over fair compensation for participants caused the Nakoda to boycott the event. The organizing committee became frustrated with the amount of work and the lack of support from businesses in Banff. It is also worth noting that in 1992 the Buffalo Nations Cultural Society revived the festival at a local ranching venue near the Nakoda reserve at Morley. Under the name Tribal Days, the event received relatively little attention from local tourists. Since 2005, a small three-day Nakoda gathering has annually occurred in Banff. This initiative is jointly led by Nakoda leaders and Parks Canada. Rollinmud, interview, 1 Nov. 2008.
64 *Crag and Canyon*, 28 July 1971, 4.

Chapter 6: Looking Back and Pushing Ahead

1 Although there are diverse experiences and regional variations associated with sweat lodges, they can be considered spiritual purification ceremonies. For Nakoda peoples, they consist of several rounds that include ritualized forms of various cultural practices. As a Euro-Canadian guest to these ceremonies, I am not qualified or permitted to speak specifically about sweat-lodge experiences.
2 See Crosby, 1992; Collins, 1998; Smith, 2004; and Harding, 2004, 2006.
3 Lenny Poucette, personal interview, 9 Oct. 2009.
4 Roland Rollinmud, personal interview, 14 Nov. 2008.
5 Poucette, interview, 9 Oct. 2009.

6 Roland Rollinmud, telephone interview, 2 Mar. 2012.

7 Idle No More emerged as a protest movement against the federal Conservative government's omnibus Bill C-45. Along with other measures, the bill proposed to alter the Navigable Waters Protection Act of 1882. Indigenous leaders anticipated that the bill would facilitate natural-resource development on their lands. Although it was inspired by Attawapiskat Chief Theresa Spence's hunger strike, the ongoing movement expanded to include several forms of peaceful public protest, social media platforms, and expressions of resistance through national and international Indigenous solidarity campaigns.

References

Alexander, Rob. 2010. *The History of Canmore*. Banff: Summerthought.

Alfred, Gerald R. 1995. *Heeding the Voices of Our Ancestors: Kahnawake Mohawk Politics and the Rise of Native Nationalism*. Toronto: Oxford University Press.

Alfred, Taiaiake. 2005. *Wasáse: Indigenous Pathways of Action and Freedom*. Toronto: University of Toronto Press.

Alfred, Taiaiake. 2009a. "Colonialism and State Dependency." *Journal of Aboriginal Health* 5: 42–60.

Alfred, Taiaiake. 2009b. *Peace, Power and Righteousness: An Indigenous Manifesto*. Toronto: Oxford University Press.

Allen, Robert S. 1983. "A Witness to Murder: The Cypress Hills Massacre and the Conflict of Attitudes towards the Native Peoples of the Canadian-American West during the 1870s." In Ian A.L. Getty and Antoine S. Lussier, eds, *As Long as the Sun Shines and the Water Flows: A Reader in Canadian Native Studies*, 229–46. Vancouver: UBC Press.

Andrews, David L. 1993. "Desperately Seeking Michel: Foucault's Genealogy, the Body, and Critical Sport Sociology." *Sociology of Sport Journal* 10, 2: 148–67.

Andrews, David L. 2000. "Posting Up: French Poststructuralism and the Critical Analysis of Contemporary Sporting Cultures." In Jay Coakley and Eric Dunning, eds, *Handbook of Sport Studies*, 106–37. London: Sage.

Anzaldua, Gloria. 1987. *Borderlands/La Frontera: The New Mestiza*. San Francisco: Spinsters/Aunt Lute.

Arac, Jonathan. 1991. *After Foucault: Humanistic Knowledge and Postmodern Challenges*. New Brunswick, NJ: Rutgers University Press.

Armstrong, Christopher, Matthew Evenden, and H.V. Nelles. 2009. *The River Returns: An Environmental History of the Bow*. Montreal: McGill-Queen's University Press.

Arndt, Grant. 2005. "Ho Chunk 'Indian Powwows' of the Early Twentieth Century." In Clyde Ellis, Luke Eric Lassiter, and Gary H. Dunham, eds, *Powwows*, 46–67. Lincoln: University of Nebraska Press.

Barker-Ruchti, Natalie. 2009. "The Media as an Authorizing Practice of Femininity: Swiss Newspaper Coverage of Karin Thürig's Bronze Medal Performance in Road Cycling." In Pirkko Markula, ed., *Olympic Women and the Media*, 214–31. New York: Palgrave Macmillan.

Bartlett, Richard H. 1980. *The Indian Act of Canada*. Saskatoon: Native Law Centre.

Battiste, Marie, and J. (Sa'k'ej) Youngblood Henderson. 2000. *Protecting Indigenous Knowledge and Heritage: A Global Challenge*. Saskatoon: Purich Press.

Baudrillard, Jean. 1977. *Forget Foucault*. New York: Semiotext(e).

Bella, Leslie. 1987. *Parks for Profit*. Montreal: Harvest House.

Bhabha. Homi. 1994. *The Location of Culture*. London: Routledge.

Binnema, Theodore, and Melanie Niemi. 2006. "'Let the line be drawn now': Wilderness, Conservation, and the Exclusion of Aboriginal People from Banff National Park in Canada." *Environmental History* 11: 724–50.

Biolsi, Thomas. 2001. *Deadliest Enemies: Law and the Making of Race Relations On and Off the Rosebud Reservation*. Berkeley: University of California Press.

Biolsi, Thomas. 2004. "Race Technologies." In David Nugent and John Vincent, eds, *A Companion to the Anthropology of Politics*, 400–17. Oxford: Blackwell Publishing.

Bishop, Russell. 2005. "Freeing Ourselves from Neocolonial Domination in Research." In Norman K. Denzin and Yvonna S. Lincoln, eds, *The Sage Handbook of Qualitative Research*, 109–38. Thousand Oaks: Sage Publishing.

Blundell, Valda. 1993. "Aboriginal Empowerment and the Souvenir Trade in Canada." *Annals of Tourism Research* 20: 64–87.

Booth, Douglas. 2001. *Australian Beach Cultures: The History of Sun, Sand and Surf*. London: Frank Cass.

Booth, Douglas. 2005. *The Field: Truth and Fiction in Sport History*. London: Routledge.

Bouchier, Nancy, and Ken Cruikshank. 1997. "'Sportsmen and Pothunters': Environment, Conservation, and Class in the Fisheries of Hamilton Harbour." *Sport History Review* 28: 1–18.

Bracken, Christopher. 1997. *The Potlatch Papers: A Colonial Case Study*. Chicago: University of Chicago Press.

Bradford, Tolly. 2005. "A Useful Institution: William Twin, 'Indianess,' and Banff National Park, c. 1860–1940." *Native Studies Review* 16, 2: 77–98.

Brah, Avtar. 1992. "Difference, Diversity, and Differentiation." In J. Donald and A. Rattansi, eds, *Race, Culture and Difference*, 126–45. London: Sage.

Brayton, Sean, and Ted Alexander. 2007. "Dunky the Frog and the Politics of Irony." *Sociology of Sport Journal* 24, 3: 241–60.

Brown, Robert Craig. 1970. "The Doctrine of Usefulness: Natural Resources and the National Park Policy in Canada, 1887–1914." In J.G. Nelson, ed., *Canadian Parks in Perspective*, 46–64. Montreal: Harvest House Ltd.

Bruner, Edward M. 2001. "The Maasai and the Lion King: Authenticity, Nationalism, and Globalization in African Tourism." *American Ethnologist* 28, 4: 881–908.

Bruner, Edward M. 2005. *Culture on Tour: Ethnographies of Travel*. Chicago: University of Chicago Press.

Bugmann, Marlies. 2008. *Savage to Saint: The Karl May Story*. New York: Book-Surge Publishing.

Burnham, Philip. 2000. *Indian Country, God's Country: Native Americans and the National Parks*. Washington, DC: Island Press.

Butchart, A. 1998. *The Anatomy of Power: European Constructions of the African Body*. London: Zed Books.

Butler, Judith. 1990. *Gender Trouble: Feminism and the Subversion of Identity*. New York: Routledge.

Butler, Judith. 1992. "Contingent Foundations," In J. Butler and J. Scott, eds, *Feminists Theorize the Political*, 3–21. New York: Routledge.

Butler, Judith. 1993. *Bodies That Matter: On the Discursive Limits of "Sex."* New York: Routledge.

Butler, Richard, and Tom Hinch. 1996. *Tourism and Indigenous Peoples*. London: International Thomson Business Press.

Butler, Richard, and Tom Hinch. 2007. *Tourism and Indigenous Peoples: Issues and Implications*. Burlington: Butterworth-Heinemann.

Cahn, Susan. 1995. *Coming on Stong: Gender and Sexuality in Twentieth-Century Women's Sport*. Cambridge: Harvard University Press.

Cameron, Jenny, and Katherine Gibson. 2005. "Participatory Action Research in a Postructuralist Vein." *Geoforum* 36, 3: 315–31.

Cardinal, Harold. 1969. *The Unjust Society: The Tragedy of Canada's Indians*. Edmonton: Hurtig.

Catton, Theodore. 2006. *National Park, City Playground: Mt. Rainier and the Twentieth Century*. Seattle: University of Washington Press.

Chatty, Dawn, and Markus Colchester. 2002. *Conservation and Mobile Indigenous Peoples: Displacement, Forced Settlement, and Sustainable Development*. Oxford: Berghahn Books.

Cheong, So-Min, and Marc L. Miller. 2000. "Power in Tourism: A Foucauldian Observation." *Annals of Tourism Research* 27, 2: 371–90.

Cheong, So-Min, and Marc L. Miller. 2004. "Power Dynamics in Tourism: A Foucauldian Approach." In Sharon Bohn Gmelch, ed., *Tourists and Tourism: A Reader*, 239–52. Long Grove, IL: Waveland.

Choko, Marc H., and David L. Jones. 2004. *Posters of the Canadian Pacific*. Toronto: Firefly Books.

Clark, Ella Elizabeth. 1960. *Indian Legends of Canada*. Toronto: McClelland & Stewart.

Cole, C.L. 1996. "American Jordan, P.L.A.Y., Consensus, and Punishment." *Sociology of Sport Journal* 13, 4: 366–97.

Cole, C.L., Michael D. Giardina, and David L. Andrews. 2004. "Michael Foucault: Studies of Power and Sport." In R. Giulianotti, ed., *Sport and Modern Social Theorists*, 207–23. New York: Palgrave Macmillan.

Collins, Patricia Hill. 1998. "Some Group Matters: Intersectionality, Situated Standpoints, and Black Feminist Thought." In *Fighting Words: Black Women and the Search for Justice*, 101–18. Minneapolis: University of Minnesota Press.

Colpitts, George. 1998. "Wildlife Promotions, Western Canadian Boosterism and the Conservation Movement, 1890–1914." *American Review of Canadian Studies* 28, 1–2: 103–30.

Colpitts, George. 2002. *Game in the Garden: A Human History of Wildlife in Western Canada to 1940*. Vancouver: UBC Press.

Craig-Dupont, Olivier. 2011. "Hunting, Timber Harvesting, and Precambrian Beauties: The Scientific Reinterpretation of La Maurice National Park's Landscape History, 1969–1975." In Claire Elizabeth Campbell, ed., *A Century of Parks Canada, 1911–1921*, 179–204. Calgary: University of Calgary Press.

Cronon, William. 1996. *Uncommon Ground: Rethinking the Human Place in Nature*. New York: Norton & Company.

Crosby, Christina. 1992. "Dealing with Differences." In J. Butler and J. Scott, eds, *Feminists Theorize the Political*, 130–43. New York: Routledge.

Cruikshank, Julie. 1994. "Oral Tradition and Oral History: Reviewing Some Issues." *Canadian Historical Review* 75, 3: 403–18.

Cruikshank, Julie. 2005. *Do Glaciers Listen? Local Knowledge, Colonial Encounters, and Social Imagination*. Vancouver: UBC Press.

Dallaire, Christine. 2003. "'Not Just Francophone': The Hybridity of Minority Francophone Youths in Canada." *International Journal of Canadian Studies* 28: 163–99.

Dallaire, Christine. 2006. "'I Am English Too': Francophone Youth Hybridities in Canada." In Pam Nilan and Carles Feixa, eds, *Global Youth: Hybrid Identities, Global Worlds*, 32–52. London: Routledge.

Deloria, Philip J. 1998. *Playing Indian*. New Haven: Yale University Press.

Deloria, Philip J. 2004. *Indians in Unexpected Places*. Lawrence: University of Kansas Press.

Dempsey, Hugh. 1997. *Indian Tribes of Alberta*. Calgary: Glenbow Museum Institute.

Dempsey, Hugh. 1998. *Indians in the Rocky Mountain Parks*. Calgary: Fifth House.

Dyck, Noel. 1991. *What Is the Indian "Problem"? Tutelage and Resistance in Canadian Indian Administration*. St John's: Institution of Social and Economic Research.

Farnell, Brenda. 1995. *Do You See What I Mean? Plains Indian Sign Talk and the Embodiment of Action*. Lincoln: University of Nebraska Press.

Farnell, Brenda. 2004. "The Fancy Dance of Racializing Discourse." *Journal for Sport and Social Issues* 28,1: 30–55.

Fedje, Daryl W., James M. White, Michael C. Wilson, Earle Nelson, John S. Vogel, and John R. Southon. 1995. "Vermilion Lakes Site: Adaptations and Environments in the Canadian Rockies during the Latest Pleistocene and Early Holocene." *American Antiquity* 60, 1: 81–108.

Field, Les W. 2008. *Abalone Tales: Collaborative Explorations of Sovereignty and Identity in Native California*. Durham, NC: Duke University Press.

Forsyth, Janice, and Kevin Wamsley. 2006. "'Native to Native We'll Recapture Our Spirits': The World Indigenous Nations Games and North American Indigenous Games as Cultural Resistance." *International Journal of History of Sport*, 23, 2: 294–314.

Forsyth, Janice, and Michael Heine. 2008. "Sites of Meaning, Meaningful Sites? Sport and Recreation for Aboriginal Youth in Inner City Winnipeg, Manitoba." *Native Studies Review* 17, 2: 99–113.

Foster, Janet. 1978. *Working for Wildlife: The Beginning of Preservation in Canada*. Toronto: University of Toronto Press.

Foucault, Michel. 1970 (1966). *The Order of Things: An Archaeology of the Human Sciences*. Trans. A.M. Sheridan. New York: Pantheon Books.

Foucault, Michel. 1972 (1969). *The Archaeology of Knowledge and the Discourse on Language*. London: Tavistock Publications.

Foucault, Michel. 1977 (1975). *Discipline and Punish: The Birth of the Prison*. Trans. A.M. Sheridan. New York: Vintage Books.

Foucault, Michel. 1978 (1976). *The History of Sexuality, Volume I: An Introduction*. New York: Vintage Books.

Foucault, Michel. 1980. *Power/Knowledge: Selected Interviews and Other Writings, 1972–1977*. Ed. C. Gordan. Harlow: Harvester.

Foucault, Michel. 1984. *The Foucault Reader*. Ed. Paul Rabinow. New York: Pantheon Books.

Foucault, Michel. 1985. *The History of Sexuality, Volume II: The Use of Pleasure*. London: Penguin Books.

Foucault, Michel. 1986. *The History of Sexuality, Volume III: The Care of the Self*. New York: Pantheon.

Foucault, Michel. 1987. "The Ethic of Care for the Self as a Practice of Freedom." In J. Bernauer and D. Rasmussen, eds, *The Final Foucault*, 1–20. Cambridge: MIT Press.

Foucault, Michel. 1988 (1961). *Madness and Civilization: A History of Insanity in the Age of Reason*. Trans. R. Howard. New York: Vintage Books.

Foucault, Michel. 1994 (1963). *The Birth of the Clinic: An Archaeology of Medical Perception*. Trans. A.M. Sheridan. New York: Vintage Books.

Francis, Margot. 2011. *Creative Subversions: Whiteness, Indigeneity, and the National Imaginary*. Vancouver: UBC Press.

Frith, Simon. 1996. "Music and Identity." In Stuart Hall and Paul du Gay, eds, *Questions of Cultural Identity*, 108–27. London: Sage Publications

Fumoleau, René. 1973 *As Long as This Land Shall Last: A History of Treaty 8 and 11, 1870–1939*. Calgary: University of Calgary Press.

Furniss, Elizabeth. 1995. *Victims of Benevolence: The Dark Legacy of the Williams Lake Residential School*. Vancouver: Arsenal Pulp Press.

Furniss, Elizabeth. 1999. *The Burden of History: Colonialism and the Frontier Myth in a Rural Canadian Community*. Vancouver: UBC Press.

Gadd, Benn. 1989. *Bankhead: The Twenty Year Town*. Toronto: Coal Association of Canada.

Giles, A.R. 2005. "A Foucaultian Approach to Menstrual Practices in the Dehcho, Northwest Territories, Canada." *Arctic Anthropology* 24, 2: 9–21.

Giles, A.R. 2008. "Beyond 'Add Women and Stir': Politics, Feminist Development, and Dene Games." *Leisure/Loisir* 32, 2: 489–512.

Giles, A.R. 2012. "Women's and Girls' Participation in Dene Games in the Northwest Territories." In Janice Forsyth and Audrey R. Giles, eds, *Aboriginal Peoples and Sport in Canada: Historical Foundations and Contemporary* Issues, 145–59. Vancouver: UBC Press.

Gillespie, Greg. 2002. "'I Was Well Pleased with Our Sport among the Buffalo': Big Game Hunters, Travel Writing and Cultural Imperialism and the British North American West, 1847–1872." *Canadian Historical Review* 83: 555–84.

Gilroy, Paul. 2005. *Postcolonial Melancholia*. New York: Columbia University Press.

Greenstein, Ran. 1995. "History and the Production of Knowledge." *South African History* 32: 217–32.

Greenwald, Emily. 2002. *Reconfiguring the Reservation: The Nez Perces, Jicarilla Apaches, and the Dawes Act*. Albuquerque: University of New Mexico Press.

Greenwood, Davydd J. 2004. "Culture by the Pound: An Anthropological Perspective on Tourism and Cultural Commoditization." In Sharon Bohn Gmelch, ed., *Tourists and Tourism: A Reader*, 157–70. Long Grove, IL: Waveland.

Grieveson, Lee. 1998. "Fighting Films: Race Morality, and the Governing of Cinema, 1912–1915." *Cinema Journal* 38, 1: 40–72.

Hall, M. Ann. 2009. *The Girl and the Game: The History of Women's Sport in Canada*. Toronto: University of Toronto Press.

Hall, M. Ann. 2012. "Towards a History of Aboriginal Women in Canadian Sport." In Janice Forsyth and Audrey R. Giles, eds, *Aboriginal Peoples and Sport in Canada: Historical Foundations and Contemporary Issues*, 64–94. Vancouver: UBC Press.

Hall, Stuart. 1996. "Who Needs 'Identity?'" In Stuart Hall and Paul du Gay, eds, *Questions of Cultural Identity*, 2–17. London: Sage Publications.

Hall, Stuart. 1997. "Old and New Identities, Old and New Ethnicities." In Anthony D. King, ed., *Culture, Globalization and the World-System: Contemporary Conditions for the Representation of Identity*, 41–68. Minneapolis: University of Minnesota Press.

Harding, Sandra. 2004. "Introduction: Standpoint Theory as a Site of Political, Philosophical and Scientific Debate." In Sandra Harding, ed., *A Feminist Standpoint Theory Reader: Intellectual and Political Conversations*, 1–16. London: Routledge.

Harding, Sandra. 2006. "Transformation vs. Resistance Identity Projects: Epistemological Resources for Social Justice Movements." In Linda Martín Alcoff, Michael Hames-García, Satya P. Mohanty, and Paula M.L. Moya, eds, *Identity Politics Reconsidered*, 246–63. Basingstoke: Palgrave Macmillan.

Hargreaves, John. 1987. "The Body, Sport and Power Relations." In J. Home, D. Jary, A. Tomlinson, eds, *Sport, Leisure and Social Relations*, 139–59. London: Routledge.

Harkin, M. 2003. "Staged Encounters: Postmodern Tourism and Aboriginal People." *Ethnohistory* 50, 3 : 575–85.

Hart, E.J. 1979. *Diamond Hitch: The Pioneer Guides and Outfitters of Banff and Jasper*. Banff: Summerthought Ltd.

Hart, E.J. 1983. *The Selling of Canada: The CPR and the Beginning of Canadian Tourism*. Banff: Altitude Publishing.

Hart, E.J. 1999. *The Place of Bows: Exploring the Heritage of the Banff–Bow Valley*. Banff: EJH Literary Enterprises Ltd.

Hart, E.J. 2003. *The Battle for Banff: Exploring the Heritage of the Banff–Bow Valley, Part II*. Banff: EJH Literary Enterprises Ltd.

Hart, E.J. 2009. *J.B. Harkin: Father of Canada's National Parks*. Edmonton: University of Alberta Press.

Hart, Elisa. 1995. *Getting Started in Oral Traditions Research*. Occasional Papers of the Prince of Wales Northern Heritage Centre, No. 4, Government of the Northwest Territories, Yellowknife, NT.

Hartsock, Nancy. 1990. "Foucault on Power: A Theory for Women?" In L. Nicholson, ed., *Feminism/Postmodernism*, 155–75. London: Routledge.

Heine, Michael. 1991. "The Symbolic Capital of Honour: Gambling Games and the Social Construction of Gender in Tlingit Indian Culture." *Play & Culture* 4: 346–58.

Henderson, Stuart. 2005. "'While there is still time ...': J. Murray Gibbon and the Spectacle of Difference in Three CPR Folk Festivals, 1928–1931." *Journal of Canadian Studies* 39, 1: 140–69.

Hertzberg, Hazel W. 1971. *The Search for an American Indian Identity: Modern Pan-Indian Movements*. Syracuse, NY: Syracuse University Press.

Hildebrandt, Walter, Dorothy First Rider, Sarah Carter, and Treaty 7 Elders and Tribal Councils. 1996. *The True Spirit and Original Intent of Treaty 7*. Montreal: McGill-Queen's University Press.

Hokowhitu, Brendan. 2003. "Physical Beings: Stereotypes, Sport and the 'Physical Education' of New Zealand Māori." *Culture, Sport and Society* 6, 2: 192–218.

Hokowhitu, Brendan. 2004. "Tackling Māori Masculinity: A Colonial Genealogy of Savagery and Sport." *The Contemporary Pacific* 16, 2: 259–284.

Hokowhitu, Brendan. 2005. "Rugby and *Tino Rangatiratanga*: Early Māori Rugby and the formation of Māori Masculinity." *Sporting Traditions: Journal of the Australian Society for Sports History* 21, 2: 75–95.

Hokowhitu, Brendan. 2013. "Foucault, Genealogy, Sport and Indigeneity." In Murray Phillips and Richard Pringle, eds, *Critical Sport Histories: Paradigms, Power and the Postmodern Turn*, 225–48. Morgantown, WV: F.I.T. Publishers.

Hollinshead, Keith. 1994. "The Unconscious Realm of Tourism." *Annals of Tourism Research* 21: 387–91.

Hollinshead, Keith. 1999. "Surveillance of the Worlds of Tourism: Foucault and the Eye of Power." *Tourism Management* 20: 7–23.

Hughes, George. 1995. "Authenticity in Tourism." *Annals of Tourism Research* 22, 2: 781–803.

Hungry Wolf, Adolf, and Beverly Hungry Wolf. 1989. *Indian Tribes of the Northern Rockies*. Skookumchuck, BC: Good Medicine Books.

Hutcheon, Linda. 2002. *The Politics of Postmodernism*. New York: Routledge.

Jacoby, Karl. 2001. *Crimes against Nature: Squatters, Poachers, Thieves and the Hidden History of American Conservation*. Berkeley: University of California.

Jacoby, Russell. 1995. "Marginal Returns: The Trouble with Postcolonial Theory." *Lingua Franca*, September/October: 30–7.

Jessup, Lynda. 2002. "The Group of Seven and the Tourist Landscape in Western Canada, or The More Things Change ..." *Journal of Canadian Studies* 37, 1: 144–79.

Jette, Shannon. 2006. "Fit for Two? A Critical Discourse Analysis of Oxygen Fitness Magazine." *Sociology of Sport Journal* 23: 331–51.

Jiwani, Yasmin. 2006. *Discourses of Denial: Mediations of Race, Gender, and Violence*. Vancouver: UBC Press.

Johns, D.P., and J.S. Johns. 2000. "Surveillance, Subjection and Technologies of Power: An Analysis of the Discursive Practice of High-Performance Sport." *International Review for the Sociology of Sport* 35: 219–34.

Johnston, Allison M. 2006. *Is the Sacred for Sale? Tourism and Indigenous Peoples*. London: EarthScan.

Jonker, Peter. 1988. *The Song and the Silence: Sitting Wind – the Life Story of Stoney Indian Chief Frank Kaquitts*. Edmonton: Lone Pine Publishing.

Kaplan, Martha. 1995. "Panopticon in Poona: An Essay on Foucault and Colonialism." *Cultural Anthropology* 10, 1: 85–98.

Kasson, Joy S. 2000. *Buffalo Bill's Wild West: Celebrity, Memory, and Popular History*. New York: Hill and Wang.

Keller, Robert H., and Michael F. Turek. 1999. *American Indians and National Parks*. Tucson: University of Arizona Press.

Kelm, Mary-Ellen. 2011. *A Wilder West: Rodeo in Western Canada*. Vancouver: UBC Press.

King, Richard C. 2005. *Native Athletes in Sport and Society*. Lincoln: University of Nebraska.

King, Thomas. 2003. *The Truth about Stories: A Native Narrative*. Toronto: House of Anansi Press.

Kirshenblatt-Gimblett, Barbara. 1998. *Destination Culture: Tourism, Museums, and Heritage*. Berkeley: University of California Press.

Kordan, Bohdan. 2002. *Enemy Aliens, Prisoners of War: Internment in Canada during the Great War*. Montreal: McGill-Queen's University Press.

Kordan, Bohdan, and Peter Melnycky. 1991. *In the Shadow of the Rockies: Diary of the Castle Mountain Internment Camp*. Edmonton: CIUS Press.

Kovach, Margaret. 2009. *Indigenous Methodologies: Characteristics, Conversations, and Contexts.* Toronto: University of Toronto Press.

Krech, Shepard. 1999. *The Ecological Indian: Myth and History*. New York: W.W. Norton.

Langemann, Gwyn E. 2004. "Zooarchaeological Research in Support of a Reintroduction of Bison to Banff National Park, Canada." In Roel C.G.M. Lauwerier and Ina Plug, eds, *The Future from the Past: Archaezoology in Wildlife Conservation and Heritage Management*. Oxford: Oxbow Books.

Langemann, Gwyn E. 2011. "Archeology in the Rocky Mountain National Parks: Uncovering an 11,000 Year-Long Story." In Claire Elizabeth Campbell, ed., *A Century of Parks Canada, 1911–1921*, 303–31. Calgary: University of Calgary Press.

Liao, Judy, and Pirkko Markula. 2009. "Reading Media Texts in Women's Sport: Critical Discourse Analysis and Foucauldian Discourse Analysis." In Pirkko Markula, ed., *Olympic Women and the Media*, 30–49. New York: Palgrave Macmillan.

Little, Walter E. 2004. *Mayas in the Marketplace: Tourism, Globalization, and Cultural Identity*. Austin: University of Texas Press.

Locke, Harvey. 2009. "Civil Society and Protected Areas: A Lesson from the Canadian Experience." *George Wright Forum* 26, 2: 101–28.

Loo, Tina. 2006. *States of Nature: Conserving Canada's Wildlife in the Twentieth Century*. Vancouver: UBC Press.

Loomba, Ania. 2005. *Colonialism/Postcolonialism: The New Critical Idiom*. New York: Routledge.

Louter, David. 2006. *Windshield Wilderness: Cars, Roads and Nature in Washington's National Parks*. Seattle: University of Washington Press.

Lutz, Catherine A., and Jane L. Collins. 1993. *Reading National Geographic*. Chicago: University of Chicago Press.

Luxton, Eleanor G. 1974. *Banff: Canada's First National Park*. Banff: Summerthought.

MacEachern, Alan. 2001. *Natural Selections: National Parks in Atlantic Canada, 1935–1970*. Montreal: McGill-Queen's University Press.

MacEachern, Alan. 2011. "M.B. Williams and the Early Years of Parks Canada." In Claire Elizabeth Campbell, ed., *A Century of Parks Canada, 1911–1921*, 22–52. Calgary: University of Calgary Press.

Mackey, Eva. 1999. *The House of Difference: Cultural Politics and National Identity in Canada*. London: Routledge.

MacLaren, I.S. 2011. "Rejuvenating Wilderness: The Challenge of Reintegrating Aboriginal Peoples into the 'Playground' of Jasper National Park." In Claire Elizabeth Campbell, ed., *A Century of Parks Canada, 1911–1921*, 333–70. Calgary: University of Calgary Press.

Magoc, Chris J. 1999. *Yellowstone: The Creation and Selling of an American Landscape: 1870–1903*. Albuquerque: University of New Mexico Press.

Manry, Kathryn. 2010. *West on One: The Stories behind the Scenery*. Kelowna, BC: Sandhill Book Marketing.

Markula, Pirkko. 1995. "Firm but Shapely, Fit but Sexy, Strong but Thin: The Postmodern Aerobicizing Female Bodies." *Sociology of Sport Journal* 12: 424–53.

Markula, Pirkko. 2003. "The Technologies of the Self: Sport, Feminism and Foucault." *Sociology of Sport Journal* 20: 87–107.

Markula, Pirkko. 2004. "'Turning into One's Self': Foucault's Technologies of the Self and Mindful Fitness." *Sociology of Sport Journal* 21: 302–21.

Markula, Pirkko. 2009. *Olympic Women and the Media*. New York: Palgrave Macmillan.

Markula, Pirkko, and Richard Pringle. 2006. *Foucault, Sport and Exercise: Power, Knowledge and Transforming the Self*. London: Routledge.

Markula, Pirkko, and Courtney W. Mason. 2013. "Doing Foucauldian Sport History." In Murray Phillips and Richard Pringle, eds, *Examining Sport Histories: Power, Paradigms and Reflexivity*, 193–224. Morgantown, WV: F.I.T. Publishers.

Martin, Brad. 2011. "Negotiating a Partnership of Interests: Inuvialuit Land Claims and the Establishment of Northern Yukon (Ivvavik) National Park." In Claire Elizabeth Campbell, ed., *A Century of Parks Canada, 1911–1921*, 273–301. Calgary: University of Calgary Press.

Marty, Sid. 1978. *Men for the Mountains*. Toronto: McClelland & Stewart.

Marty, Sid. 1984. *A Grand and Fabulous Notion: The First Century of Canada's National Parks*. Toronto: NC Press.

Mason, Courtney W. 2005. "Rethinking the Revival of the Glengarry Highland Games: Modernity, Identity, and Tourism in Rural Canada, 1880–1948." *Sport History Review* 36, 2: 130–53.

Mason, Courtney W. 2007. "The Glengarry Highland Games, 1948–2003: Problematizing the Role of Tourism, Scottish Cultural Institutions, and the Cultivation of Nostalgia in the Construction of Identities." *International Journal of Canadian Studies* 34: 13–38.

Mason, Courtney W. 2008. "The Construction of Banff as a 'Natural' Environment: Sporting Festivals, Tourism, and Representations of Aboriginal Peoples." *Journal of Sport History* 35, 2: 221–39.

Mason, Courtney W. 2009. "The Buffalo Nations/Luxton Museum: Tourism, Regional Forces and Problematizing Cultural Representations of Aboriginal Peoples in Banff, Canada." *International Journal of Heritage Studies* 15, 4: 351–69.

Mason, Courtney W. 2010. "Imagining the Canadian Rocky Mountains: Discourses of Indigeneity, Sport and Foucault's Conceptions of Power Relations." *Biopolitica* 11, 2: 4–27.

Mason, Courtney W. 2012. "Consuming the Physical and Cultural Practices of Aboriginal Peoples: Spaces of Exchange, Conflict and (Post)colonial Power Relations." In John Hughson, Clive Palmer, and Fiona Skillen, eds, *The Role of Sports in the Formation of Personal Identities: Studies in Community Loyalties*, 157–81. London: Edwin Mellen Press.

Mason, Courtney W., and Josh Koehli. 2012. "Barriers to Physical Activity for Aboriginal Youth: Implications for Community Health, Policy and Culture." *Pimatisiswin: Journal of Aboriginal and Indigenous Community Health* 10, 1: 97–108.

Mason, Kaley. 2004. "Sound and Meaning in Aboriginal Tourism." *Annals of Tourism Research* 31, 4: 837–54.

McKay, Ian. 1994. *The Quest of the Folk: Antimodernism and Cultural Selection in Twentieth Century Nova Scotia*. Montreal and Kingston: McGill-Queen's University Press.

McNamee, Kevin 1993. "From Wild Places to Endangered Spaces: A History of Canada's National Parks." In Philip Dearden and Rick Rollins, eds, *Parks and Protected Areas in Canada*, 15–44. Oxford: University of Oxford Press.

Medicine, Beatrice. 2001. *Learning to Be an Anthropologist and Remaining "Native."* Chicago: University of Illinois Press.

Meijer-Drees, Laurie. 1991. "Making Banff a Wild West: Norman Luxton, Indians and Banff Tourism, 1902–1945." MA thesis, University of Calgary.

Meijer-Drees, Laurie. 1993. "'Indians' Bygone Past: The Banff Indian Days, 1902–1945." *Past Imperfect* 2: 7–28.

Mitchell, Timothy. 1991. *Colonizing Egypt*. Berkeley: University of California Press.

Moses, L.G. 1996. *Wild West Shows and the Images of American Indians, 1883–1933*. Albuquerque: University of New Mexico Press.

Murphy, Peter J. 2008. "Homesteading the Upper Athabasca Valley to 1910." In I.S. MacLaren, ed., *Culturing Wilderness in Jasper National Park: Studies in Two Centuries in the Human History of the Upper Athabasca River Watershed*, 123–54. Edmonton: University of Alberta Press.

Nadasdy, Paul. 2003. *Hunters and Bureaucrats: Power, Knowledge and Aboriginal-State Relations*. Vancouver: UBC Press.

Nelson, J.G. 1970. "Man and Landscape Change in Banff National Park: A National Park Problem in Perspective." In J.G. Nelson, ed., *Canadian Parks in Perspective*, 63–98. Montreal: Harvest House Ltd.

Nesper, Larry. 2003. "Simulating Culture: Being Indian for the Tourists in Lac du Flambeau's Wa-Swa-Gon Indian Bowl." *Ethno-History* 50, 3: 447–72.

Neufeld, David. 2011. "Kluane National Park Reserve, 1923–1974: Modernity and Pluralism." In Claire Elizabeth Campbell, ed., *A Century of Parks Canada, 1911–1921*, 235–72. Calgary: University of Calgary Press.

Neumann, Roderick P. 1998. *Imposing Wilderness: Struggles over Livelihood and Nature Preservation in Africa*. Berkeley: University of California Press.

Nicol, J.I. 1970. "The National Parks Movement in Canada." In J.G. Nelson, ed., *Canadian Parks in Perspective*, 19–34. Montreal: Harvest House Ltd.

Palmer, Andie Diane. 2005. *Maps of Experience: The Anchoring of Land to Story in Secwepemc Discourse*. Toronto: University of Toronto Press.

Pannekoek, Frits. 1996. *A Snug Little Flock: The Social Origins of the Riel Resistance of 1869–1870*. Winnipeg: J. Gordan Shillingford Publishing Inc.

Paraschak, Victoria. 1996. "Racialized Spaces: Cultural Regulation, Aboriginal Agency and Powwows." *Avante* 2, 1: 7–18.

Paraschak, Victoria. 1997. "Variations in Race Relations: Sporting Events for Native Peoples in Canada." *Sociology of Sport Journal* 14: 1–21.

Paraschak, Victoria. 2000. "Knowing Ourselves through the 'Other': Indigenous Peoples in Sport in Canada." In Robyn Jones and Kathleen Armour, eds, *Sociology of Sport: Theory and Practice*, 153–66. Essex: Longman.

Paraschak, Victoria, and Janice Forsyth. 2010. "Aboriginal Women 'Working' at Play: Canadian Insights." *Ethnologies* 31, 1: 157–73.

Parker, Patricia. 1990. *The Feather and the Drum: The History of Banff Indian Days, 1889–1978*. Calgary: Consolidated Communications.

Peyto, David W. 2002. *Banff Town Warden: The Journals of Walter H. Peyto Rocky Mountains Park, 1914–1922*. Calgary: Peyto Lake Books.

Peyto, David W. 2004. *Banff Town Warden 2: The Journals of Walter H. Peyto Rocky Mountains Park, 1923–1928*. Calgary: Peyto Lake Books.

Prakash, G. 1994. "Postcolonial Criticism and Indian Historiography." In L. Nicholson and S. Seidman, eds, *Social Postmodernism: Beyond Identity Politics*, 87–100. Cambridge: Cambridge University Press.

Pratt, Mary Louise. 1992. *Imperial Eyes: Travel Writing and Transculturation*. London: Routledge.

Pringle, Richard, and Pirkko Markula. 2005. "No Pain Is Sane After All: A Foucauldian Analysis of Masculinities and Men's Experiences in Rugby." *Sociology of Sport Journal* 22: 472–97.

Pringle, Richard. 2005. "Masculinities, Sport, and Power." *Journal of Sport and Social Issues* 29, 3: 256–78.

Rabinow, Paul. 1984. *The Foucault Reader*. Ed. Paul Rabinow. New York: Pantheon Books.

Rail, Genevieve, and Jean Harvey. 1995. "Body at Work." *Sociology of Sport Journal* 12, 2: 164–79.

Rangarajan, Mahesh. 1996. *Fencing the Forest: Conservation and Ecological Change in India's Central Provinces, 1860–1914*. Delhi: Oxford University Press.

Reichwein, PearlAnn. 1996. "'Hands Off Our National Parks': The Alpine Club of Canada and Hydro-development Controversies in the Canadian Rockies, 1922–1930." *Journal of the Canadian Historical Association* 6: 129–55.

Reichwein, PearlAnn. 2005. "Holiday at the Banff School of Fine Arts: The Cinematic Production of Culture, Nature, and Nation in the Canadian Rockies, 1945–1952." *Journal of Canadian Studies* 39, 1: 49–73.

Reilly, John. 2010. *Bad Medicine: A Judge's Struggle for Justice in a First Nations Community*. Calgary: Rocky Mountain Books.

Richardson, Bonham C. 1992. *The Caribbean in the Wider World, 1492–1992: A Regional Geography*. Cambridge: University of Cambridge Press.

Rinehart, Robert. 1998. "Born-again Sport: Ethics in Biographical Research." In Genevieve Rail, ed., *Sport in Postmodern Times*, 36–43. Albany: State University of New York Press.

Robidoux, M.A. 2004. "Narratives of Race Relations in Southern Alberta: An Examination of Conflicting Sporting Practices." *Sociology of Sport Journal*, 21, 3: 281–301.

Robidoux, M.A. 2006. "The Nonsense of Native American Sport Imagery: Reclaiming a Past That Never Was." *International Review for the Sociology of Sport* 41, 2: 201–19.

Robidoux, M.A. 2012. *Stickhandling through the Margins: First Nations Hockey in Canada*. Toronto: University of Toronto Press.

Robins, Kevin 1996. "Interrupting Identities: Turkey/Europe." In Stuart Hall and Paul du Gay, eds, *Questions of Cultural Identity*, 61–86. London: Sage Publications.

Robinson, Bart. 1973. *Banff Springs: The Story of the Hotel*. Banff: Summerthought.

Robinson, Zac. 2007. "Off the Beaten Path? Ski Mountaineering and the Weight of Tradition in the Canadian Rockies, 1909–1940." *International Journal of the History of Sport* 24, 10: 1320–43.

Rojek, Chris. 1985. *Capitalism and Leisure Theory*. London: Tavistock.

Rojek, Chris. 1992. "The 'Eye of Power': Moral Regulation and the Professionalization of Leisure Management." *Society and Leisure* 15: 355–73.

Ross, Luana. 1994. "Race, Gender, and Social Control: Voices of Imprisoned Native American and White Women." *Wicazo Sa Review* 10: 17–40.

Ross, Luana. 1998. *Inventing the Savage: The Social Construction of Native American Criminality*. Austin: University of Texas Press.

Rudin, Ronald. 2009. *Remembering and Forgetting in Acadie: A Historian's Journey through Public Memory*. Toronto: University of Toronto Press.

Rudin, Ronald. 2011. "Kouchibouguac: Representations of a Park in Acadian Popular Culture." In Claire Elizabeth Campbell, ed., *A Century of Parks Canada, 1911–1921*, 205–33. Calgary: University of Calgary Press.

Said, Edward W. 1978. *Orientalism*. New York: Random House.

Said, Edward W. 1991. "Michel Foucault, 1926–1984." In Jonathan Arac, ed., *After Foucault: Humanistic Knowledge and Postmodern Challenges*, 1–11. New Brunswick, NJ: Rutgers University Press.

Said, Edward W. 1993. *Culture and Imperialism*. New York: Random House.

Sandlos, John. 2005. "Federal Spaces, Local Conflicts: National Parks and the Exclusionary Politics of the Conservative Movement in Ontario, 1900–1 935." *Journal of Canadian Historical Association* 16, 1: 293–318.

Sandlos, John. 2007. *Hunters at the Margin: Native People and Wildlife Conservation in the Northwest Territories*. Vancouver: UBC Press.

Sandlos, John. 2008. "Not Wanted in the Boundary: The Expulsion of the Keeseekoowenin Ojibway Band from Riding Mountain National Park." *Canadian Historical Review* 89, 2 (June): 189–221.

Sandlos, John. 2011. "Nature's Playgrounds: The Parks Branch and Tourism Promotion in the National Parks, 1911–1929." In Claire Elizabeth Campbell, ed., *A Century of Parks Canada, 1911–1921*, 53–78. Calgary: University of Calgary Press.

Scace, Robert C. 1970. "Banff Townsite: An Historical and Geographical View of Urban Development in a Canadian National Park." In J.G. Nelson, ed., *Canadian Parks in Perspective*, 187–208. Montreal: Harvest House Ltd.

Scanlon, K. 1990. "Der Wilde Westen." *Equinox* 53: 57–66.

Schama, Simon. 1996. *Landscape and Memory*. New York: Vintage Books.

Scott, Chic. 2000. *Pushing the Limits: The Story of Canadian Mountaineering*. Surrey, BC: Rocky Mountain Books.

Scott, Chic. 2005. *Powder Pioneers: Ski Stories from the Canadian Rockies and Columbia Mountains*. Surrey, BC: Rocky Mountain Books.

Scott, Chic. 2009. *Deep Powder Steep Rocks: The Life of Mountain Guide Hans Gmoser*. Banff: Assiniboine Publishing Ltd.

Sen, Amartya. 2006. *Identity and Violence: The Illusion of Destiny*. New York: W.W. Norton.

Shogan, Debra. 1999. *The Making of High Performance Athletes*. Toronto: University of Toronto Press.

Shogan, Debra. 2002. "Characterizing Constraints of Leisure: A Foucauldian Analysis of Leisure Constraints." *Leisure Constraints* 21: 27–38.

Sivaramakrishnan, K. 2004. "Postcolonialism." In David Nugent and John Vincent, eds, *A Companion to the Anthropology of Politics*, 367–82. Oxford: Blackwell Publishing.

Sloop, John, M. 1997. "Mike Tyson and the Perils of Discursive Constraints: Boxing, Race, and the Assumption of Guilt." In A. Baker and T. Boyd, eds, *Out of Bounds: Sports, Media, and the Politics of Identity*, 102–22. Bloomington: University of Indiana Press.

Smith, Dorothy E. 2004. "Women's Perspective as a Radical Critique of Sociology." In Sandra Harding, ed., *A Feminist Standpoint Theory Reader: Intellectual and Political Conversations*, 21–34. London: Routledge.

Smith, Keith. 2009. *Liberalism, Surveillance and Resistance: Indigenous Communities in Western Canada, 1877–1927*. Edmonton: Athabasca University Press.

Snow, John. 2005. *These Mountains Are Our Sacred Places: The Story of the Stoney Indians*. Toronto: Fifth House Publishing.

Spence, Mark David. 1999. *Dispossessing the Wilderness: Indian Removal and the Making of National Parks*. New York: Oxford University Press.

Spivak, Gayatri Chakravorty. 1988. "Subaltern Studies: Deconstructing Historiography." In Ranajit Gahu and Gayatri Chakravorty Spivak, eds, *Selected Subaltern Studies*, 3–32. Oxford: University of Oxford Press.

Springwood, Charles Fruehling. 2001. "Playing Indian and Fighting (for) Mascots: Reading the Complications of Native American and Euro-American Alliances." In Richard C. King and Charles Fruehling Springwood, eds, *Team Spirits: The Native American Mascot Controversy*, 304–27. Lincoln: Nebraska University Press.

Stanley, George F.G. 1983. "As Long as the Sun Shines and the Water Flows: An Historical Comment." In Ian A.L. Getty and Antoine S. Lussier, eds, *As Long as the Sun Shines and the Water Flows: A Reader in Canadian Native Studies*, 1–26. Vancouver: UBC Press.

Stewart-Harawira, Makere. 2005. *The New Imperial Order: Indigenous Responses to Globalization*. London: Zed Books.

Stoler, Ann Laura. 1995. *Race and the Education of Desire: Foucault's History of Sexuality and the Colonial Order of Things*. Durham, NC: Duke University Press.

Sweet, Jill D. 2004. "'Let 'em Loose': Pueblo Indian Management of Tourism." In Sharon Bohn Gmelch, ed., *Tourists and Tourism: A Reader*, 289–302. Long Grove, Illinois: Waveland.

Tester, Frank James, Paule McNicoll, and Jessie Forsyth. 1999. "With an Ear to the Ground: The CCF/NDP and Aboriginal Policy in Canada, 1926–1993." *Journal of Canadian Studies* 334, 1: 52–74.

Thorpe, Holly. 2008. "Foucault, Technologies of the Self, and the Media." *Journal of Sport and Social Issues* 32, 2: 99–129.

Tierney, William G. 2003. "Undaunted Courage: Life History and the Postmodern Challenge." In Norman K. Denzin and Yvonna S. Lincoln, eds, *Strategies of Qualitative Inquiry*, 292–317. London: Sage Publications.

Tobias, John L. 1983. "Protection, Civilization, Assimilation: An Outline History of Canada's Indian Policy." In Ian A.L. Getty and Antoine S. Lussier, eds, *As Long as the Sun Shines and the Water Flows: A Reader in Canadian Native Studies*, 39–55. Vancouver: UBC Press.

Tuhiwai Smith, Linda. 1999. *Decolonizing Methodologies: Research and Indigenous Peoples*. London: Zed Books Ltd.

Tuhiwai Smith, Linda. 2005. "On Tricky Ground: Researching the Native in the Age of Uncertainty." In Norman K. Denzin and Yvonna S. Lincoln, eds, *The Sage Handbook of Qualitative Research*, 85–108. Thousand Oaks, CA: Sage Publishing.

Urion, Josephine Celeste. 1999. "The Construction of Wilderness in the Formation of Glacier National Park, Montana." MA thesis, University of Alberta.

Urry, John. 1990. *The Tourist Gaze: Leisure and Travel in Contemporary Societies*. London: Sage.

Veijola, S., and E. Jokinen. 1994. "The Body in Tourism." *Theory, Culture and Society* 11: 125–51.

Vertinsky, Patricia. 1994a. *Eternally Wounded Women: Women, Doctors and Exercise in the Late Nineteenth Century*. Manchester: Manchester University Press.

Vertinsky, Patricia. 1994b. "The Social Construction of the Gendered Body: Exercise and the Exercise of Power." *International Journal of the History of Sport* 11, 2: 147–71.

Waiser, Bill. 1995. *Park Prisoners: The Untold Story of Western Canada's National Parks, 1915–1946*. Saskatoon: Fifth House.

Waiser, Bill. 2011. "'A Case of Special Privilege and Fancied Right': The Shack Tent Controversy in Prince Alberta National Park." In Claire Elizabeth Campbell, ed., *A Century of Parks Canada, 1911–1921*, 103–31. Calgary: University of Calgary Press.

Wakeham, Pauline. 2008. *Taxidermic Signs: Reconstructing Aboriginality*. Minneapolis: University of Minnesota Press.

Wall, Karen L. 2012. *Game Plan: A Social History of Sport in Alberta*. Edmonton: University of Alberta Press.

Warry, Wayne. 2007. *Ending Denial: Understanding Aboriginal Issues*. Toronto: Broadview Press.

Wearing, B. 1995. "Leisure and Resistance in an Aging Society." *Leisure Studies* 14: 263–79.

Wearing, Stephen, and Matthew McDonald. 2002. "The Development of Community- based Tourism: Re-thinking the Relationship between Community Operators and Development Agents as Intermediaries in Rural and Isolated Area Communities." *Journal of Sustainable Tourism* 10, 3: 191–206.

Weber-Pillwax, Cora. 2004. "Indigenous Researchers and Indigenous Research Methods: Cultural Influences or Cultural Determinants of Research

Methods." *Pimatisiwin: A Journal of Aboriginal and Indigenous Community Health* 2, 1: 77–90.

Wetherell, Margaret, Jonathan Potter. 1992. *Mapping the Language of Racism: Discourse and the Legitimation of Exploitation*. New York: Harvester Wheatsheaf.

Whyte, Jon. 1985. *Indians in the Rockies*. Banff: Altitude Publishing.

Williams, Mabel B. 1922. *The Heart of the Rockies*. Hamilton: H.R. Larson Publishing Co.

Williams, Mabel B. 1936. *Guardians of the Wild*. London: T. Nelson and Sons.

Williams, Mabel B. 1948. *The Banff Jasper Highway, Descriptive Guide*. Hamilton: H.R. Larson.

Williams, Raymond. 1980. *Problems of Materialism and Culture*. London: Verso.

Willig, Carla. 2001. *Introducing Qualitative Research in Psychology: Adventures in Theory and Method*. Houston: Open University Press.

Wilson, Alexander. 1991. *The Culture of Nature: North American Landscape from Disney to the Exxon Valdez*. Toronto: Between the Lines.

Wilson, Shaun. 2001. "What Is Indigenous Research Methodology?" *Canadian Journal of Native Education* 25, 2: 175–79.

Winter, Caroline. 2007. "Tourism, Nation and Power: A Foucauldian Perspective of Australia's Ghan Train." In Andrew Church and Tim Coles, eds, *Tourism, Power and Space: Contemporary Geographies of Leisure, Tourism and Mobility*, 101–22. New York: Routledge.

Yeo, William B. 1990. "Making Banff a Year-Round Park." In E.A. Colbert and A.W. Rasporich, eds, *Winter Sports in the West*, 87–98. Calgary: Historical Society of Alberta.

Young, David C. 1996. *The Modern Olympics: A Struggle for Revival*. Baltimore: Johns Hopkins University Press.

Young, Robert. 1995. *Colonial Desire: Hybridity in Theory, Culture and Race*. London: Routledge.

Zezulka-Mailloux, Gabrielle. 2008. "Laying the Tracks for Tourism: Paradoxical Promotions and the Development of Jasper National Park." In I.S. MacLaren, ed., *Culturing Wilderness in Jasper National Park: Studies in Two Centuries in the Human History of the Upper Athabasca River Watershed*, 233–59. Edmonton: University of Alberta Press.

Zhan, Mei. 2005. "Civet Cats, Fried Grasshoppers, and David Beckham's Pajamas: Unruly Bodies after SARS." *American Anthropologist* 107, 1: 31–42.

Index

www.ingramcontent.com/pod-product-compliance
Lightning Source LLC
Chambersburg PA
CBHW030811300925
33189CB00010B/193